AF324663

# PATTERNS OF CONSTITUTIONAL DESIGN

# Patterns of Constitutional Design
## The Role of Citizens and Elites in Constitution-Making

*Edited by*

JONATHAN WHEATLEY

FERNANDO MENDEZ

*both at Centre for Research on Direct Democracy (c2d),*
*Centre for Democracy Studies Aarau (ZDA) at the University of Zurich,*
*Switzerland*

ASHGATE

Published by
Ashgate Publishing Limited
Wey Court East
Union Road
Farnham
Surrey, GU9 7PT
England

Ashgate Publishing Company
110 Cherry Street
Suite 3-1
Burlington, VT 05401-3818
USA

www.ashgate.com

**British Library Cataloguing in Publication Data**
Patterns of constitutional design : the role of citizens and elites in constitution-making.
   1. Constitutional law--Africa. 2. Constitutional law--Europe. 3. Constitutional law--South America. 4. Political participation--Africa. 5. Political participation--Europe.
   6. Political participation--South America. 7. Elite (Social sciences)--Political activity--Africa. 8. Elite (Social sciences)--Political activity--Europe. 9. Elite (Social sciences)--Political activity--South America.
   I. Wheatley, Jonathan. II. Mendez, Fernando, 1972–
   342'.02-dc23

**The Library of Congress has cataloged the printed edition as follows:**
Patterns of constitutional design : the role of citizens and elites in constitution-making / by Jonathan Wheatley and Fernando Mendez.
   p. cm.
   Includes bibliographical references and index.
   ISBN 978-1-4094-6088-6 (hardback) -- ISBN 978-1-4094-6089-3 (ebook) -- ISBN 978-1-4724-0775-7 (epub) 1. Constitutional law--Political aspects. 2. Constitutional law--Social aspects. 3. Constitutional law--Citizen participation. 4. Conflict management--Political aspects. 5. Democratization. 6. Political participation--Social aspects. I. Wheatley, Jonathan, 1964– II. Mendez, Fernando, 1972–
   K3165.P374 2013
   342.02--dc23

2013000258

ISBN 9781409460886 (hbk)
ISBN 9781409460893 (ebk – PDF)
ISBN 9781472407757 (ebk – ePUB)

Printed in the United Kingdom by Henry Ling Limited, at the Dorset Press, Dorchester, DT1 1HD

# Contents

# List of Figures

# List of Tables

# Notes on Contributors

**Andreas Auer** graduated in Switzerland (University of Neuchâtel) and the United States (Southern Methodist University, Dallas) and has been Professor of Constitutional Law at the University of Geneva Law School (1980–2008) before joining the University of Zurich in 2008. He was formerly Dean of the Geneva Law School (2000–2003) and is currently Director of the Centre for Democracy Studies Aarau (ZDA) as well as of the Centre for Research on Direct Democracy (c2d) which he founded in 1993. Professor Auer has taught courses in constitutional law at the University of Antananarivo, Madagascar (1988, 1991, 1993, 1995), was a member of the Public Law Jury of the Conseil Africain et Malgache de l'Enseignement Superieur (CAMES; concours d'agregation 1993, 1995, 1997, 1999) and has been a constitutional expert for the Organisation internationale de la francophonie (OIF) on missions in Senegal, Benin, Togo, Chad and Mali.

**Micha Germann** is a doctoral researcher at the University of Zurich, ETH Zurich, and the Centre for Democracy Studies Aarau. He is currently engaged in a Swiss National Science Foundation project dealing with referendums on sovereignty issues. His focus is on the relationship between ethno-nationalist referendums and ethnic conflict. His research interests include direct democracy, civil war, and state repression. He is also interested and has conducted research on voting advice applications (VAAs).

**Nina Massüger Sánchez Sandoval** studied law at the University of Zurich and the Université François Rabelais in Tours (France). After a research stay at the Instituto de Investigaciones Jurídicas of the Universidad Nacional Autonóma de México (UNAM) in Mexico City as a holder of a scholarship offered by the Emil Boral Foundation and the Swiss National Foundation, she is currently finishing her PhD thesis on the constitution-making processes in Venezuela (1999), Bolivia (2006–2009) and Ecuador (2007–2008). She is also currently doing an internship at the Office of Waste, Water, Energy and Air of the Canton of Zurich.

**Fernando Mendez** is a Senior Researcher at the Centre for Research on Direct Democracy and Director of the e-Democracy centre (eDC), both based at the University of Zurich. He is a Lecturer in Political Science on the Masters Programme at the University of Zurich and the Swiss Federal Institute of Technology (ETH) since 2007. Dr. Mendez holds a PhD in Political Science from the European University Institute, Florence. He has led various projects funded by the Swiss National Science Foundation (SNF) on aspects of direct democracy and constitutional change. Dr. Mendez's academic interests include direct democracy, comparative federalism, European integration, and comparative public policy. He has published across these various fields in journals such as the *Journal of European Public Policy*; *Publius: The Journal of Federalism; Representation; Journal of Balkan and Near Eastern Studies*; *Public Law*; and has co-authored a book on the 'European Union and e-voting'. His most recent book, *Referendums and the European Union*, (co-authored with Mario Mendez and Vicky Triga) will be published with Cambridge University Press in 2013.

**Ana Tornic** graduated in law at the University of Zurich and subsequently worked as an assistant researcher at the Centre for Research on Direct Democracy (c2d) and as an assistant at the Law Faculty of the University of Zurich at the Chair of Public Law of Prof. Dr. Andreas Auer. Her research interests lie in the fields of comparative constitutional law, national and international human rights protection and the consolidation of democracy and the rule of law in states of transition. As holder of a scholarship of the Swiss National Foundation, she is currently completing a research visit at the Law Faculty of the University of Zagreb in order to finish the research for her doctoral on access rights of individuals to the Constitutional Courts of the Successor States of the former Yugoslavia.

**Yanina Welp** is currently the Regional Director for Latin America at the Center for Research on Direct Democracy (c2d) and Academic Program Manager of the doctoral program 'The Dynamics of Transcultural Governance and Management in Latin America' (Universities of St. Gallen, Bern and Geneva, and the Graduate Institute). Dr. Welp's main areas of research are democratization, mechanisms of direct and participatory democracies and e-democracy. Among recent publications, she has co-edited the books *Caleidoscopio de la Innovación Democrática en América Latina* (with Laurence Whitehead, 2011, FLACSO) and *Armas de doble Filo. La participación ciudadana en la encruciajada* (with Uwe Serdült, Prometeo, 2009) and is also author of chapters of books, reports, working papers and articles published in various countries.

**Jonathan Wheatley** is a senior researcher at the Centre for Research on Direct Democracy (c2d). He is also lecturer at the University of Zurich and the Swiss Federal Institute of Technology at Zurich (ETH). Dr Wheatley's research interests include democratization, state-building, parties and party systems in developing democracies and the impact of new forms of media and information-communication technologies on party systems in established democracies. In addition to publishing a number of scholarly articles, Wheatley has also published a book entitled *Georgia from National Awakening to Rose Revolution: Delayed Transition in the Former Soviet Union* (Ashgate, 2005), an analysis of the political regime in Georgia from 1988 to 2004.

# Prologue
# Constitutional Conventions, Constitutional Change and Democracy

Andreas Auer

The research on which this book is based was made possible by a generous Swiss National Science Foundation grant. As the project director, one of the animating features which drove me to put together the research proposal was the dearth of literature on the specific institution of the constitutional convention (in the sense of a body specifically mandated to draft a constitution). Of course, much has been written about the most famous constitutional convention which met in Philadelphia in 1787 but apart from this celebrated case little was known about the phenomenon from a more comparative perspective. In the course of their research, the investigators working on the project adopted a broader conception of the constitution making process, partly in order to also compare constitutional conventions with other forms of constitution making. One notable feature that comes out of this research is that constitutional convention (and variants thereof) is much more common than is readily acknowledged. In this short prologue I would like to return to the animating spirit of the original proposal – the constitutional convention.

The world's oldest and the world's (to date probably) youngest constitution were both drafted by constitutional conventions and approved by the people. While the Constitution of the Commonwealth of Massachusetts of 15 June 1780 is still in force at this day, the Constitution of the Republic and canton of Geneva of 14 October 2012 will enter into force in June 2013. Of course, two hundred and thirty-three years of constitution making around the globe have seen many other techniques of writing and ratifying constitutions. But constitutional conventions and constitutional referendums remain common features, at all times and in all continents, for trying to build up a solid legitimacy to constitutional schemes designed to create new chains of legality.

Straddling the gap between past and future, constitutional conventions, whatever their name, are unique and quite curious bodies both in law and politics. With regard to law, they live through and suffer from an inescapable contradiction. They are extra-legal as they are convened to break up the precedent legality; they are supra-legal as they set basic rules for future lawmaking; they are infra-legal as they need a legal basis for coming into existence and functioning. They are called upon to conclude a new social contract, to create a new chain of legality, to shape new institutions, to legitimate new rulers. They put in motion a set of regulations that will not apply to them, as they act only to disappear. They define the rules of a game that they will never be playing. Yet their will and intentions will be taken as guidelines, maybe for decades or centuries, by all those who are called to interpret the constitutional rules and concepts they had framed.

As political bodies, constitutional conventions are exposed to many threats and challenges, internal as well as external. Between the faithful transcription of given power structures into legal rules designed to survive the dominant political actors of the moment – the conservative approach – and the prophetic vision of new institutional designs and ideological goals capable of overcoming existing stalemates and dogmas – the radical view – there are many ways for combining both or failing to attend either. The difficulty is all the more frustrating as the chosen way, be it the one or the other, and the means to get there, radical or conservative, risk at any time being blocked from outside through politically inspired manoeuvres on which the body and its members have hardly any influence. Egypt's monumental yet agonizing constitutional convention – alternatively challenged by courts, parliament, president, parties and the street – is a (still) living example of the inherent political fragility of constitutional conventions.

Such fragility is by no means a weakness that should or could be avoided, but an inherent characteristic of an institution sitting on two stools, one standing on legal and the other on political grounds, that cannot stop moving and therefore ever threatens to fall in between. Because the interactions of one with the other are so numerous, manifold and unpredictable, lawyers as well as political scientists are rather unfit and, to put it bluntly, helpless to make any serious scientific statement with regard to the possible failure or success of acting constitutional conventions or to causal relationships between given institutional parameters and political outcomes. The patterns of constitutional change can occasionally be evaluated and measured by looking back at isolated experiences that have more or less failed or succeeded. If comparing them even in the past is already hazardous, because dependent on so many factors, foreseeing them and even more controlling them for the future seems simply out of the question. As soon as a possible rational connection seems to take shape, reality shows its power by overriding it at the next occasion.

Yet another characteristic is worth noting. Constitutional conventions are mere drafters of constitutions or constitutional amendments, but usually they have no power to enact them formally and even less to ensure they enter into force. In order for their product to become law it needs a positive decision by another entity – the people, parliament, the president or whoever. In all their omnipotence – what greater power is there than to write a new constitution? – constitutional conventions are impotent bodies. By themselves, they are nothing. Unable to come into existence, to live and to have effect by their own means, they need to be somehow institutionalized by somebody else and followed by others. They do not have and are not the *'pouvoir constituant'*; they merely, yet significantly, have the power to determine the contents of the rule that the *'pouvoir constituant'* may or may not ratify and put into force. There is a curious relationship of mutual dependence between the constitutional convention and the constitution making power.

Constitutional conventions are closely tied to democracy, even though there is no guarantee that its end result will be able to promote democracy effectively. First, constitution-making bodies are, in many cases, children of democracy. Their election is often preceded by a consultation of the citizens as to the opportunity to work out a new constitution by an elected convention. Thus it may be a referendum that leads to the election of a constitutional convention. This has been experienced since the very first experiences with conventions in New England, in revolutionary France, but also in recent years in a series of Swiss cantons as well as in Latin America.

Second, in democratic societies, constitutional conventions are *per se* mechanisms of democratic government. Not only but especially when, as is often the case, their members are directly elected by the people. Even in case of designation by another state organ, constitutional conventions typically have some scent of democracy, stemming probably from the specific legitimacy they are enjoying over all other authorities of the state. It is the very fact that the writing of a new constitution is taken out of the hands of the existing bodies of authority that confers to the constitutional convention a position that, in a way, resembles the one granted to the people in direct democracies: the supreme normative power.

Third, in countries with experience of direct democracy, constitutional conventions can strengthen this experience. They not only create constitutions, they not only tend to favour democratic institutions, they often give birth to direct democracy, or strengthen it in a significant way. One reason behind this link between constitutional conventions and direct democracy might be some kind of twofold dependency. Just like handing over the responsibility to write a constitution from the classical state organs to a constitutional convention needs a special legitimacy that direct democratic institutions can best provide, instituting the people as an organ of the state that is given other powers than to elect, every four or five years, its representatives in parliament needs a stronger legitimacy than the one available to the classic political organs.

# Acknowledgements

The editors would like to thank all the researchers and staff at the Centre for Direct Democracy (c2d) in Aarau, Switzerland for supporting the project. A special thanks goes to the c2d Director, Andreas Auer, who provided the encouragement as well as institutional and intellectual support that made the volume possible. Last but by no means least, we are extremely grateful to the Swiss National Science Foundation (grant no. 100015-120040 and grant no. 1000015_135127/1) for supporting the research project on which this volume is based.

# Introduction

Fernando Mendez and Jonathan Wheatley

The comparative study of constitutions is one of the oldest fields in the social sciences; the first known contribution to this field can be found in Aristotle's *Politics* in which the Greek philosopher develops a typology of constitutions (πολιτειων) as a way of organizing the offices of the city-state and goes on to compare the constitutions of different city-states. However, despite such early beginnings, it is surprising how poorly understood the phenomenon of constitution making remains. Thus far, the only systematic attempt to empirically investigate the impact of constitution making processes is a recent (2009) work *The Endurance of National Constitutions*, by Zachary Elkins, Tom Ginsburg and James Melton of the Comparative Constitutions Project (CCP) based at the University of Illinois. The CCP assembled the largest constitutional dataset that encompasses most constitutions made between 1789 and the present day. One of the main research goals of the CCP and *The Endurance of National Constitutions* was to explain the variance in the lifespan of national constitutions. In a similar vein, Donald Lutz's *Principle of Constitutional Design* (2007) also adopts a large-N approach to his study of the content of a constitution and its impact on democracy.

It is the aim of this study to build on this literature by further exploring the impact of constitution-making on modern polities, not only in terms of the survival of the constitutional order, but also in terms of its capacity to foster democracy and the peaceful resolution of conflict. The focus of this book is on the influence of the constitution-making process not on only the constitutional text (and its subsequent evolution) but also on the development of informal norms of *constitutionalism* or unwritten constitutional principles that come to define the polity as much as the formal legal framework. To this end, the book contributes to further research in the field in a number of ways.

First, it helps to bridge the gap between law and politics. The constitution-making process is a unique phenomenon in both fields. To a lawyer, constitution-making is of interest because of its peculiar relationship to the existing legal framework. It is extra-legal as its outcome is to break up the preceding legality; it is supra-legal as it sets basic rules for future lawmaking; it is infra-legal as it needs a legal basis for functioning (see the Prologue by Andreas Auer). To a political scientist, the constitution-making process is interesting because it is a unique moment in high politics: it aims to conclude a new social contract, to shape new institutions and to legitimate new rulers.

A second distinctive feature of the book is that it focuses on both procedure and context. While its primary goal is to explore the relevance of constitution-making procedures, one of its conclusions is that the (often informal) institutional context may condition both procedures and outcomes. Both the informal institutions of constitutionalism, as well as the formal rules of the constitution as a document, are relevant here; an informal consensus on the desirability of democratic principles is needed to ensure that the constitution-making process moves beyond a raw struggle for power in which the winner takes all.

Finally, the book also bridges the gap between a number of different subdisciplines. The comparative method that it uses relies on the discipline of comparative politics, while the emphasis on procedures owes much to constitutional law. The study of informal institutional constraints draws from a subfield of political science called new institutionalism, while the emphasis on the development of an (informal) democratic consensus is highly relevant to students of democratization. Finally, the book also explores the role of constitution-making in conflict resolution. In short, the book draws together strands of research that are not commonly juxtaposed.

The first part of the book begins with an overview of existing theoretical approaches to constitution-making (Chapter 1 'The Constitution-Making Process: An Analytical Framework' by Fernando Mendez and Jonathan Wheatley). It derives from the literature a number of tentative hypotheses as to the relationship between the constitution-making process and two particular outcomes that we are interested in: democracy and conflict resolution. Chapters 2 and 3 ('Patterns of Constitution-Making over Time and Space' by Fernando Mendez and Jonathan Wheatley 'Outcomes of Constitution-Making. Democratization and Conflict Resolution' by Jonathan Wheatley and Micha Germann) employ a large-N approach to identify interrelationships and dependencies between the constitution-making process on the one hand and a number of clearly defined outcomes on the other. Chapter 2 compares 160 constitution-making events, and focuses on the interrelationships between certain features of the process. It concludes that in order to investigate the outcomes of constitution-making we need to focus on two key variables: the mode of representation of the constitution-making body (i.e. how it is appointed) and the mode of legitimation (i.e. how the constitution is ratified). Chapter 3 then explores how these two variables impact on the persistence (or collapse) of authoritarian regimes, on the one hand, and the resolution of violent conflict, on the other. To investigate the persistence of authoritarianism, it uses a method called Qualitative Comparative Analysis (QCA) to identify certain configurations of factors (constitution-making and otherwise) that are associated with continuing authoritarianism. In order to study the role of constitution-making in conflict resolution three 'mini case studies' are used (Switzerland, India and South Africa).

The second part of the book uses small-N comparative case studies to shed more light on the puzzles identified in the first part. In contrast to the first part, it adopts a qualitative approach that is better tuned to revealing the processes linking the constitution-making process to outcomes. Chapter 4 ('Constitution-Making in West Africa: Keeping the President in Check' by Jonathan Wheatley) focuses on five West African countries that all passed new constitutions in the early 1990s and, at least formally, began a transition process from authoritarian rule. It attempts to explain why in some cases, the constitution has remained more or less unchanged since its adoption and at least minimum standards of democracy have been observed, while in others the political leadership subsequently violated the constitutional principles of limited government by amending the constitution to impose strong-arm presidential rule. Chapter 5 ('Transitions from Above: The Constitution-Making Process and the Consolidation of Democracy' by Yanina Welp) also focuses on constitution-making in the context of democratic transition by exploring three cases in which a democratic consensus has been achieved (albeit gradually) in the context of a kind of pact-making process that involved the drafting of a new constitution. The chapter focusses on the cases of Spain, Brazil and Poland, in which negotiations between the incumbent leadership and opposition forces eventually resulted in a democratic constitution that defined the new regime in each case. Chapter 6 ('Legality and Legitimacy: Constituent Power in Venezuela, Bolivia and Ecuador' by Nina Massüger Sánchez Sandoval and Yanina Welp) looks at three more recent cases of constitution-making – Venezuela in 1999, Ecuador in 2008 and Bolivia in 2009. It attempts to explain the paradox of why, despite the fact that the constitution was elaborated in the most participatory manner possible in each case, a lack of consensus amongst the main players led to the violation of the existing law and sometimes even the violation of the rules that had been set up specifically to regulate the constitution-making process.

The second part of the book concludes with two chapters that focus on different levels of constitution-making: the sub-national and the supra-national level. Chapter 7 ('Constituent Assemblies in Swiss Cantons' by Ana Tornic and Nina Massüger Sánchez Sandoval) explores the extent to which constitution-making in the Swiss cantons in general, and constitution-making by constituent assemblies in particular, has changed in the course of the past 180 years. Specifically, it examines the evolution of constituent assemblies from their first appearance as a revolutionary means of constitution-making in some liberal cantons in the 1830s to a constitutional means later on and shows the impact of such assemblies on the development of the constitutional order and democracy in the cantons. Chapter 8 ('Popular Input, Territoriality, and the Constitution-Making Process: Comparative Reflections on the European Union's Supranational Experience' by Fernando Mendez) explores the European Union's experience with constitution-making from a comparative perspective. Specifically, it compares modes of constitutional change in the European Union with other systems governed by the territorial principle and asks how this principle can be reconciled with that of popular sovereignty.

The concluding chapter (Chapter 9, 'Conclusions: On the role of Popular Participation and Constitution-Making' by Jonathan Wheatley) ties up some of the main threads that emerge throughout the book. In particular, it offers an overview of the role of popular participation in constitution making exercises and some of the problems involved with popular input, especially in conflict cases.

# PART 1
# Theoretical Framework

Chapter 1
# The Constitution-Making Process:
# An Analytical Framework

Fernando Mendez and Jonathan Wheatley

The central focus of this book can be stated simply. To what extent does the constitution-making process matter. Such a broadly formulated question will immediately raise two ancillary questions. First, what do we understand by a constitution-making process? And, second, in relation to which outcomes might a constitution-making process matter? For the benefit of the later discussion, let us clarify some of these terms. What is of particular relevance to our research inquiry into the constitution-making process is the nature of the constitution-making body and the various ways in which such bodies can be formed and legitimized. Who decides on undertaking a constitution-making exercise and which operational procedures are to govern the process. Also of relevance is the way decisions are reached within that body and whether the wider public participates in these decisions in any meaningful way. The case studies in some of the later chapters of this book will be devoted, in part at least, to this aspect of decision making. Crucially, we must also consider the end product of the process, the constitution itself, and the way it is ratified. Are the people directly involved or is ratification achieved via intermediary institutions such as legislatures?

The second point of clarification relates to the relevance of constitution-making. In short, what is the impact (if any) of the constitution-making process on the political framework of the entity concerned? There are at least three aspects of the post-constitution political environment that are relevant. The first is stability: is the new constitutional order stable, or does it break down after a few years? Of particular interest here is whether the constitutional text itself endures, or whether it is amended or rewritten within a relatively short time frame as a result of political intrigue. The second aspect is conflict: does the new constitutional order bring about an environment more or less conducive to conflict resolution? Some constitutions are drawn up as a part of a peace settlement after a civil war (for example, Namibia and Bosnia-Herzegovina), and the expectations are that the constitution contains within it a number of crucial mechanisms for conflict resolution. On the other hand, there are also instances in which new constitutions inadvertently sow the seeds of discord (an example here is the 1921 Constitution of Yugoslavia). The third and final aspect of the post-constitution environment that we are interested in is democracy: is the new order more or less democratic than the old? Constitution-making can be an integral part of the process of transition from an authoritarian regime to a democracy, so an intended outcome of the new constitutional order is a democratic regime. Linz and Stepan, for instance, have argued that the constitution-making environment during a period of transition has a critical impact on the future regime that emerges (Linz and Stepan 1996, 81–3).

Our main concern is to investigate potential causal chains between the constitution-making process, on the one hand, and the outcomes of the process in terms of stability, conflict and democracy, on the other. A variety of methods, some quantitative and others more qualitative, will be deployed to try to unfold some of these relations. There are two main steps to the analysis. A first step is to identify patterns of association with regard to forms of constitution-making both over time and space. The second is to link particular forms of constitution-making with substantive outcomes. Our principal unit of analysis will be constitution-making events, primarily at the level of the nation-state, but some of the chapters will also focus on other levels of political aggregation: the sub-state level (Switzerland) and the supranational level (the European Union). All chapters, whether relying on a larger number cases or smaller subsets of cases, employ the comparative method of analysis. In the next section we provide a brief overview of some of the main contributions from the literature before outlining a conceptual framework for analysing our guiding research questions.

**The State-of-the-art**

Given its centrality it is surprising how poorly understood the phenomenon of constitution-making is. To be sure, there has been much commentary and speculation about the impact of different forms of constitution-making but the empirical record is unclear (for a review see Ginsburg 2009, Ginsburg and Dixon 2011). In recent years this has begun to change as scholars try to assess the impact of constitution-making processes. A number of research programs have begun to collect data on constitution-making processes over time and across different regions of the globe.[1] What is of interest in the emerging research programmes is their interdisciplinary nature which typically involves bringing constitutional scholars and political scientists together. Furthermore, such programmes provide ample scope for deploying combined methodologies in innovative ways (see for instance Elkins et al. 2009, Ginsburg and Dixon 2011).

The comparative study of constitutions is, of course, one of the oldest fields in the 'social sciences'. Not only is this the case for lawyers but for political scientists too. One need only mention the first 'social scientific' exercise in the

---

1 Three international research programmes can be singled out. The Comparative Constitution Project involving researchers from the University of Texas and University of Chicago; The Constitution Writing and Conflict Resolution programme at the Princeton University; and the Centre for Research on Direct Democracy constitutional convention project at the University of Zurich.

Western tradition, Aristotle's *Politics*, which was based on a comparative analysis of around 150 constitutions from ancient Greece. Constitutional design has, in short, occupied scholars throughout the ages. However, there is a sense in which the field has moved towards a more theory grounded and empirically focused analysis of constitutions, broadly understood. This involves a growing concern with categorization and measurement of concepts and has begun to generate the collection of relatively large datasets. A number of factors have helped spur the empirical turn towards larger n studies of constitutions. On the demand side, a crucial driver has been the process of democratization with its accompanying regime changes across many nations since the 1980s. At a more practical level, the democratization process has raised important questions about constitutional design. Further demand for expertise in constitutional engineering has occurred in many post-conflict settings and as solutions for divided societies.

On the supply side there have been a number of major intellectual changes since the 1980s too. Much of this can be grouped under the label of institutionalism or, as it has come to be referred to, new institutionalism. The new institutionalist wave has impacted on most of the social sciences and, in particular, the fields of constitutional political economy and comparative politics. Prior to the institutionalist turn, scholars had been largely preoccupied with broader structural features of the environment. Although the study of institutions had always been a core concern for students of constitutions, the new turn in the social sciences meant a greater concern for the 'rules of the game'. Indeed, as the Nobel laureate economic historian and pioneer in institutional analysis, Douglass North, put it, institutions are best conceived as the 'rules of the game', that is those 'humanly devised constraints that structure human interaction'. For North this meant paying attention to 'the formal constraints (e.g. rules, laws, constitutions), informal constraints (e.g. norms of behaviour, conventions, self-imposed codes of conduct), and their enforcement characteristics' (North 1994: 360). In many respects the new intellectual shift attempted to reconcile elements of the age-old structure-agency debate by moving beyond a preoccupation with environmental determinants and abstract systems theorizing. Especially among analysts working in the fields of constitutional political economy, new institutional economics, and comparative politics, a core concern was with who gets to set the rules, when, under what conditions, and with what effects. The comparative study of constitutional design was a subject matter ideally suited to the intellectual concerns of new institutionalists.

One of the pioneers in agency-oriented studies of constitution-making, Jon Elster, made some important contributions to our understanding of constitutional negotiations and constitutional waves (Elster 1995, 1999). With respect to the latter, Elster argued that constitution-making comes in waves and went on to identify a number of distinct waves of constitution-making in the modern age (Elster 1995). These waves include some of the first constitution-making exercises at the close of the eighteenth century in Europe and North America. Other constitutional waves were identified such as those in the aftermath of the 1848 revolutions, the post-Versailles constitutions, in the immediate aftermath of the First World War, the decolonization period, and more recently with the transitions from authoritarianism and the collapse of communisms. In total he identifies seven waves of constitution-making (Elster 1995: 368–9). Interestingly, a detailed historical comparative analysis of two key examples of the very first wave, the convention in the United States (Philadelphia) and the constituent assembly in France (French Revolution) led Elster to postulate a number of hypotheses about the style of constitution-making and the role of public debate therein. He argued, quite persuasively, that constitution-making in deliberative settings under the gaze of the public was unlikely to produce enduring constitutional settlements (Elster 1995).

Elster's pioneering work has set the scene for more extensive, and collaborative, attempts to empirically investigate the impact of constitution-making processes too. The most prominent attempt thus far is that undertaken by the US-based research consortium behind the Comparative Constitutions Project. The research consortium has assembled the largest constitutional dataset that encompasses most constitutions made between 1789 and the present day. Included in the dataset are all significant constitutional events; namely revisions/amendments, suspensions and enactments of both new and interim constitutions. The project will no doubt inject a new empirical turn into the large n study of constitutional engineering, the fruit of interdisciplinary collaboration between constitutional scholars and political scientists. One of the main research goals of the Comparative Constitutions Project was to explain the variance in the lifespan of national constitutions (Elkins et at 2009). Possible explanations include 'environmental factors' and 'design factors'. In line with much institutionalist thinking, Elkins et al. (2009) emphasize the design side. They identify three generic type principles that are said to account for constitutional endurance: flexibility (rules regarding revision), inclusion (more rather than fewer actors), and specificity (more rather than less details). These are important findings from a sophisticated quantitative analysis of one of the most extensive data gathering exercises.

Our two main concerns with regard to the CCP project findings (especially in Elkins et al. 2009), relate to how they define inclusion, on the one hand, and constitutional flexibility, on the other. In terms of the first of these, Elkins et al. (2009) argue that inclusive drafting processes and inclusive constitutional provisions enhance the possibilities for constitutional endurance. Indeed, constitutions 'that generate much debate and discussion among citizens will be those that are likely to be enforced and maintained when pressures for breach arise' (Elkins et al. 2009: 81). Our main issue with their conceptualization insofar as the constitution-making process is concerned relates to how they measure inclusion. They do so by means of a complex proxy which combines elements of the drafting process, the ratification process, and the degree of inclusiveness of the final constitutional document measured in terms of constitutional provisions for instruments of direct democracy. All of these dimensions – both ex-ante and ex-post – are combined into a single indicator which purports to measure inclusiveness. We are also interested in investigating the degree of inclusiveness during the constitution-making process but base our analysis on the measurement of various, separate dimensions, of the constitutional design process (see discussion below) rather than a single composite indicator. In other words, our focus is squarely on the ex-ante process of constitution-making.

Second, central to Elkins et al.'s notion of constitutional flexibility is the distinction they draw between amendment and replacement of the constitution. Amendment, they argue, is when 'actors claim to follow the amending procedure of the existing constitution', while replacement occurs 'when they undertake revision without claiming to follow such procedure' (Elkins et al. 2009: 55). They also make the rather self-evident statement that constitutions endure (i.e. are not replaced) when they are relatively easy to amend, and use ease of amendment as a proxy for constitutional flexibility. As indicators for this variable, they use both the observed amendment rate and the formal amendment procedures of the relevant constitution (Elkins et al. 2009: 100). Our problem here is that often – as our case studies from West Africa later in the book will show – constitutions are amended in such a way as to undermine the key constitutional principles of limited government and separation of powers, typically by giving almost unlimited authority to an executive president. Such amendments, we argue, fit their notion of 'constitutional death' far more readily than a constitutional replacement that remains loyal to more fundamental constitutional principles. A truly flexible constitution is not one that can be amended beyond all recognition.

The CCP project has drawn attention to what we call the *outputs* of the constitution-making process, especially with regard to provisions contained in the text and their subsequent institutionalization (Elkins et al. 2009). This has also been the subject of Lutz's (2007) large-N study of the principles of constitutional design in which the focus is on the actual 'content' of constitutions and how this impacts on what Lutz calls constitutional democracy. The principle of constitutionalism is that of limited government, or in Charles McIlwain's words 'a legal limitation on government ... the antithesis of arbitrary rule' (McIlwain 1939: 21). Constitutionalism means adherence to fundamental constitutional principles, such as respect for human rights, multi-party democracy, separation of powers and rule of law. In modern democracies (normally written) constitutions are expected to embody the shared values of a society. While democracy is not a prerequisite of constitutionalism as non-democratic regimes can also be regulated by constitutional laws and principles, constitutionalism is a necessary condition for democracy as it establishes a set of self-binding procedures to regulate and limit the exercise of political power (Linz and Stepan 1996: 10). In most democracies, written constitutions are designed on the one hand to establish a system of checks and balances between government institutions and on the other to establish a set of fundamental civil and political rights for citizens (Gargarella 2003: 148). Thus, the crafting of new or revised constitutions is often an aspect of democratic transition and consolidation. Indeed, the establishment of broad consensus over the principles of the constitution both within the political elite and within society in general is viewed as one of the preconditions for a stable and consolidated democracy (Weingast 1997).

However, such a consensus may or may not involve a new constitution, while constitutions may or may not be the result of a consensus. First, formal constitutional changes may embody a historic compromise based on consensus, but these changes may, at best, take the form of a relatively minor constitutional amendment. In Sweden what Rustow terms the 'Great Compromise' of 1907 between conservatives (representing landowners, bureaucrats and industrialists) and liberals and radicals (representing the urban working and lower middle classes as well as agrarian constituencies) on voting reform was enshrined in the constitution by means of a little-known amendment enacted in 1909 (Rustow 1970). Similarly, in the Netherlands the compromise reached between the various Christian parties and liberals that allowed manhood suffrage (and five years later universal suffrage) in exchange for constitutional equality for religious schools was enshrined in a constitutional amendment (in 1917), not a new constitution. We must also bear in mind that for democracy to become consolidated over time an informal, but widely-shared consensus may be more important than any formal constitutional change that may have preceded or enabled it. In the case of Sweden, Rustow argues that the acceptance of the new democratic system by all sectors of society, including conservatives, took a generation (Rustow 1970). Finally, new constitutions do not require any far-reaching democratic consensus to be enacted; if such a consensus is absent, constitutions may still be amended and replaced, but they will reflect the will of the powerful, rather than a compromise that encompasses all, or even most sectors of society.

Such considerations mean that we must take a rather nuanced approach to how we investigate the impact of constitutional compromises on the prospects for consolidating democracy. Most importantly, if we are to conduct a large-n study, in the manner of Elkins et al., on the relationship between constitution-making and democratization, we must first be aware that the existence or non-existence of the kind of consensus identified in the previous paragraph may shape *both* the constitution-making process *and* the prospects for consolidation of democracy. We must also bear in mind that constitutionally enshrined compromises that lay the framework for such a consensus are rare and may not easily be identified in a large-N study. The more nuanced case studies of Poland, Spain and Brazil in Chapter 5 and of the Swiss cantons in Chapter 7 will better illustrate how such compromises become institutionalized in democracies.

Turning now to the dynamics of the constitution-making process and its impact, if any, on the consolidation (or non-consolidation) of democracy, we need to investigate how the bargains and deals made between elite actors during constitution-making can best be translated into a broader consensus on democratic constitutional principles that encompasses most, if not all, sectors of society. Advocates of participatory constitution-making hold that public participation in constitution-making is essential for this to occur. Hart (2001: 4) emphasizes the notion of public ownership of the constitution that can come about as a result of participatory constitution-making; Elster, Offe and Preuss argue that 'the perceived legitimacy of the [constitution-making] process will be one determinant of the extent to which the rules are actually obeyed' (Elster, Offe and Preuss 1998: 64); Moehler examines whether citizens' participation in constitution-making is associated with stronger democratic values (Moehler 2008); while Ghai argues that a more participatory process empowers citizens 'by promoting knowledge and respect for the principles of constitutionalism' (Ghai 2006: 3). For Weingast, constitutional restrictions are required in order to ensure that that there are incentives for power-holders to uphold the democratic order rather than subvert it. These restrictions will 'become self-enforcing when citizens hold [them] in high enough esteem that they are willing to defend them by withdrawing support from the sovereign when he attempts to violate [them]' (Weingast 1997: 251). From these discussions, we would expect that the more the public are involved in the constitution-making process, in terms of electing the constitution-making body, participating in its discussions and approving the final constitutional draft by referendum, the more citizens will internalize constitutional norms and defend them from authoritarian abuse.

However, it is also possible to present the counter-argument that it is political elites, not citizens, that play the main role in the success or failure of the constitution-making process. There is much in the literature about the role of pact-making during the process of transition to democracy in which rival elites take centre stage and strike a deal that determines the subsequent power-sharing arrangement (Karl 1990, Karl and Schmitter 1991, O'Donnell and Schmitter 1986). Such pacts depend for their success on the capacity of their makers to reach a deal behind closed doors without the clamour of popular demands forcing them to take the hard line demanded by some of their most vehement supporters. The implication of an elite-centred perspective is that constitution-making is a particular kind of elite pact and, like all pacts, the arrangements and compromises made between the relevant elites will be the main determinant of the future prospects for democratization. According to this rival hypothesis, the *less* the public input into the constitution-making process, at all stages of the process, the greater the chances of consolidating democracy. A more broadly-based consensus on the principles of constitutionalism would come later, as the masses, as well as elites, gradually internalize the rules of the game in such a way that they become self-enforcing.

Constitutional engineering has also been the focus of another group of institutional analysts whose focus is on the role of constitution-making in the management of conflict. In the 1980s and 1990s a number of important studies on constitutional engineering in difficult political settings fuelled a vigorous debate between advocates of 'accommodation' versus supporters of 'integration' as the optimal principles of constitutional design in deeply divided societies. The advocates of accommodation or 'consociationalists' argue for a constitutional design based on the principles of executive power sharing through grand coalitions, segmental autonomy in the cultural sector, proportionality in the voting system and in public sector employment and the minority veto (Lijphart 1977). Adherents of 'integration', on the other hand, prioritize the strengthening of cross-communal ties and reject the separation that they believe the consociational model engenders. They prefer a preferential electoral system based on territorial constituencies, such as the Alternative Vote or the Single Transferable Vote, as the best means of promoting inter-ethnic cooperation through broad-based parties and of excluding extremists who appeal to a narrow sectarian constituency (Horowitz 1985, Sisk 1996, Reilly 2001).

As well as the *content* of the constitution, there is also a debate about the impact of the *constitution-making process* on the prospects for conflict resolution. Empirical research on this topic has recently been carried out by the Princeton based research group on Constitution Writing and Conflict Resolution, who have analysed constitution writing in post-conflict settings.[2] Their analysis is based on a dataset of 195 cases of constitution writing between 1975 and 2002 and examines variables such as the type of constitution-making body and whether or not there has been any significant public consultation in terms of whether they have any impact on conflict resolution. Their research suggests that constitutional bargains struck in a conflict resolution setting cannot be conducted according to participatory ideals. Another important finding is that in conflict resolution cases the use of interim arrangements is preferable to full-scale efforts to draft a new constitution (Widner 2008). Only later when passions have diminished is it possible to address the process in a more logical manner and thereby increase the possibility that the eventual product will create a framework for accountable government (Widner 2008).

Overall, many of the same questions arise when looking at the relationship between constitution-making and conflict resolution as crop up when we explore the linkages between constitution-making and the consolidation of democracy. In both studies, we are interested in crafting a compromise between a number of parties engaged in conflict and ensuring that such a compromise forms the basis for an enduring consensus. The only difference is that in our so-called 'conflict resolution' cases a) the intensity of the conflict typically spills over into violence, and b) the consensus achieved may be limited to preventing the recurrence of violence and may not include a deeper democratic compromise. However, in certain cases the resolution of a violent conflict also involved democratization; our vignettes in Chapter 3 on the 1848 constitution in Switzerland, the 1950 constitution in India and the 1997 constitution in South Africa are all examples of how conflict-resolution and the crafting of democratic principles can go hand in hand.

Methodologically too, we face many of the same problems exploring the link between constitution-making and conflict resolution as we do in exploring the link between constitution-making and the consolidation of democracy. First, many instances of conflict resolution involved compromises that did not require wholesale replacement of the constitution; in a number of cases simply changing

---

2   http://www.princeton.edu/~pcwcr/.

the election law may suffice. Even the so-called Taif Agreement of 1989 that saw an end to the war in Lebanon was implemented through a constitutional amendment, rather than by replacing the entire constitution. Second, constitutions that are enacted in the aftermath of a conflict may be intended not as a mechanism for resolving the conflict, but instead as a means of institutionalizing the gains of the strongest party. In such cases the constitution is a product of the conflict dynamic, rather than a solution, and it is likely to fail as a long-term instrument for solving conflict.

## Constitution-Making: A Framework of Analysis

In this section we try to elaborate a framework for the analysis of constitution-making process. We begin with the observation that since constitutions prescribe a political order and establish the basic rules of institutional engagement, bargaining over constitutional design is likely to be a highly salient political event. Although the constitution-making process is sometimes dominated by a single individual, such as Solon in the Athenian polis or De Gaulle with the French Fifth Republic, as we hinted in the previous section it is sometimes the result of a specific political bargain between disparate and competing elites. In fact the concept of a constitutional bargain has been fruitfully explored by William Riker in his seminal analysis of federations (1964). Riker was particularly interested in the constraints under which territorial elites negotiated a federal bargain. We also look at constitutional events that involve explicit political bargains, but our analysis is not restricted to federations even though in the case studies we do cover some federal systems (e.g. Chapters 7 and 8). Our main interest, however, is the many different ways in which political elites create constitution-making bodies during politically salient constitutional moments. A first issue to address will be to distinguish between the different types of constitutional events and specify the type of constitutional event at the core of our inquiry.

The focus of our investigation is both on foundational constitutional events that define an entirely new polity and on transformational constitutional events that introduce significant constitutional transformation within a given polity. Our investigation will consist of two parts. First (in Chapter 2) we shall look at the broader universe of events across the world and develop a typology of these events in terms of how the various aspects of the constitution-making process relate to each other. Having developed our typology we then (in Chapter 3) explore the differential impact of these types of event on the twin processes of democratization and conflict resolution. The total number of constitutional events we explore stands at 160. Despite the misgivings expressed in the previous section that many cases of constitutional amendment can be as fundamental in scope as replacement of the entire constitution, in this (large n) study we will restrict our subset of events to those defined by Elkins et al. as replacement events. Such events are those in which constitution-makers undertake a revision of the constitution without following the amending procedure of the existing constitution. This is because in such a large sample of events it is impossible to distinguish between fundamental or 'first order' constitutional amendments and less significant, cosmetic amendments.

In the second part of this book, we take a more nuanced approach by looking more closely at how actors and institutions interact in a number of selected constitution-making events in West Africa (Chapter 4), Spain, Poland and Brazil (Chapter 5), Ecuador, Venezuela and Bolivia (Chapter 6), in the Swiss cantons (Chapter 7) and at the supranational level of the European Union (Chapter 8). While our focus here is still on fundamental constitutional change, we also cover (in Chapter 4 on West Africa) changes that do not formally count as replacement, but still represent a significant transformation of the constitutional order. The nuanced approach that our small n case studies permit also allows us to explore not only the interactions between the constitution-making processes and outcomes, but also the pre-existing political and legal context. Of particular interest here is the more informal understanding of constitutionalism that we touched upon in the previous section and that shapes both processes and outcomes. Finally, it will allow us to look in greater depth at what we mean by the stability of a constitution by relating the notion of stability less to procedural features and more to the extent to which the constitution adheres to principles of constitutionalism such as limited government and separation of powers.

The constitution-making process is a dynamic one, involving a series of complex interactions amongst and between political leaders and citizens. For the analyst, this implies focusing on the role of the key political actors involved and their specific mandates, the input of the public or the lack thereof, as well as the process by which acquiescence is achieved on the final constitutional package. In this connection the following three operational dimensions can be identified:

*a) Mode of Representation*

Since universal participation is in most cases impracticable, representation procedures have to be established in order to select the type of body entrusted with negotiating and drafting a new constitution. Here we draw a distinction between three distinct modes of representation. First, governing elites may appoint themselves as the principal constitutional designers. A common method is for the Executive to appoint a Constitutional Committee or a variant thereof. In other cases it is the legislature that appoints the committee. The crucial point is that regular parliaments are not elected for this purpose and the decision of a legislature to convert itself into a constitution-making body is a decision taken by the political elite. Such modes of representation we refer to as *elite appointment*. This can be contrasted with a body that is directly elected with the express purpose of elaborating a new constitution, whether or not it carries out other legislative functions at the same time. This mode of representation, we refer to as *direct election*. Between the poles there are other modes of representation, such as bodies that consist of delegates selected to represented territorial units, electoral colleges or a national conferences. In such intermediate cases, we describe the mode of representation as *indirect selection*.

### b) Style of the Constitution-Making Process

Two extremes can be defined in terms of whether the process is broadly open and participatory or whether it is an exclusive and largely closed affair. An *open* style is one in which citizens not only have the theoretical right to comment upon the constitution-making process and submit suggestions, but actually exercise that right, while a *closed* style refers to a 'behind-closed-doors' scenario in which public consultation and public input is minimal. This generates two conflicting modes of communicative interaction; the more closed the process the more likely a bargaining style of negotiation will dominate. On the other hand, the more open the process the more likely a deliberative style of debate can emerge. A closed bargaining setting induces a style of personalized negotiation and potential horse-trading (which can be necessary during a conflict resolution setting for instance). In a more public and open deliberative setting, discursive interaction tends to be shaped by the need to argue (rather than bargain) in terms of the common good.

### c) Mode of Legitimation

This refers to how the constitution is to be ratified and become law. Another continuum can be identified here that ranges from instances in which the final product of a constitution-making process is ratified by political elites (e.g. the state executives themselves) to an alternative ratification mechanism involving a *popular vote* by the citizens. In the first case, the constitution-making body itself ratifies the draft constitution whilst in the second case the constitutional draft is ratified by the people in a referendum. The first mode of legitimation we refer to as *elite adoption*. There is of course an intermediate mode that we refer to as *institutional ratification* in which a parallel institutional body, such as the Parliament or a Constitution Court, has to approve the constitutional draft.

How the three dimensions are configured give rise to multiple models of constitution-making processes. One of our research goals is to investigate patterns of association in terms of the three dimensions outlined above (we do this in Chapter 2). Another goal is to examine linkages between the three dimensions of constitution-making and various substantive outcomes (this is done in Chapter 3 and the various case study chapters in Part 2 of the book).

## An Historical Example

Our framework has identified three main dimensions along which it is possible to examine the constitution-making processes. These include the mode of representation (political leaders versus an elected assembly), the type of communicative interaction (bargaining versus deliberative settings), and legitimation procedures (ratification by state executive versus popular vote), and various intermediate positions along each continuum. As with most social science concepts, these categories are not fixed and a blurred area exists between them. We further develop the dimensions and their operationalization in Chapter 2. At this stage, however, our aim is to provide an illustrative overview of the types of patterns we wish to investigate. We do this by means of comparative *vignette* of two well-known historical examples: the Philadelphia Convention in the United States and the French Revolutionary Assemblies.

Both the Philadelphia Convention of 1787 and the French Revolutionary Assemblies (Constituent Assembly of 1789–1791 and the National Convention of 1792–1795) occurred at roughly the same time and ushered in constitutional transformations of the first order. In terms of their origins, both experiences occurred at a time of deep conflict, though the French case took place in the midst of revolution and external war. Thus, from a comparative perspective the delegates meeting in post-revolution America worked under less pressure and in a less hostile environment (Bowen 1966, Jillson 1988) than the French Assemblée Constituante, under the threatening menace of the Parisian mob (Mitchell 1988, Fitzsimmons 1994). The significance of the constitutional packages (various constitutions in the case of revolutionary France) also differed considerably. While the convention in Philadelphia gave birth to the most durable and arguably the most successful constitution of the modern era, the French context produced an unstable constitutional order that fuelled the reign of terror and the ascendancy of Napoleon. Our analytical concern, however, is with the operational procedures of these two historic 18th-century constitution-making experiences rather than the contextual origins. Let us now focus on the three operational dimensions that we identified above.

In terms of the mode of representation the two cases differed. One immediate difference is that in the US case the delegates were sent to the convention by the states with a mandate to reform the Articles of Confederation rather than draw up a new constitutional order. From the citizens' perspective, the delegates were elected or appointed by the states' representative institutions (legislature and/ or executive). It was not the state leaders who negotiated the new constitutional package but rather the indirectly appointed delegates. In France's first constituent assembly of 1789, the delegates represented functional interests (i.e. the three estates) rather than territorial interests. In terms of the mode of representation the most interesting case is France's second experience with a convention type body. In the midst of social turmoil and imminent civil war, the National Convention of 1792–1795 was directly elected by the people and entrusted with drawing up a new constitutional settlement. It was, in this regard, France's first election by universal male suffrage. In contrast to 1789, the delegates considered themselves representatives of the nation of France rather than a particular territorial or functional constituency.

It appears that the mode of representation had a direct effect on the second dimension, what we refer to as the style of constitution-making and its corollary, the mode of communicative interaction. In the French cases the proceedings, which involved at times more than a thousand delegates, were open and under the glare of publicity, whereas in Philadelphia the debates took place behind closed doors and were kept secret. Elster (1999) has convincingly argued that these distinct settings produced diverging modes of debating: speakers in France argued in terms of the common good and lofty philosophical ideals while their American counterparts bargained from positions of self-interest. The outcome, according to Elster, was a false and unstable consensus in France and a viable negotiated compromise in the US. Yet these two cases cannot constitute a 'recipe' since, as we will see in subsequent chapters, other countries followed similar processes with the inverse end-results.

Our last dimension is that of legitimation. How is a constitutional package to be ratified and adopted? In the US, the ratification procedure was approved by the institutional organs of the states (legislatures and state conventions). There was one exception in which the legitimacy of a popular vote was sought however. Intriguingly, it was precisely in the case of Rhode Island where the US constitution was rejected by a referendum. In France the constituent assembly had discussed whether to ratify by popular vote but in the end the constitution was submitted to the King in 1791, who accepted it. Two years later the National Convention, whose first act was to abolish the monarchy, produced France's first republic constitution of 1793. In the midst of the reign of terror the constitution was ratified by a popular vote. However, despite being ratified, France's first historic republican constitution was eventually never applied.

The two historical cases present notable variation in terms of distinct operational procedures of the constitution-making process. It should be noted that the French assemblies also morphed into legislative and executive organs, though the context of civil strife and war helps to explain such dynamics. From a normative perspective, the French revolutionary assemblies come closest to a 'pure' regime in terms of democratic criteria such as direct election, open and deliberative discussion, as well as democratic legitimation through popular vote. Incidentally, they combined three features of modern democratic theory that are emphasized to varying degrees by competing representative, deliberative, and participatory models of democracy (Fung 2007).

The vignette of these two celebrated historical cases of constitutional transformation has served to illustrate the importance of the three dimensions of constitution-making that form the basis of our large n approach. The next chapter will elaborate on this theme. But the historical example also serves another purpose, which is to underscore, albeit in brief form, the comparative method at the core of our enquiry. This is best understood as the focus on the presence or absence of specific characteristics by means of a comparison of multiple cases. In matching and contrasting the cases, our aim is to identify common features that may be linked to some of the substantive outcomes. In Chapter 3, we do this by employing the techniques of Qualitative Comparative Analysis, which allows for the comparison of a more extensive subset of cases, typically between 30–60 cases. However, the logic of the comparative method is most extensively deployed in the in-depth case studies that form Part 2 of the book. The conclusion then ties back our general findings to the dimensions, and substantive outcomes, discussed in this chapter.

# Chapter 2
# Patterns of Constitution-Making over Time and Space

Fernando Mendez and Jonathan Wheatley

**Introduction**

In Chapter 1 we reviewed the state-of-the-art in terms of theoretical approaches to the constitution-making process and its outcomes. In doing so we derived from the literature a number of tentative hypotheses as to the relationship between this process and two particular outcomes that we are interested in: democracy and conflict resolution. We then identified three key variables that we deemed to be defining features of the constitution-making process: the mode of representation, the style of the process and the mode of legitimation. Finally, we used two well-known historical examples (those of France and the USA) to illustrate ways in which these three variables may be associated.

In this chapter we investigate in a more comprehensive manner the patterns of association between the three features of constitution-making identified in Chapter 1. We will leave it to Chapter 3 to explore how the constitution-making process may or may not affect the substantive outcomes we are interested in: transition to democracy (or entrenchment of authoritarianism) and the resolution (or escalation) of conflict.

In order to carry out the tasks we have set ourselves, we will proceed as follows. First, in order to obtain a picture of how constitution-making events are distributed over time, we shall further refine Elster's typology of waves of constitution-making described in Chapter 1, by identifying our own constitution-making waves. Next, we shall use our wave-based chronological distribution of constitution-making events as well as a geographically-based distribution that is based on sub-continents to derive a representative sample of events across space and time. The third step will be to introduce a typology of constitution-making bodies based on what we earlier identified as the mode of representation. From there we will identify a number of 'clusters' in which the same forum of constitution-making is used in geographically or temporally proximate events. Fourth, we will operationalize the key independent variables that we will use for our subsequent analysis: the mode of representation, the style and the mode of legitimation. We will then look at the patterns of association between these variables and, in doing so, challenge the assumption of the CCP project that all three variables can be reduced to a single underlying variable of inclusion. We show that while the mode of representation and the style are rather closely correlated positively, the mode of representation and the mode of legitimation are actually negatively correlated with one another. We conclude that in order to investigate the outcomes of the constitution-making process we need to focus on two independent variables: the mode of representation and the style of deliberation on the one hand and the mode of legitimation on the other. The chapter ends with a short conclusion to summarize the findings.


## Waves of Constitution-Making

As mentioned in Chapter 1, Elster (1995) identifies seven distinct waves of constitution-making in the modern age. He identifies the first wave with the making of the first modern constitutions (various individual North American states, the United States, Poland and France) between 1780 and 1791, while with the second wave he associates constitution-making in the aftermath of the 1848 revolutions in Europe. The post-Versailles constitutions after the First World War constitute the third wave, while the fourth occurred after the Second World War when Japan, Germany and Italy adopted new constitutions under the strict supervision of the victorious allies. Elster classifies the decolonization process in the former British and French colonial empires as a fifth wave which began immediately after the Second World War and reached its apogee in the 1960s. Finally, the sixth and seventh waves are characterized by constitution-making in the aftermath of transition from authoritarian rule: the sixth being associated with the so-called third wave of democratization in Southern Europe in the 1970s and the seventh and final wave occurring in the beginning of the 1990s after the collapse of communism in Eastern and Central Europe (Elster 1995: 368–9).

For the purposes of this book, we will adapt Elster's waves somewhat. First we will extend the first wave into the 1840s so as to include the wave of constitution-making that is associated with the independence of most Latin American states and the associated constitution-making activity in the 1820s and 1830s. Also, for reasons of simplicity we will delimit waves by clear time intervals as this will make analysis easier. Our seven waves are the following:

> Wave 1: 1780–1844. First Wave: Early constitutions of Europe, the USA and Latin America.
> Wave 2: 1845–1899. This period begins with the 1848 revolutions in Europe and includes constitution-making processes in the latter part of the nineteenth century.
> Wave 3: 1900–1939. This wave reaches its apogee in 1918–1922 with the elaboration of the constitutions of newly-created (or recreated) states in Europe after the Treaty of Versailles.
> Wave 4: 1940–1954. This wave not only includes the making of post-War constitutions in Germany, Italy and Japan, but also the making of the first decolonialization constitutions in India, Burma and Sri Lanka.

Wave 5: 1955–1969. This wave includes the bulk of the constitutions drawn up for former British and French colonies in Africa and Asia. It also includes the making of second constitutions in many of these countries, as often the independence constitutions were short-lived and soon made way for new constitutional arrangements.

Wave 6: 1970–1989. This wave includes the constitutions elaborated in Southern Europe and Latin America during the process of transition to democracy after a period of authoritarian rule.

Wave 7: 1990-present day. This wave includes the constitutions that were elaborated following the fall of communism in Central and Eastern Europe and the collapse of the USSR. Also included is the wave of constitution-making in Africa that occurred in the immediate aftermath of the Cold War as authoritarian leaders either fell from power or themselves initiated some kind of transition process.

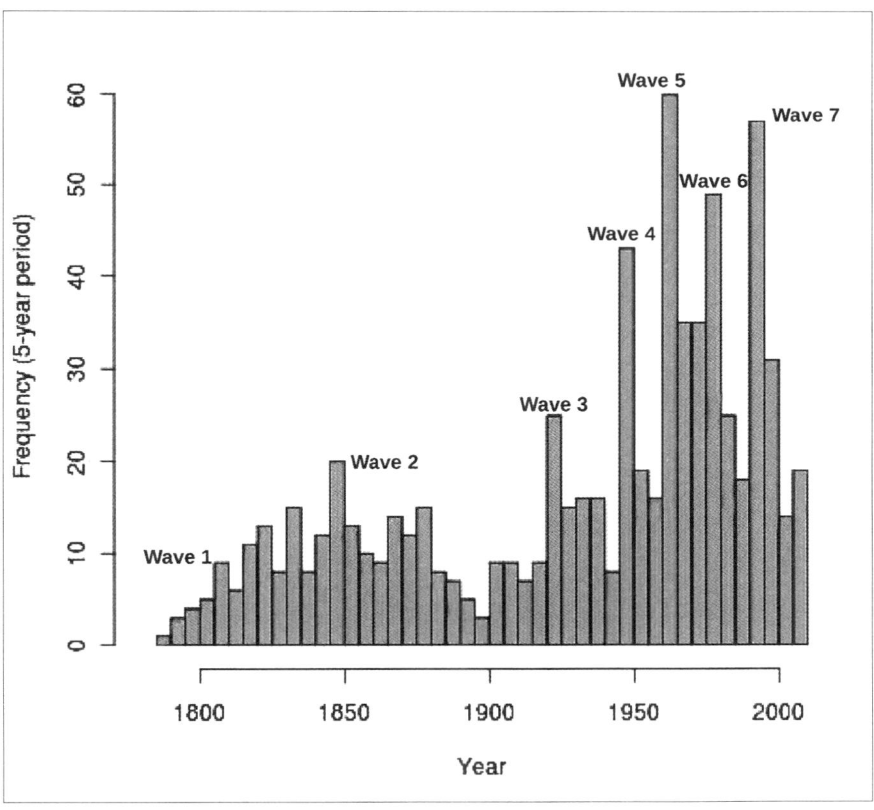


**Figure 2.1    Waves of constitution-making (global sample)**

Throughout the world as a whole the wave-like nature of constitution-making is illustrated in Figure 2.1. Using data from the Comparative Constitutions Project based at the University of Illinois[1] and adding supplementary data from other sources, we were able to identify 746 cases in which new constitutions were drafted at national (state) level since 1780. Figure 2.1 shows the distribution of these events in each five-year time period.

## Creating a Representative Sample of Constitution-Making Bodies

It would be our ideal to examine all 746 constitution-making events and identify the type of constitution-making body for each event. As the relevant data is simply not available, we were obliged to be far less ambitious and focus on a representative sample of 160 events (just over 20 per cent of the total). The events were selected according to time (i.e. the wave of constitution-making, see above) and space (subcontinent). Due to the proliferation of short-lived and temporary constitutions in Latin America and Western Europe during the nineteenth century (96 of 184 Latin American constitutions and 66 out of 96 Western European constitutions were drafted before 1900) and the consequent risk that our sample may be skewed, it was decided to correct for this by (i) removing from the sample constitutions that endured for less than five years (leaving just 635 out of 746 constitutions) and (ii) giving a weighting for selection within each time period (wave) that reflects the total number of sovereign states that existed at the time. For a precise explanation of how the sampling procedure was carried out, see the Appendix to this chapter. Corresponding to the sampling criteria, 12 events were sampled from Wave 1, 14 events from Wave 2, 16 events from Wave 3, 12 events from Wave 4, 27 from Wave 5, 37 from Wave 6 and 42 from Wave 7. In terms of sub-continent, 15 cases were selected from Western Europe, 14 from Eastern Europe, nine from the (former) Soviet Union, 47 from Africa, two from North America,[2] 30 from Latin America, four from Oceania, seven from South Asia, thirteen from East Asia, nine from the Middle East and ten from the West Indies.

## A Typology of Constitution-Making Bodies

The classification of constitution-making bodies is complicated by the diversity of such bodies as well as the ambiguous terminology that is sometimes used in the field of constitution-making. Thus, the term 'constitutional convention' on the one hand describes a certain type of constitution-making body (see below),

---

1   Source:   Comparative   Constitutions   Project   at   <http://www. comparativeconstitutionsproject.org>, accessed 1 February 2012.

2   By 'North America' we mean the United States and Canada.

but on the other has a quite different meaning in that it may refer not to any sort of body but instead to a set of informal procedural agreements that have constitutional force in countries such as the United Kingdom (Marshall 1987: 3). The aim of this section is not to invent a generic term for all constitution-making bodies, but instead to develop a clear and unambiguous *typology* of such entities.

Within the literature, terms such as 'constitutional convention', 'constitutional assembly' and 'constituent assembly' are often used to refer to ideal types of constitution-making bodies that are based on principles of representation and democracy. Jon Elster's typology is illustrative here. Elster distinguishes between three (or possibly four) types of constituent assembly. First he identifies 'constitutional conventions', which are 'assemblies called into being exclusively for [the] purpose [of constitution-making] and devoting themselves exclusively to that task'. He then distinguishes constitutional conventions from constituent legislatures, which are 'bodies that have combined constituent and legislative functions'. He further distinguishes between mandated constituent assemblies, which are created with the explicit mandate of writing a constitution, and self-created assemblies, which are created for other purposes but arrogate to themselves constitution-making functions (Elster 2006: 182). Finally he identifies a subset of constitutional conventions that convert themselves into ordinary legislatures once the constitution is passed. He refers to these 'former constitutional conventions' as self-created legislating assemblies, although these should not be considered as constitution-making bodies as they are no longer vested with constitution-making powers. As all constituent conventions are mandated, this leaves us with three types of constituent assemblies: 1) constitutional conventions, or pure constituent assemblies that undertake exclusively constitution-making tasks and do not simultaneously function as a legislature; 2) mandated constituent legislatures that are set up explicitly for constitution-making, but simultaneously carry out other legislative activities; and 3) self-created constituent legislatures, typically regular parliaments that decide subsequent to their election to vest themselves with constitution-making powers. In this third type citizens remain somewhat uncoupled from the constitution-making process to the extent that during the elections in which the assembly is chosen, voters have no idea that they are voting for a constitution-making body.

However, there are several weaknesses to Elster's typology. First, the terms he uses are not defined clearly enough and do not sufficiently distinguish between types of constitution-making body that are fundamentally different. Thus, within the genus 'constitutional convention' no distinction is made between the directly elected assemblies recently established in Colombia, Venezuela, Bolivia and Ecuador and indirectly elected bodies such as the Indian Constituent Assembly of 1946. Second, these terms exclude many other types of constitution-making body that are also of interest to researchers. As well as elected constituent assemblies and legislatures, the Princeton University team researching constitution writing and conflict resolution identify *national conferences* as another possible forum for constitution-making (Widner 2007). National conferences are 'unelected but nonetheless representative' bodies that consist of a large number of delegates from a wide range of political and societal organizations and featured prominently in the transition process in much of Africa (particularly Francophone Africa) in the early 1990s. Finally, some constitution-making bodies are hardly representative of the population at all. Ginsburg et al. (2009) identify a subset of cases in which constitutions are drafted in an executive-centred process in which representative bodies play little or no role. Similarly, there are even cases in which no formally-constituted constitution-making body exists at all and instead the principles of the constitutions are drawn up through ad hoc meetings between various elite representatives, while the text itself is elaborated by legal specialists hired by these leaders. Such a process was common in elaborating the constitutions of many of the newly-independent colonies of Africa during the post-war period.

As mentioned previously, the typology that this book employs draws a clear distinction between three broad types of constitution-making body, according to what we term the mode of representation: bodies that are directly elected, those that are indirectly selected in a broadly representative manner, and those that are appointed by elites with little regard for representativeness. In addition there is a residual category for cases in which no formal constitution-making body is constituted. Finer distinctions can now be drawn within each broad category according to how the body is formed, allowing the identification of the following ten types of constitution-making body:

*Elite appointed*
0.  Residual category. No constitution-making body. The constitution is elaborated as a result of face-to-face meetings between members of elites.
1.  Executive Committee: The constitution-making body is a committee appointed by the executive.
2.  Executive-appointed Assembly: A nominally representative body appointed by the executive that has been deliberately stacked in its composition to reflect the interests of incumbent power-holders.
3.  Round Table: A body that unites the leaders of all main parties and/or factions, but these factions are represented equally irrespective of electoral support.
4.  Parliament or a committee thereof. This corresponds to Elster's notion of the self-created constituent legislature. Regular parliaments, although directly elected, are not directly elected *as constituent assemblies* and the decision to convert the parliament or a committee thereof into a constitution-making body *is a decision taken by the political elite itself.*

*Indirectly selected*
5.  Delegates from states: Delegates representing territorial units within a federal state along the model of the Federal Convention of the USA.

6. National conference (identified above): Large, broad-based body drawn from all sectors of society, including members of most or all elected bodies, civic/economic organizations, professional associations, traditional leaders, women's groups and/or religious organizations.
7. Electoral college: Body indirectly selected from at least one representative body (local councils, lower house, upper house) designed to represent each party or grouping in proportion to its popular support as expressed by the election to the relevant body. The Indian constitution-making body convened in 1946 (see above) is an example of this.

*Directly elected*
8. Mandated constituent legislature (identified by Elster, see above): A parliament that is specially elected to draft a new constitution but also carries out other legislative functions.
9. Pure Constituent Assembly: Directly elected body that only performs constitution-making functions, corresponding to Elster's notion (see above) of a constitutional convention, although unlike Elster's constitutional convention, assemblies belonging to this type *must* be directly elected. Typically they exist in parallel to a separate legislative body.

Of the 160 constitution-making events identified in the previous section, in fifteen cases there was no constitution-making body (i.e. the event corresponded to the 'residual category' identified above). In 55 further cases, the constitution-making body was elite-appointed: 21 bodies were classified as executive committees, 13 as executive appointed assemblies, nine bodies were round tables and in 11 cases it was the regular parliament that elaborated the constitution. In one case the body included features of more than one type of body, but was still classified as elite-appointed. In 28 cases, the constitution-making body was indirectly selected: eight of these bodies consisted of delegates from states, eight were national conferences and ten were electoral colleges. In two cases the body included features of more than one type body but was still classified as indirectly selected  In 62 cases, the body was directly elected: in 35 cases it also assumed legislative powers and was therefore a mandated constituent legislature, while in 23 cases it was a pure constituent assembly. In two cases, insufficient information was available to decide whether the body was a mandated constituent legislature or a pure constituent assembly, while in another two cases the body included features of different types, but direct election was the dominant form. These findings are summarized in Table 2.1.

**Table 2.1      Types of constitution-making body**

| Type of constitution-making body | Frequency |
| --- | --- |
| Elite, non-constitution-making body | 15 |
| Executive committee | 21 |
| Executive-appointed assembly | 13 |
| Round Table | 9 |
| Parliament | 11 |
| Delegates from states/cantons | 8 |
| National conference | 8 |
| Electoral college | 10 |
| Constituent assembly as parliament | 35 |
| Pure constituent assembly | 23 |
| Mixed (elite appointed) | 1 |
| Mixed (indirectly selected) | 2 |
| Mixed (directly elected) | 4 |
| Total | 160 |

Looking at the geographical distribution of constitution-making events, as well as their spread across time, we see that a number of events that are characterized by particular types of constitution-making body are clustered in time and space. Of the 15 events in which no constitution-making body was established and the constitution was elaborated as a result of face-to-face meetings between members of elites, nine out of 15 events occurred during the period 1955–1969 (Wave 5) and seven occurred in Africa. This confirms our earlier assertion that this type of process was most commonly used in elaborating the constitutions of newly-independent colonies during the post-war period.

The use of elite-appointed executive committees was also prevalent in Africa during the post-colonial period, although events using this forum tended to occur somewhat later. Ten out of 21 such events occurred in Africa, 11 occurred during 1970–1989 (Wave 6) and six occurred subsequently (Wave 7). As we shall see in Chapter 3, this group of events is typically associated with modern-day, non-democratic regimes, especially in Africa.

The use of another type of elite-appointed forum, the round table, is also prevalent in post-colonial Africa. Six out of nine events involving a round table were located in Africa, all after 1960. This probably reflects a need to bring together rival elite factions, but is also symptomatic of a tendency to exclude the masses from the constitution-making process.

Probably the most interesting clusters of events are those that involve a directly-elected forum for constitution-making. The French Constitutional Convention that elaborated the 1793 constitution can be held up as a prototype for an open type of participatory constitution-making body that was based on the notion of popular sovereignty and was elected by universal male suffrage. This model was later adopted in a number of Western European and Latin American countries later on during Wave 1, including foundational constitutions in Norway (1814), Portugal (1821), Mexico (1823) and Uruguay (1830). Directly elected constitution-making bodies (asambleas constituyentes) were used frequently in Latin America during the nineteenth century (Waves 1 and 2) as political instability and frequent coups d'état meant that one short-lived constitution followed the next in many countries. Both types of directly elected body (mandated constituent legislatures and pure constituent assemblies) were used.

During Wave 3 in Europe, directly elected constitution-making bodies, typically mandated constituent legislatures, predominated. In the elaboration of the post-World War I constitutions in Germany (1919), Austria (1920), Georgia (1921), Poland (1921), Turkey (1921), Yugoslavia (1921), Latvia (1922), Lithuania (1922) and Spain (1931) the format of a mandated constituent legislatures was used. In all, ten out of 16 cases in Wave 3 used this type of body to elaborate a constitution. Pure constituent assemblies, on the other hand, are particularly prevalent in Latin America. Altogether 12 out of 23 constitution-making events that used this forum are located in Latin America. Early examples include Mexico (1857), Venezuela (1864) and Peru (1867), and, although the use of this forum diminished somewhat during the first half of the twentieth century, it became more prevalent again after 1970 and was used in the recent events in Venezuela (1999), Ecuador (2008) and Bolivia (2009), which are the subject of Chapter 6.

While bodies consisting of delegates from states or cantons are relatively rare fora for constitution-making, even in federal states, those that do exist have a clear pedigree and were most commonly used in the earlier waves. The Philadelphia Constitutional Convention (1788) that gathered together representatives of constituent states in a federal system provided the prototype for other similar constitution-making events in the nineteenth century (especially Wave 2), including Venezuela (1830), Switzerland (1848), Argentina (1853), Canada (1867), and Australia (where a constitutional convention was convened in 1891 but initially failed to pass a constitution).

Finally, the French Constituent Assembly that drafted the 1791 French Constitution was based on representatives from the Three Estates (nobility, clergy and commoners) and while this model was rarely used subsequently in the same form, a version of it was adopted by the national conferences in Francophone Africa in the early 1990s (Wave 7), when representatives of a number of different social groups were included in the constitution-making process. This resemblance has already been noted by Pearl Robinson. For Robinson, the intellectuals that shaped the National Conferences in Francophone Africa 'were the strategists who perceived that the Estates-General provided an appealing framework for structuring a democratic transition' (Robinson 1994). All eight cases from our representative sample in which this forum were used are located in Africa (Francophone Africa in seven out of the eight cases) and all events occurred after 1990 during the post-Cold War period of democratization.

The existence of these clusters appears to demonstrate that ideas and ideological movements play a major role in determining how the constitution-making process unfolds. The French Revolution appears to have brought about a 'contagion effect' in terms of the liberal, republican and democratic ideals that emerged from the various intellectual currents inspired by it, which impacted upon the constitution-making process in the early nineteenth century both in Europe and in the newly-independent states of Latin America. Despite Napoleon's tyranny, his subsequent defeat and the restoration of the monarchy in France, these ideals experienced a revival with the Paris revolution of July 1830. In Chapter 7, we will see how the 1830 revolution and the ideas it embodied inspired the liberal revival movement in the Swiss cantons, which in turn led many cantons to renew their constitutions by means of a directly elected constituent assembly. They also continued to inspire the constitution-making process in Latin America and elsewhere.

In their analysis of the impact of design factors on the endurance of constitutions, Elkins et al. warn of the potential pitfall of 'unavoidable endogeneity'. They argue that '[b]ecause many of the key design elements will be a product of choices of constitutional designers, they are likely to reflect underlying conditions that may themselves be conducive to constitutional endurance' (Elkins et al. 2009: 78). In terms of our own investigation into the impact of the constitution-making process on the political regime, we must make a similar caveat: namely that *both* the process of constitutional design (including the body that is entrusted with the process) *and* the post-constitution outcome in terms of the evolution of the political regime may reflect the prevailing ideological trend. Both process and output may be swayed by 'winds of change' that alter our conception of the relationship between citizens and the state.

In Chapter 1, we suggested that the capacity of a society to reach a minimal consensus on the limits of government may shape *both* the constitution-making process *and* the prospects for the consolidation of democracy. Here we make a similar point in terms of ideology. Returning to the central question of this book – whether or not the constitution-making process matters – we are now armed with a couple of hypotheses as to why it may *not* matter, or, at least, may not matter so much. 'Vaccinated' in such a way against a temptation to assume an automatic link between the constitution-making process and outcomes, it is now time to return to the central aim of the book, which is to explore whether such links do indeed exist. In order to do so, we must first attempt to define and operationalize our key independent variable – the constitution-making process.

## Operationalization

In Chapter 1 we provided an overview of the three dimensions at the core of our analysis of the constitution-making process. These were the mode of representation, which could vary from little or virtually no representation, as in the case of a body directly appointed by a president, to a fully representative, directly-elected constitution-making body. In terms of style of constitution-making, the distinction was between open processes and closed styles. Lastly, for the mode of legitimation we distinguished between three types of ratification mechanisms in terms of the degree of popular input. This ranged from little or no popular input when the constitution was adopted by elites, to an intermediate stage whereby some form of institutional ratification was conducted, and lastly a mode which maximized popular input through the mechanism of a ratification referendum.

In the above-cited work that seeks to explain why constitutions endure, Elkins et al. identify what they term 'inclusion' as a potential independent variable. They define inclusion as 'the breadth of participation in formulating the constitutional agreement and in the ongoing enforcement of it' (Elkins et al. 2009: 78). Inclusion therefore involves not only the constitution-making process itself, but also the manner in which the constitution, once adopted, operates. They use the following indicators to operationalize this variable: i) whether a publicly elected body deliberates, ii) whether the ratification procedure involves a public referendum, iii) whether the public is involved in the election of the head of state and first chamber of the legislature, iv) whether the constitution involves mechanisms of direct democracy and v) whether the public can challenge the constitutionality of the legislation (Elkins et al. 2009: 98). Testing the hypothesis that 'constitution-making processes that are highly open and inclusionary ... increase citizens' awareness and regard for the document as well as their confidence that *other* citizens have developed the same awareness and respect' (Elkins et al. 2009: 97) and that therefore inclusion is likely to contribute positively to the possibility that the constitution will endure, they show that 'constitutions written under inclusive conditions and that also seem to incorporate inclusive provisions, are more likely to survive than those that do not' (Elkins et al. 2009: 139).

However, 'inclusion' is a complex concept and we are yet to be convinced that the five indicators listed in the previous paragraph indeed constitute a single underlying variable. Given that the focus of this book is the constitution-making *process* rather than the subsequent functioning of the constitution, we limit our analysis to exploring whether or not the first two indicators that Elkins et al. identify with inclusion (whether a publicly elected body elaborates the constitution and whether the constitution is ratified by a public referendum) belong to the same underlying variable. We also add a third indicator, which could perhaps also be a manifestation of inclusiveness: the possibility of the public to participate in the constitution-making process, either actively (by reviewing or proposing provisions) or passively (by being informed of the process through the media or other channels). In this section, therefore, we look at the interrelationships between the three variables we identified earlier as the mode of representation, the mode of legitimation and the style with a view to testing the hypothesis of Elkins et al. that these variables are fundamentally manifestations of a single variable: inclusion. Before we explore these interrelationships, however, we must first operationalize the three variables.

The mode of representation is relatively easy to operationalize on the basis of the analysis provided above. We assign a value of 1.0 to the mode of representation if the constitution-making body is directly elected (i.e. a mandated constituent legislature or a pure constituent assembly), we assign a value of 0.5 if it is indirectly selected (made up of delegates from states, a national conference or an electoral college) and we assign a value of 0.0 if the body is appointed by elites (including the other four types of constitution-making body as well as the residual category). The mode of legitimation is also easy to operationalize; we assign a value of 1.0 to this variable if the constitution was ratified by referendum, 0.5 if it was ratified by a state institution other than the constitution-making body or the executive (institutional ratification) and 0.0 if it was promulgated by the executive (e.g. an executive president) or by the constitution-making body itself.

Possibly the most problematic variable to operationalize is the style of constitution-making. This is because for a number of events that occurred in the more distant past it is difficult to obtain sufficient information in order to gauge the degree of public input into the process; historical records of how the deliberation process was conducted is incomplete. Lack of information meant that it was only possible to code 88 of the 160 events for style. For style we give the variable a value of 1.0 if the deliberation process of the constitution-making body was: a) widely publicized and transparent and b) open to input from members of the public. On the other hand, we assign a value 0.0 to style if the process was held behind closed doors with a minimum of publicity. We also assign an intermediate value of 0.5 if the public was passively involved in the constitution-making process by virtue of the fact that the process was transparent and widely discussed in the media, but at the same time the possibility of real public input into the process was strictly limited.

## Dilemmas of Constitutional Design

As noted above, we identified a representative sample of 160 constitution-making events that spanned the length and breadth of the globe and over two centuries of time. This enables us to look more closely at how our three variables – mode of legitimation, mode of representation and style – are related. More specifically, it allows us to judge whether, as Elkins et al. suggest, it is valid to aggregate them into a single variable, or whether, instead they are independent features of the constitution-making process.

We begin by focussing on two indicators that Elkins et al. themselves define as belonging to the 'inclusion' variable: the mode of representation and the mode of legitimation. To this end, we first identify nine models of constitution-making on a two dimensional map in which one axis (the x-axis) represents the mode of representation and the other (the y-axis) represents the mode of legitimation, according to the values (0.0, 0.5 and 1.0) of the two indicators in question (Figure 2.2). From here we match each constitution-making event with the model to which it corresponds (Table 2.2). Of the 160 events, three were not included in the mapping (Indonesia in 1959, Pakistan in 1949 and Russia in 1918), by virtue of the fact that the process was terminated before the constitution-making body had finalized a draft. In addition, the 1997 Constitution of Eritrea was approved but never implemented (denoted by the † symbol in Table 2.2), and the constitutions of Australia (1891) and Kenya (2005) were rejected by the ratifying body (the people by means of a referendum in Kenya and the state parliaments in Australia, denoted by the * symbol in Table 2.2). For all other events, the dates shown in brackets refer to the date the constitution came into force.

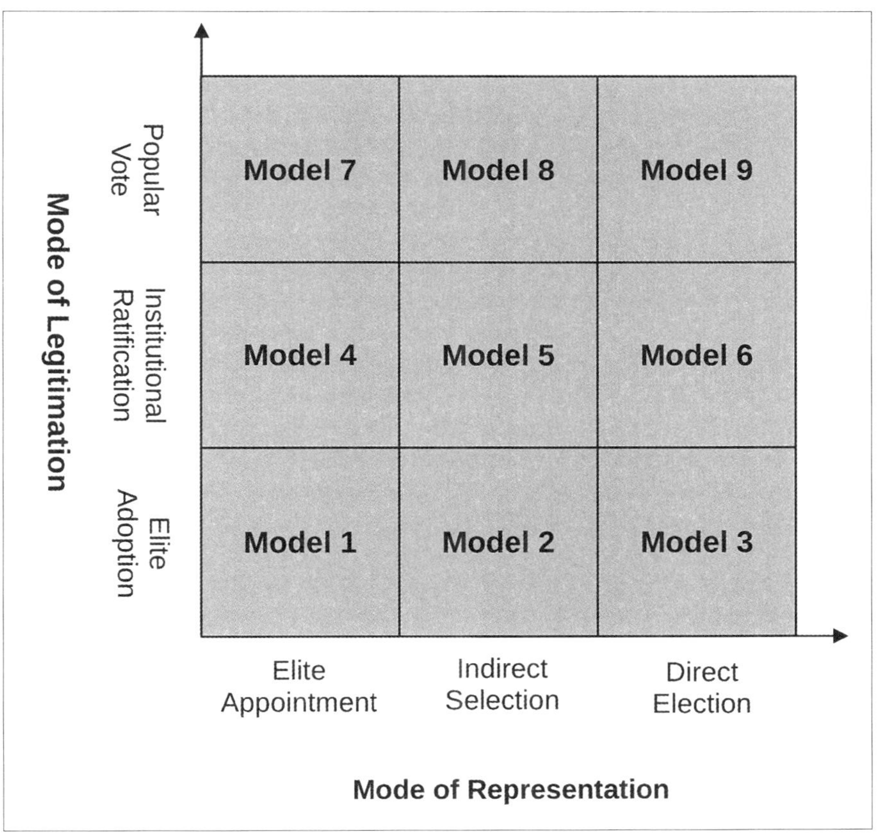


**Figure 2.2　　Models of constitution-making**

**Table 2.2     Models of constitution-making by country**

| Model 7 (n=27) | | Model 8 (n=8) | Model 9 (n=11) | |
|---|---|---|---|---|
| Albania (1998) | Ivory Coast (2000) | Benin (1990) | Australia (1901) | |
| Armenia (1995) | Kazakhstan (1995) | Chad (1996) | Bolivia (2009) | |
| Azerbaijan (1995) | Liberia (1986) | Congo-Brazzaville (1992) | Ecuador (2008) | |
| Burma (2008) | Mali (1974) | Estonia (1992) | Haiti (1987) | |
| Cameroon (1960) | Morocco (1962) | Kenya (2005)* | Iraq (2005) | |
| Chad (1989) | Philippines (1987) | Madagascar (1992) | Peru (1993) | |
| Chile (1981) | Poland (1997) | Mali (1992) | Romania (1991) | |
| Cuba (1976) | Qatar (2005) | Niger (1992) | Samoa (1962) | |
| Djibouti (1992) | Russia (1993) | | Somalia (1961) | |
| Ecuador (1979) | Rwanda (2004) | | Spain (1978) | |
| Ethiopia (1987) | Sierra Leone (1978) | | Venezuela (1999) | |
| Ghana (1960) | Somalia (1979) | | | |
| Haiti (1964) | Uruguay (1967) | | | |
| Iran (1979) | | | | |
| **Model 4 (n=21)** | | **Model 5 (n=9)** | **Model 6 (n=9)** | |
| Afghanistan (1977) | Hungary (1949) | Australia (1891)* | Brazil (1946) | |
| Afghanistan (1987) | Ivory Coast (1960) | Canada (1867) | Cambodia (1993) | |
| Albania (1976) | Japan (1890) | Gabon (1991) | Costa Rica (1949) | |
| Brazil (1824) | Kenya (1964) | Germany (1949) | Ethiopia (1995) | |
| China (1954) | Mauritius (1968) | Ghana (1979) | Iran (1906) | |
| Congo (1964) | Malawi (1966) | Jamaica (1965) | Kuwait (1963) | |
| Croatia (1990) | Malawi (1994) | Switzerland (1848) | Mexico (1857) | |
| Dominican Rep. (2010) | Tanzania (1977) | Thailand (1997) | Philippines (1973) | |
| Eritrea (1997)† | Uruguay (1952) | USA (1788) | South Africa (1997) | |
| Georgia (1995) | | | | |
| Greece (1975) | | | | |
| Guinea-Bissau (1984) | | | | |

| Model 1 (n=22) | | Model 2 (n=10) | Model 3 (n=40) | |
|---|---|---|---|---|
| Bosnia-Herzegovina (1995) | Nigeria (1960) | Argentina (1853) | Austria (1920) | Mexico (1824) |
| Central African Republic (1976) | Paraguay (1967) | Bulgaria (1879) | Bangladesh (1972) | Mexico (1917) |
| China (1913) | Seychelles (1979) | Colombia (1886) | Belgium (1831) | Namibia (1990) |
| Dominican Rep. (1887) | Singapore (1965) | Czechoslovakia (1920) | Brazil (1988) | Nicaragua (1987) |
| Ethiopia (1955) | Sweden (1809) | France (1791) | Bulgaria (1991) | Norway (1814) |
| Ghana (1957) | Tangyanika (1962) | India (1950) | Chile (1823) | Peru (1867) |
| Grenada (1974) | Tonga (1875) | Nigeria (1979) | Colombia (1991) | Peru (1980) |
| Guyana (1966) | Uganda (1962) | Nigeria (1989) | Cuba (1940) | Poland (1921) |
| Haiti (1806) | Zambia (1973) | Pakistan (1956) | Dominican Rep. (1858) | Portugal (1822) |
| Lesotho (1993) | Zimbabwe (1979) | Venezuela (1830) | East Timor (2002) | Portugal (1976) |
| Libya (1951) | | | France (1848) | São Tomé e P. (1975) |
| Malaya (1957) | | | Georgia (1921) | South Korea (1948) |
| | | | Germany (1919) | Spain (1931) |
| | | | Guatemala (1986) | Sri Lanka (1972) |
| | | | Honduras (1965) | Tunisia (1959) |
| | | | Honduras (1982) | Turkey (1921) |
| | | | Ireland (1922) | Uganda (1995) |
| | | | Italy (1948) | Uruguay (1830) |
| | | | Latvia (1922) | Venezuela (1864) |
| | | | Lithuania (1922) | Yugoslavia (1921) |

Probably the most important finding from this analysis is that there appears to be a negative relationship between the mode of representation and the mode of legitimation. The most frequently adopted models are Models 3 and 7 in which we have *either* direct elections to the constitution-making body, but no popular ratification of the constitution (e.g. Model 3) *or* popular approval by referendum of a constitutional text cooked up by elites (Model 7). Furthermore, if we apply a Spearman's rho correlation on the sample based on the two variables (mode of representation and mode of legitimation), we observe a *negative* correlation of –.300, which is significant at the $p<0.01$ level. This would appear to refute the assertion by Elkins et al. (2009) that the mode of representation and the mode of legitimation are fundamentally manifestations of a single 'inclusion' variable. On the contrary, there appears to be a trade-off at the heart of constitutional design. This could have important implications for how a given constitution-making exercise is configured to promote popular participation.

Our analysis suggests that popular input during constitutional events can be sequenced in a variety ways. Popular participation can be introduced into the mode of representation whereby the citizens directly elect the body responsible for drafting a new constitution. Alternatively, popular participation can be introduced into the mode of legitimation whereby the citizens have a direct say on the adoption of a new constitution by means of a referendum. This relationship is represented in Figure 2.3 which identifies a number of channels for introducing popular participation. In the first channel, represented by the letter B, popular input into a constitution-making process is achieved through various devices such as specially convoked elections to a Constituent Assembly. In a second channel, popular input is generated through a direct consultation of the people on the constitutional product – i.e. the proposed new constitution – represented by the letter A. What our analysis reveals is that at the aggregate level and across the global sample there is a trade-off between the two. This is represented by the downward sloping line in Figure 2.3. Evidently there are other possible channels, which lie outside the line. These are represented by the letter C, where popular participation is low on both axes. This is characteristic of conflict resolution contexts, for instance the Dayton Peace Agreement of 1995 in Bosnia-Herzegovina, and is quite common during a decolonization setting (see Model 1 in Table 2.2). There are also examples of activating popular participation during a constitution-making process in terms of both the mode of representation and the mode of legitimation. In these cases, represented by the letter D, a directly elected Constituent Assembly drafts the constitution which is subsequently submitted to the people for ratification (see Model 9). In some rather rare cases, such as Venezuela and Ecuador, a triple popular input mechanism has been used whereby the people also decide by referendum on whether to engage in a constitutional process and elect a Constituent Assembly in the first place. Overall, analysis of our sample reveals a common trade-off facing constitutional designers given the need to legitimate a constitution-making exercise through some degree of popular input. Notwithstanding some important outlier conditions, as discussed above, most cases can be placed along the downward slopping curve in Figure 2.3.

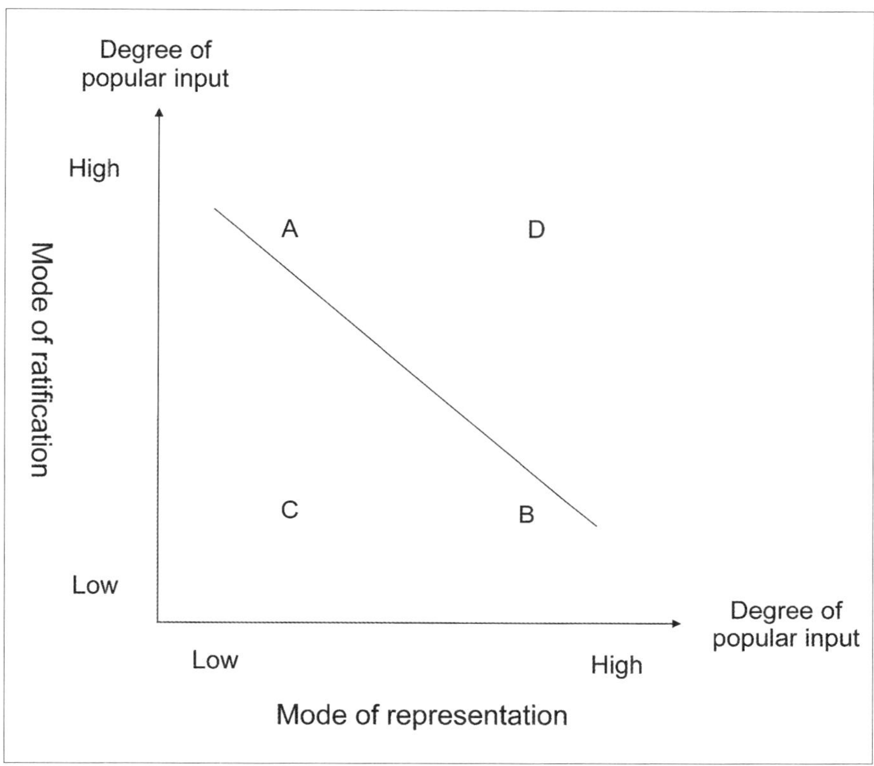


**Figure 2.3　A trade-off**

Turning now to the style of constitution-making, as we explained in the previous section, data was not always available on this variable, especially in the case of many of the early constitution-making events for which information is sparse. Just 88 of the 160 events could be coded for style. Three coding categories were used: open (coded as 1.0), partly open (0.5) and closed (0.0). While there is no clear link between the mode of legitimation and the style (see Table 2.3), there is a clear positive correlation between the mode of representation and the style (Table 2.4)[3] – a Spearman's rho correlation coefficients of 0.380 is significant at the p<0.01 level. This observation is entirely expected. For instance, constitution-making exercises that occur in a conflict resolution context or during initial periods of decolonization are frequently negotiated by elites in a closed setting. In order to foster favourable conditions for bargaining and compromise, public

---

3　Indonesia (1958) is also included in this sample as a constitution-making body was established, even though the constitution was never legitimized. This event is marked by the symbol ‡ in Table 2.4 on p.40.

input or media access to the negotiations is usually absent or minimal. At a later stage, the constitution-making process can be opened up to a broader range of stakeholders. There is therefore a direct relationship between the mode of representation and the style of constitution-making and debating. Different modes of representation generate diverging models of debating and negotiating constitutions. Where delegates are elected, especially in large numbers, or selected to reflect a broad range of societal groups, deliberative discussions and open public participation are more likely. A bargaining model of negotiation that is generally more closed prevails where the process is controlled by a committee of governing elites. This is also reflected in our earlier comparison (see Chapter 1) of the U.S. and French constitution-making processes at the end of the eighteenth century.

**Table 2.3    Comparative findings: Style and mode of legitimation**

<table>
<tr><td rowspan="2" colspan="2"></td><td colspan="2" align="center">n=15</td><td align="center">n=3</td><td align="center">n=12</td></tr>
<tr></tr>
<tr>
<td rowspan="13">Popular Vote</td>
<td>
Armenia (1995)<br>
Azerbaijan (1995)<br>
Burma (2008)<br>
Cameroon (1960)<br>
Chad (1989)<br>
Chile (1981)<br>
Djibouti (1992)<br>
Haiti (1987)<br>
Iraq (2005)<br>
Ivory Coast (2000)<br>
Kazakhstan (1995)<br>
Mali (1974)
</td>
<td>
Morocco (1962)<br>
Russia (1993)<br>
Spain (1978)
</td>
<td>
Estonia (1992)<br>
Ethiopia (1987)<br>
Peru (1993)
</td>
<td>
Albania (1998)<br>
Australia (1901)<br>
Benin (1990)<br>
Bolivia (2009)<br>
Chad (1996)<br>
Cuba (1976)<br>
Ecuador (1979)<br>
Ecuador (2008)<br>
Kenya (2005)*<br>
Niger (1992)<br>
Rwanda (2004)<br>
Venezuela (1999)
</td>
</tr>
<tr><td colspan="2" align="center">n=17</td><td align="center">n=3</td><td align="center">n=5</td></tr>
<tr>
<td rowspan="2">Institutional Ratification</td>
<td>
Afghanistan (1977)<br>
Albania (1976)<br>
Cambodia (1993)<br>
Canada (1867)<br>
Croatia (1990)<br>
Dominican Rep. (2010)<br>
Georgia (1995)<br>
Germany (1949)<br>
Greece (1975)
</td>
<td>
Ivory Coast (1960)<br>
Japan (1890)<br>
Kenya (1964)<br>
Mauritius (1968)<br>
Malawi (1994)<br>
Switzerland (1848)<br>
Tanzania (1977)<br>
USA (1788)
</td>
<td>
Ethiopia (1995)<br>
Jamaica (1965)<br>
Mexico (1857)
</td>
<td>
Afghanistan (1987)<br>
China (1954)<br>
Eritrea (1997)†<br>
South Africa (1997)<br>
Thailand (1997)
</td>
</tr>
<tr><td colspan="2" align="center">n=18</td><td align="center">n=6</td><td align="center">n=8</td></tr>
<tr>
<td>Elite Adoption</td>
<td>
Argentina (1853)<br>
Bosnia-Herzegovina (1995)<br>
Central African Republic (1976)<br>
Dominican Rep. (1887)<br>
Ethiopia (1955)<br>
France (1848)<br>
Georgia (1921)<br>
Ghana (1957)<br>
Grenada (1974)
</td>
<td>
Guyana (1966)<br>
Ireland (1922)<br>
Namibia (1990)<br>
Nigeria (1989)<br>
Paraguay (1967)<br>
Singapore (1965)<br>
Sri Lanka (1972)<br>
Tonga (1875)<br>
Zimbabwe (1979)
</td>
<td>
East Timor (2002)<br>
India (1950)<br>
Nigeria (1979)<br>
Peru (1980)<br>
Spain (1931)<br>
Zambia (1973)
</td>
<td>
Brazil (1988)<br>
Colombia (1991)<br>
France (1791)<br>
Lesotho (1993)<br>
Nicaragua (1987)<br>
Portugal (1976)<br>
Turkey (1921)<br>
Uganda (1995)
</td>
</tr>
<tr><td colspan="2"></td><td colspan="2">Closed</td><td>Partly Open</td><td>Open</td></tr>
</table>

*Mode of Legitimation* (left vertical axis)

**Style**

**Table 2.4     Comparative findings: Style and mode of representation**

<table>
<tr><th rowspan="2">Mode of Representation</th><th>Direct Election</th><th>n=9<br>Cambodia (1993)<br>France (1848)<br>Georgia (1921)<br>Haiti (1987)<br>Ireland (1922)<br>Iraq (2005)<br>Nigeria (1989)<br>Switzerland (1848)<br>USA (1788)</th><th>n=7<br>East Timor (2002)<br>Ethiopia (1995)<br>Indonesia (1958)‡<br>Mexico (1857)<br>Peru (1980)<br>Peru (1993)<br>Spain (1931</th><th>n=11<br>Australia (1901)<br>Bolivia (2009)<br>Brazil (1988)<br>Colombia (1991)<br>Ecuador (2008)<br>Nicaragua (1987)<br>Portugal (1976)<br>South Africa (1997)<br>Turkey (1921)<br>Uganda (1995)<br>Venezuela (1999)</th></tr>
<tr><th>Indirect Selection</th><td>n=6<br>Argentina (1853)<br>Canada (1867)<br>Germany (1949)<br>Nigeria (1989)<br>Switzerland (1848)<br>USA (1788)</td><td>n=4<br>Estonia (1992)<br>India (1950)<br>Jamaica (1965)<br>Nigeria (1979)</td><td>n=6<br>Benin (1990)<br>Chad (1996)<br>France (1791)<br>Kenya (2005)*<br>Niger (1992)<br>Thailand (1997)</td></tr>
<tr><th>Elite Appointment</th><td>n=35<br>Afghanistan (1977)  Grenada (1974)<br>Albania (1976)  Guyana (1966)<br>Armenia (1995)  Ivory Coast (1960)<br>Azerbaijan (1995)  Ivory Coast (2000)<br>Bosnia-Herzegovina  Japan (1890)<br>(1995)  Kazakhstan (1995)<br>Burma (2008)  Kenya (1964)<br>Cameroon (1960)  Malawi (1994)<br>Central African Republic  Mali (1974)<br>(1976)  Mauritius (1968)<br>Chad (1989)  Morocco (1962)<br>Chile (1981)  Paraguay (1967)<br>Croatia (1990)  Russia (1993)<br>Djibouti (1992)  Singapore (1965)<br>Dominican Rep. (1887)  Tanzania (1977)<br>Dominican Rep. (2010)  Tonga (1875)<br>Ethiopia (1955)  Zimbabwe (1979)<br>Georgia (1995)<br>Ghana (1957)<br>Greece (1975)</td><td>n=2<br>Ethiopia (1987)<br>Zambia (1973)</td><td>n=8<br>Afghanistan (1987)<br>Albania (1998)<br>China (1954)<br>Cuba (1976)<br>Ecuador (1979)<br>Eritrea (1997)†<br>Lesotho (1993)<br>Rwanda (2004)</td></tr>
<tr><td></td><td></td><td>*Closed*</td><td>*Partly Open*</td><td>*Open*</td></tr>
<tr><td></td><td></td><td colspan="3" align="center">**Style**</td></tr>
</table>

## Conclusion

The relationship identified in the previous section between the mode of representation and the mode of legitimation would appear to challenge the hypothesis of Elkins and al. that both of these are features of a single 'inclusion' variable. What we appear to have instead are two basically independent variables that are frequently inversely correlated with one another. On the one hand, we have the mode of representation, which correlates strongly with the style of constitution-making. On the other hand we have the mode of legitimation, which refers to the degree of public participation in the ratification process and which is determined, above all, by whether or not the constitution is approved by referendum.

The analysis in this chapter has brought to light a number of phenomena that would, at a first glance appear anti-intuitive, but can be explained by a more in-depth look at certain cases. The first revelation is that there is a distinct tendency for constitutions that have been elaborated behind closed doors by elites to be legitimized by means of a referendum (as in Model 7 in Figure 2.2, on p.33). Conversely most constitutions that are drawn up by a directly elected body such as a constituent assembly tend to be adopted by the assembly itself and are not submitted to a referendum (Model 3). There therefore seems to be a trade-off between what we term the mode of legitimation and the mode of representation. Although the literature on participatory constitution-making stresses the normative value of building popular attachment to the constitution *both* through participation in the drafting process itself *and* through ratification by referendum, Ghai argues that 'referendum as a method of people's participation is less effective than prior participation' (Ghai 2006). What we find in our analysis in subsequent chapters is that referendums can often be used as a substitute for genuine participatory constitution-making. In some of the worse cases, referendums are cynically manipulated by autocrats to promote their own interests through a constitutional formula that is carefully tailored to shore up their own power base. It is to these issues we will turn in Chapter 3.

# Appendix

The representative sample of 160 critical cases of constitution-making was extracted from the larger sample of constitution-making events in the following way. First, the number of sovereign states that actually existed in the middle of each "wave" was calculated as follows:

**Table A2.1   Number of sovereign states**

| Wave | Dates | No. of States |
| --- | --- | --- |
| 1 | Up to 1844 | 25 |
| 2 | 1845–1899 | 33 |
| 3 | 1900–1939 | 49 |
| 4 | 1940–1954 | 66 |
| 5 | 1955–1969 | 111 |
| 6 | 1970–1989 | 154 |
| 7 | Post 1990 | 190 |

This formed the basis for "weighting" the number of events that would be drawn from each wave. It was felt that to weight each wave directly according to the number of states that existed at the time would reduce excessively the number of nineteenth-century constitution-making events sampled, but at the same time to give each wave equal weight would lead to an over-representation of such events and would lead to the sampling of many events in certain countries. It was therefore decided to adopt an intermediate solution, in the manner shown below:

**Table A2.2  Weightings**

| Wave | Dates | No. of States | Weight based on no. of States | Weight based on Equality | Intermediate Weight |
|---|---|---|---|---|---|
| 1 | Up to 1844 | 25 | 0.279 | 1 | 0.639 |
| 2 | 1845–1899 | 33 | 0.368 | 1 | 0.684 |
| 3 | 1900–1939 | 49 | 0.546 | 1 | 0.773 |
| 4 | 1940–1954 | 66 | 0.736 | 1 | 0.868 |
| 5 | 1955–1969 | 111 | 1.237 | 1 | 1.119 |
| 6 | 1970–1989 | 154 | 1.717 | 1 | 1.358 |
| 7 | Post 1990 | 190 | 2.118 | 1 | 1.559 |
| **Average** | | | **1** | **1** | **1** |

Using data from the Comparative Constitutions Project based at the University of Illinois and adding supplementary data from other sources, we were able to identify 746 cases in which new constitutions were drafted at national (state) level since 1780. Of these we remove from the sample constitutions that endured for less than five years, leaving just 635 constitutions. Dividing these cases a) according to time (i.e. wave of constitution-making) and b) into 11 geographical regions, we obtain the distribution shown in Table A2.3.

**Table A2.3   Distribution of cases by time and region**

| Wave | Western Europe | Eastern Europe | Ex USSR | Africa | North America | Latin America | Oceania | South Asia | East Asia | Middle East | West Indies | Total |
|---|---|---|---|---|---|---|---|---|---|---|---|---|
| 1 | 32 | 4 | 0 | 0 | 1 | 32 | 0 | 0 | 0 | 0 | 4 | **73** |
| 2 | 23 | 4 | 0 | 4 | 1 | 44 | 1 | 0 | 2 | 1 | 10 | **90** |
| 3 | 12 | 15 | 11 | 2 | 0 | 24 | 1 | 2 | 5 | 5 | 7 | **84** |
| 4 | 7 | 10 | 1 | 0 | 0 | 13 | 0 | 4 | 13 | 5 | 5 | **58** |
| 5 | 5 | 5 | 0 | 49 | 0 | 12 | 2 | 5 | 8 | 9 | 8 | **103** |
| 6 | 3 | 5 | 1 | 50 | 0 | 16 | 7 | 5 | 10 | 9 | 9 | **115** |
| 7 | 3 | 14 | 17 | 46 | 0 | 7 | 2 | 6 | 8 | 6 | 3 | **112** |
| **Total** | **85** | **57** | **30** | **151** | **2** | **148** | **13** | **22** | **46** | **35** | **46** | **635** |

Multiplying all elements in each row by the respective weights given in the right-hand column of Table A2.2, we obtain the following:

**Table A2.4    Weighted distribution of cases by time and region**

| Wave | Western Europe | Eastern Europe | Ex USSR | Africa | North America | Latin America | Occania | South Asia | East Asia | Middle East | West Indies | Total |
|---|---|---|---|---|---|---|---|---|---|---|---|---|
| 1 | 20.46 | 2.56 | 0.00 | 0.00 | 0.64 | 20.46 | 0.00 | 0.00 | 0.00 | 0.00 | 2.56 | **46.67** |
| 2 | 15.73 | 2.74 | 0.00 | 2.74 | 0.68 | 30.09 | 0.68 | 0.00 | 1.37 | 0.68 | 6.84 | **61.55** |
| 3 | 9.28 | 11.60 | 8.50 | 1.55 | 0.00 | 18.55 | 0.77 | 1.55 | 3.87 | 3.87 | 5.41 | **64.94** |
| 4 | 6.07 | 8.68 | 0.87 | 0.00 | 0.00 | 11.28 | 0.00 | 3.47 | 11.28 | 4.34 | 4.34 | **50.33** |
| 5 | 5.59 | 5.59 | 0.00 | 54.81 | 0.00 | 13.42 | 2.24 | 5.59 | 8.95 | 10.07 | 8.95 | **115.22** |
| 6 | 4.07 | 6.79 | 1.36 | 67.91 | 0.00 | 21.73 | 9.51 | 6.79 | 13.58 | 12.22 | 12.22 | **156.20** |
| 7 | 4.68 | 21.82 | 26.50 | 71.71 | 0.00 | 10.91 | 3.12 | 9.35 | 12.47 | 9.35 | 4.68 | **174.60** |
| Total | **65.89** | **59.78** | **37.23** | **198.72** | **1.32** | **126.46** | **16.32** | **26.76** | **51.52** | **40.53** | **45.00** | **669.52** |

Given that we aim to select just 160 cases, we must now divide every element in the above column by 669.52/160 or 4.18 to obtain our desired distribution:

**Table A2.5    Desired distribution**

| Wave | Western Europe | Eastern Europe | Ex USSR | Africa | North America | Latin America | Oceania | South Asia | East Asia | Middle East | West Indies | Total |
|---|---|---|---|---|---|---|---|---|---|---|---|---|
| 1 | 4.89 | 0.61 | 0.00 | 0.00 | 0.15 | 4.89 | 0.00 | 0.00 | 0.00 | 0.00 | 0.61 | **11.15** |
| 2 | 3.76 | 0.65 | 0.00 | 0.65 | 0.16 | 7.19 | 0.16 | 0.00 | 0.33 | 0.16 | 1.63 | **14.71** |
| 3 | 2.22 | 2.77 | 2.03 | 0.37 | 0.00 | 4.43 | 0.18 | 0.37 | 0.92 | 0.92 | 1.29 | **15.52** |
| 4 | 1.45 | 2.07 | 0.21 | 0.00 | 0.00 | 2.70 | 0.00 | 0.83 | 2.70 | 1.04 | 1.04 | **12.03** |
| 5 | 1.34 | 1.34 | 0.00 | 13.10 | 0.00 | 3.21 | 0.53 | 1.34 | 2.14 | 2.41 | 2.14 | **27.53** |
| 6 | 0.97 | 1.62 | 0.32 | 16.23 | 0.00 | 5.19 | 2.27 | 1.62 | 3.25 | 2.92 | 2.92 | **37.33** |
| 7 | 1.12 | 5.22 | 6.33 | 17.14 | 0.00 | 2.61 | 0.75 | 2.24 | 2.98 | 2.24 | 1.12 | **41.73** |
| **Total** | **15.75** | **14.29** | **8.90** | **47.49** | **0.32** | **30.22** | **3.90** | **6.39** | **12.31** | **9.69** | **10.75** | **160.00** |

The best fit distribution to the above, which is how we chose to sample our 160 cases was as follows:

**Table A2.6   Our sample**

| Wave | Western Europe | Eastern Europe | Ex USSR | Africa | North America | Latin America | Oceania | South Asia | East Asia | Middle East | West Indies | Total |
|---|---|---|---|---|---|---|---|---|---|---|---|---|
| 1 | 5 | 0 | 0 | 0 | 1 | 5 | 0 | 0 | 0 | 0 | 1 | 12 |
| 2 | 2 | 1 | 0 | 0 | 1 | 5 | 2 | 0 | 1 | 0 | 2 | 14 |
| 3 | 4 | 4 | 3 | 0 | 0 | 1 | 1 | 0 | 1 | 2 | 0 | 16 |
| 4 | 2 | 1 | 0 | 0 | 0 | 3 | 0 | 2 | 2 | 1 | 1 | 12 |
| 5 | 0 | 0 | 0 | 13 | 0 | 4 | 1 | 1 | 3 | 3 | 2 | 27 |
| 6 | 2 | 2 | 0 | 16 | 0 | 7 | 0 | 4 | 2 | 1 | 3 | 37 |
| 7 | 0 | 6 | 6 | 18 | 0 | 5 | 0 | 0 | 4 | 2 | 1 | 42 |
| Total | 15 | 14 | 9 | 47 | 2 | 30 | 4 | 7 | 13 | 9 | 10 | 160 |

# Chapter 3
# Outcomes of Constitution-Making: Democratization and Conflict Resolution

Jonathan Wheatley and Micha Germann

In Chapter 2 we mapped and analysed a representative subset of constitution-making processes and identified two key variables that we believe are both independent from one another and essential to that process: the mode of representation and the mode of legitimation. Having done so, we are now ready to explore whether or not these features of the constitution-making process in any way shape its outcomes in terms of democratization and conflict resolution.

In Chapter 1, we argued that the establishment of a basic degree of consensus over the limits of sovereign power both within the political elite and within society in general is essential for a stable and consolidated democracy. While there does not have to be a new constitution for this kind of consensus to be established and, conversely, constitutions may be born in a context in which a broad consensus is lacking, we would suggest that constitutional reform is a likely, though far from essential, ingredient of transition to democracy. In terms of the impact of the constitution-making process, in Chapter 1 we identified two rival hypotheses as to what that impact may be. On the one hand, advocates of participatory constitution-making argue that an open and democratic constitution-making process in which there is broad public participation is likely to be more conducive to democratization than an elite-driven process that is carried out behind closed doors. On the other hand, advocates of democracy 'crafting' and pact-making would hold that isolation of the pact-makers from the clamour of the public realm is more likely to result in a successful democratic pact than a more open process.

Transitions to democracy typically involve conflict between a number of groups within society; at the very least between those who formed a part of the old regime and those who opposed it. For Rustow, a 'hot family feud' is essential to an infant democracy, but this must stop short of 'implacable hostility' (Rustow 1970: 355, 363). However, whatever position a society occupies on the spectrum between 'hot family feud' and 'implacable hostility', the establishment of new rules of the game are essential if this conflict is to be defused. These may or may not be enshrined in constitutional changes. In cases in which conflict has spilled over into violence, these rules are likely to be: a) particularly hard to craft and b) more limited in scope than they are in cases in which the conflict is non-violent. As Widner suggests (see Chapter 1), the rule-making process is likely to take on a particular dynamic in attempts to defuse violent conflict and an open participatory process is less likely to succeed. Moreover, interim arrangements may be preferable to full-scale efforts to draft a new constitution and, the establishment of a comprehensive framework such as a new constitution may lack the flexibility needed in a post-conflict setting.

This chapter will be structured as follows. It begins by exploring the interrelationship between the mode of representation and the mode of legitimation of a constitution-making event on the one hand and the persistence (or collapse) of authoritarian regimes, on the other. To do so it uses as empirical cases a smaller subset of the constitution-making events identified in Chapter 2 that were authoritarian prior to the event. In order to reveal associations between the key variables, a method called Qualitative Comparative Analysis (QCA) is used. This method shows that, paradoxically, constitution-making events that are legitimized by a referendum are often associated with entrenched authoritarian systems that are not especially amenable to democratic transition. The second part of the chapter looks at the relationship between the constitution-making process and conflict resolution with a view to testing the hypothesis that constitutional bargains struck in a conflict resolution setting cannot be conducted according to participatory ideals. However, the number of cases in which constitutions are written for the purpose of conflict resolution is small and for this reason the focus is narrowed to three specific cases: Switzerland (1848), India (1950) and South Africa (1994/97). Vignettes of these three cases are used to illustrate how constitutional bargains that are intended for the resolution of conflict can at the same time establish a consensus on democratic principles of constitutionalism and secure the gradual consolidation of democracy. Conversely, if such a consensus is not achieved, constitution-making may merely reflect the outcomes of an ongoing power struggle and will contribute neither to the consolidation of democracy, nor to the resolution of conflict.


## Constitution-Making and Democratization

The central question this section aims to address is whether the constitution-making process has any impact on the probability of a successful transition from authoritarianism to democracy. As such, its focus will be constitution-making in (post-)authoritarian settings. We will also restrict our analysis to relatively recent constitutional events coinciding with the period commonly identified by scholars of democratization as the 'third wave of democratization', which began in the 1970s. The reason for this selection is firstly that democratization during this period tended to occur (when it did occur) more rapidly than during previous waves, making it easier to isolate the role of key events, and secondly because the information available to us, both in terms of the constitution-making process and in terms of regime dynamics, is much more abundant for this period than it is for earlier periods. Moreover, post-1970 constitutions are less heterogeneous than earlier constitutions, allowing us to divert our attention away from the (democratic or not democratic) *content* of the constitution and towards the *process* of constitution-making. Most constitutions drafted after 1970 define some kind of division of powers between the executive, legislature and judiciary, as well as certain checks and balances that are meant to set the limits of each. However, in practice the democratic procedures they set down often do not function and the checks and balances prove to be ineffective.

A quick glance at Table 2.2 from the previous chapter confronts us with a paradox: regimes in which the constitution has been legitimized by means of a referendum would appear to be, if anything, less democratic than those that have been legitimized by other means. Most regimes in Model 7, which, as a result of the apparent trade-off between the mode of representation and the mode of legitimation mentioned above, is the most frequent model for events in which a popular vote gave legitimacy to the constitution, seem to have remained (or become) undemocratic after the passage of the constitution. Amongst the countries in Model 7, only Poland could be considered a stable democracy five, or even ten years after the constitution entered into force. However, models in which citizens directly elect the constitution-making body and (given the high degree of correlation between the mode of representation and the style of deliberation) participate in its activities appear to do rather better in terms of democratic evolution. This appears to be fully congruent with neither of the two rival hypotheses on democratic constitution-making outlined in the introduction to this chapter. It is time therefore to take a closer look at our cases with a view to finding out in more detail what is going on and what are the chains of events that led to the different outcomes.

In order to find out what possible configurations of factors produce the various outcomes in terms of democratization (or, rather, the lack thereof) we use a technique known as QCA (Qualitative Comparative Analysis), a method pioneered by Charles Ragin (1987) that uses Boolean algebra to compare a relatively small number of cases in qualitative studies of macro social phenomena and from there to derive putative causal relationships. The particular type of QCA used for this study is known as 'fuzzy set QCA' in which the pure Boolean logic of the method is attenuated by allowing subsets within the outcome variable that distinguish between clearcut cases of the variable in question from non clearcut cases. In our study the phenomenon we are attempting to explain is the persistence of authoritarianism after the ratification of a new constitution. For this reason we restrict our sample to states that were more or less authoritarian at a point in time five years before the constitution entered into force (t-5). We also restrict our sample to cases coinciding with the so-called 'third wave of democratization'; hence we include only cases in which the constitution was ratified in or after 1975.[1] Overall, this leaves us with 52 cases out of our original sample of 160.

Our criterion for authoritarianism is that the country scored 9 or higher on the composite Freedom House index at t-5 (See www.freedomhouse.org). Freedom House rates countries in terms of Political Rights and Civil Liberties on scales

---

1 Freedom House only began scoring in 1973 for the year 1972. In cases in which constitutions were passed in 1975 or 1976, the 1972 score is given as the t-5 score.

ranging from 1 (most democratic) to 7 (least democratic). Summing the two indices allows one to obtain a composite score between 2 (most democratic) and 14 (least democratic). In terms of our outcome variable (*aut_sur* or authoritarian survival), we attenuate the stark dichotomy between those that remain authoritarian and those that become democratic by using a five-category fuzzy set. Those cases that remain most clearly and resolutely authoritarian are those that have experienced no improvement whatsoever in their Freedom House scores five years after the constitution has entered into force (t+5) and are therefore assigned a fuzzy score of 1.0, while those that experience an improvement (i.e. reduction) in the Freedom House score of at least eight points between t-5 and t+5 are assigned a score of 0.0. These are the cases that are most clearly and unambiguously either 'inside' or 'outside' the group of authoritarian survivors. We also define a group of countries that are 'mainly inside' the authoritarian group as those in which the score has improved, but by no more than three points, as well as a group that is 'mainly outside', having experienced an improvement of between five and seven points. These two groups are assigned fuzzy scores of 0.75 and 0.25 respectively. Finally we define a group of countries that are 'neither out nor in' as those in which the Freedom House score has improved by four points. Members of this group are assigned a fuzzy score of 0.5.[2] We base our attempt to explain on 52 cases, of which 34 are more inside than outside the set of authoritarian survivors (fuzzy scores > 0.5), 12 are more outside than in (fuzzy scores < 0.5) and six are neither out nor in (fuzzy scores = 0.5). To attempt to explain the phenomenon, we employ a total of four independent variables:

1.  A dummy indicator (*pov*) for poverty that is equal to 1 if GDP per capita in parity purchasing power is less than PPP$1,000 per capita in purchasing power terms and 0 otherwise.[3] This relates to the hypothesis that democratization is more likely in more economically developed countries (Lipset 1959, 1994; Diamond 1992).
2.  Our indicator for mode of representation (*rep*), but simplified in such a way that the value of this indicator is set to 0 if the mode of representation was elite appointment and to 1 if it was either indirect selection or direct election. The idea is to test the hypothesis that constitutions that are hammered out by elites behind closed doors are less likely to lead to a new democratic order in conformity with theories on participatory constitution-making. Given the strong correlation that appears to exist between mode

---

2   For the purposes of the analysis the "neither in nor out group" is assigned a value of 0.499, as the algorithm does not work if a case is assigned a value of exactly 0.5.

3   Source: International Monetary Fund, World Economic Outlook Database, October 2010. In the few cases in which data was not available, an estimate was made using UN data from <http://data.un.org/Data.aspx?d=SNAAMA&f=grID%3A101%3BcurrID%3AU SD%3BpcFlag%3A1>, accessed 28 January 2012.

of representation and style, and given that data is not always available for style, no indicator is used in this analysis for style.

3. Our indicator for mode of legitimation (*leg*), but simplified in such a way that its value is set to 1 if the constitution was approved by a popular referendum, and to 0 otherwise.

4. An indicator (*wave*) that takes the value 1 if the constitution-making event belonged to Wave 7 (i.e. the constitution entered into force in 1990 or subsequently, see Chapter 1) and to 0 if it belonged to Wave 6 (prior to 1990, see Chapter 1). This is because the end of the Cold War is often said to represent a 'high watermark' for democracy and subsequently virtually all regimes sought to claim democratic legitimacy.

**Table 3.1      Conditions associated with the Persistence of Authoritarianism**

| Independent variables | Configuration 1 | Configuration 2 |
| --- | --- | --- |
| Poverty (GDP per capita in PPP less than PPP\$1,000) | ○ | ● |
| Mode of representation (indirect selection or direct election) | ○ | |
| Mode of legitimation (referendum) | | |
| Wave (Wave 7) | ● | ○ |
| Cases | Armenia (1995), Azerbaijan (1995), Bosnia-Herzegovina (1995), Croatia (1990), Djibouti (1992), Georgia (1995), Ivory Coast (2000), Kazakhstan (1995), Qatar (2005), Russia (1993) | Afghanistan (1987), Central African Republic (1976), Ghana (1979), Guinea-Bissau (1984), Haiti (1987), Liberia (1986), Nigeria (1989), Sierra Leone (1978), Somalia (1979), Tanzania (1977) |

The consistency cut-off point was set at 0.75. The analysis produced six distinct configurations that could be used to explain the presence of the outcome variable (i.e. persistence of authoritarianism). Using Boolean logic this was reduced to the following two simpler configurations:[4]

1.  ~pov * ~rep * wave ==> aut_sur
2.  pov * ~wave ==> aut_sur

---

4    In the formulae provided the prefix "~" means that the indicator is 0 (FALSE). Absence of this symbol means that the indicator is 1 (TRUE). The symbol * indicates the Boolean operand "AND".

which are represented in Table 3.1 (above), in which a solid circle means that the consition is present, while an empty circle means the condition is absent. No circle means that the condition is irrelevant and may either be present or absent.

The first configuration (consisting of ten cases) represents cases in which the constitution was passed during or after 1990, the country did not belong to the poorest group of countries and the constitution-making body was selected by means of elite appointment. It is worth identifying two subgroups of cases – those in which a referendum was held to pass the new constitution and those in which no such vote was held – because the political dynamic in the two subgroups was rather different. In those cases (seven) in which a referendum was used, the political leadership of the country either had consolidated or was in the process of consolidating political power had enshrined a system that was aimed at preserving power in a new constitution, and used the referendum as a kind of rubber stamp aimed at conferring legitimacy to the new state of affairs. In most cases, public input was not sought and the referendum was subject to manipulation. In the four post-Soviet cases (Azerbaijan, Kazakhstan, Armenia and Russia), new leaders were consolidating their power after independence; the presidents of Azerbaijan and Kazakhstan, in particular, were building strongly authoritarian political systems based on an all-powerful presidency and had begun doing so well before the constitution was elaborated. The new constitutions were merely a further stepping stone towards that goal. The Russian and Armenian constitutions were also designed to entrench the power of the president; the former was enshrined after a violent power struggle with the Russian Duma (which President Boris Yeltsin won) and the Armenian constitution was approved shortly after President Levon Ter Petrosian's military victory over Azerbaijan for control over the disputed enclave of Nagorno-Karabakh.

In the two African cases (Ivory Coast and Djibouti), as well as Qatar, the aim of the constitution was also to consolidate power. The constitution of Ivory Coast was passed shortly after General Robert Gueï replaced President Bédié following a military coup and included within it a controversial clause requiring that both parents of the Ivorian president must hold Ivorian citizenship; a clause deliberately designed to exclude one of his main rivals, Alassane Ouattara. In Djibouti, the constitution and referendum were organized by President Hassan Gouled Aptidon, who had already been in office as a virtual dictator since 1977. Finally, in Qatar, although the constitution (the first ever to be written) introduced a partially-elected parliament for the first time, it left the authority of the Emir untouched, bestowing on him the authority to appoint one third of MPs.

In four out of the seven cases in which a referendum was held (Azerbaijan, Djibouti, Qatar and Kazkkahstan), the 'yes' vote for the constitution was at least 90 per cent, and in a fifth case (Ivory Coast) over 85 per cent voted 'yes'. This suggests a high probability of electoral manipulation. At the very least, it suggests that no serious debates were held in public over the merits or drawbacks of the constitutional text. Even in the cases of Armenia and Russia, where the 'yes' vote was 70 per cent and 58 per cent respectively, there were credible allegations of electoral fraud (Wheatley 2008).

Overall, this subgroup of events was characterized by minimal public participation and a referendum that was no more than a fig leaf to mask authoritarian rule. Of particular importance is the fact that in all cases the political leadership gained power *before* the constitutional text was elaborated and the constitution was for them a tool to stay in power. The significance that all these events occurred after 1990 lies in the fact that in a post-Cold War environment dominated by 'democratic' forces, autocrats felt that they needed to adopt certain formal trappings of democracy to access foreign development aid, even though they had not the slightest intention of introducing real democratic reforms (Levitsky and Way 2010). Highly controlled (and manipulated) referendums were one such trapping.

Turning now to the subgroup of events within the first configuration in which no referendum was held (Croatia, Bosnia-Herzegovina and Georgia), we see that these were cases in which newly independent states emerged from a communist superstate (Yugoslavia and the USSR) and the constitutions were either written in an atmosphere of conflict, or (in the case of Croatia) conflict supervened soon after the constitution had been passed. In Croatia in 1990, the newly-elected parliament dominated by the Hrvatska Demokratska Zajednica (HDZ, Croatian Democratic Union), led by the hard-line nationalist Franjo Tudjman, took little time to draft a national constitution that provided for a strong, directly elected president. The constitution did not reflect Serb demands to name Serbs as one of the republic's constituent nations, effectively relegating them to minority status, and by the summer of 1991 conflict with Croatia's own Serbian community and the Yugoslav Federal Army led to civil war. Tudjman's government continued to give priority to national interests over democratic reforms and little progress towards democracy was made until after his death in 1999. In Bosnia-Herzegovina, the 1995 constitution was part of the internationally guaranteed Dayton Agreement and as such was effectively written under foreign supervision, its complex territorial arrangements have impeded the development of a self-sustaining functioning state and democracy has been undermined by a lack of consensus between the autonomous territorial entities. Finally, in Georgia the constitution was written against the backdrop of violent conflict, principally in the breakaway entity of Abkhazia, but also even in other parts of the country. The background of conflict and Georgia's subsequent failure to regain territorial integrity have often meant that issues of democratization have been viewed as subordinate to national goals.

Finally, the second configuration of ten events tells us little about the phenomenon we are trying to explain, namely the role of the constitution-making process on the persistence (or overturning) of authoritarian rule, because neither the mode of representation nor the mode of legitimation are defining features of this group. The constitution-making events occurred before 1990 in the poorest group of countries and eight out of ten countries are located in Africa. These countries were left largely unaffected by the wave of democratization that swept

Latin America and southern Europe in the 1970s and 1980s (even if some of them did experience pressure to democratize in Wave 7). Their low income per capita would, according to modernization theories of democracy (Diamond 1992; Lipset 1959; 1994), mean that they would be unlikely to consolidate democracy anyway. It is noteworthy that in just four out of ten cases was a referendum used to legitimate the constitution, suggesting that prior to the collapse of communism there was less pressure on regimes to show that they were (outwardly) democratic, and a referendum may therefore not have proved so necessary for legitimizing authoritarian regimes.

Our analysis appears to show that one element of the constitution-making process may be relevant for the persistence or opening up of authoritarian regimes: the mode of representation. Specifically, the chance of authoritarian entrenchment appears to be greater in cases in which the constitution-making body is appointed by elites. We do not, however, have sufficient evidence to affirm a causal relationship between these two phenomena. It is quite possible that it is an underlying authoritarian regime dynamic that determines *both* the (elite-centred) appointments to the constitution-making body *and* the failure to replace the authoritarian regime. It requires a more nuanced, qualitative study to investigate whether or not such a causal relationship exists and it is the task of subsequent chapters to provide such a qualitative study.

In terms of the role of direct democracy in constitution-making, we have seen how in many of the events identified in the previous paragraphs, a referendum was used to ratify the constitution, but that referendum was used more as a means to achieve a rubber stamp of (often bogus) legitimacy than as a genuine attempt to canvass public opinion on the constitution. Focussing on the wider universe of referendums on major constitutional changes, we find, paradoxically, that referendums are more likely to occur in less democratic societies than in more democratic societies. Using a dataset adapted from that of the Comparative Constitutions Project (CCP)[5] and Freedom House democracy scores, we find that, on average, referendums held to pass new constitutions in the period beginning in 1972 occurred in less democratic contexts than in those cases in which a new constitution was passed without a referendum. Averaging the composite Freedom House scores (from 2 to 14) in those countries in which a referendum was held to pass a new constitution for the year in which the constitution was passed, and comparing this figure with the average scores in those countries in which a constitution was passed without a referendum, we obtain average scores of 9.99 and 8.85 respectively for the two groups (N=89 for the referendum group and N=139 for the non-referendum group). Using a t-test for equality of means, we

---

5   Comparative Constitutions Project (CCP) is directed by Zachary Elkins (University of Texas, Department of Government) and Tom Ginsburg (University of Chicago, Law School), in cooperation with the Cline Center for Democracy at the University of Illinois. The project is supported by the National Science Foundation (SES0648288). <www.comparativeconstitutionsproject.org>, accessed 29 January 2012.

find this difference is significant at the 0.01 level if we do not assume equality of variance.[6] This suggests that it is actually rather common that referendums are used as weapons by non-democratic actors, especially presidents, in order to consolidate power. Indeed, as we have seen, examples abound, especially in Africa and the former Soviet Union, in which presidents have used a referendum as a weapon to augment their powers or extend the presidential term beyond the constitutionally-mandated period.

## Constitution-Making and Conflict Resolution

In order to explore what, if any, is the impact of the constitution-making process on the resolution (or non-resolution) of (violent) conflict, we first need to consider how violent conflicts are resolved. On the one hand, conflicts can be resolved when one side prevails over another, as we saw in 2009 in Sri Lanka when a twenty-six year civil war between government forces and Tamil Tiger rebels ended with the outright victory of the former over the latter. On the other hand, a war can end with a peace agreement in which no side emerges victorious, but all agree to put down their weapons in exchange for certain benefits or guarantees. The first model is based on the consolidation of power in the hands of one player, while the second involves the generation of consensus amongst most, if not all, players. If a new constitution is drafted in the first case, it will be a 'victory constitution' that is likely to reflect a unipolar power structure and favour the powers that be. Moreover, consensus will play no role in constitution-making; it will be the balance of power on the ground that will determine both the end of the fighting and the new constitution. In the second case, the new constitution is likely to formalize the peace agreement and reflect the interests of all players. Ideally, it will pave the way for a lasting peace.

Turning to our sample of 160 constitution-making events, we first identify cases in which there was an armed conflict that led up to the constitution-making process (irrespective of whether the conflict was subsequently resolved). We used the UCDP/PRIO Armed Conflict Dataset[7] to identify armed conflicts in which either: a) the government of a country was party in an intrastate armed conflict (fighting against classic rebels) or in an extrasystemic conflict (fighting against liberation movements), or b) there was, before the state's independence, an intrastate or an extrasystemic armed conflict about the particular territory of the future independent state. Given that data from this particular dataset is not available before 1946, we exclude all cases in which the constitution-making

---

6    However, the applicability of the t-test is questionable given that the two groups are not distributed normally along the Freedom House score.

7    From <http://www.prio.no/Data/Armed-Conflict>, accessed 29 January 2012.

process began before 1950. We also exclude cases in which a new constitution was not passed. This leaves us with 35 cases.[8]

Of these 35 cases, we have 13 cases in which regime incumbents consolidated power after a period of conflict and cemented their grip on power through a new constitution.[9] We also have 12 cases in which rebels won the conflict and designed a constitution more or less on their own terms. In six of these cases this occurred in the context of decolonization or secession from a superstate,[10] while in the other six cases the rebellion occurred in an already-established state.[11] In another six cases the constitution-making process and the conflict dynamic were not inter-related; a low-level conflict was endemic in these cases and therefore the constitution-making process had little relevance to conflict resolution.[12] In another case (Afghanistan in 1987), incumbents passed a new constitution despite the fact that war was raging and the constitution had little meaningful effect.

This leaves us with just three 'peacemaking constitutions', compared with twenty-five cases of 'victory constitutions' (with thirteen designed by incumbents and twelve designed by 'rebels'). These three cases are Bosnia-Herzegovina (1995), Iraq (2005) and Zimbabwe (1979). The sample of cases is clearly far too small to make any meaningful conclusions about the impact of the constitution-making process on the subsequent course of conflict resolution. The three cases themselves are, in fact, far from auspicious in terms of conflict resolution. While Bosnia has not returned to wide-scale violence, the complexity of the state territorial structures defined by the Dayton Agreement has undermined the coherence of the state itself, dependence on foreign supervision has further diminished the state's capacity to govern, and the former warring parties remain unable to reach consent on the future existence of the state. In Iraq, the new constitutional order has remained incapable even of preserving peace; inter-factional struggles have continued or even intensified and the country remains in a state of low-level civil war. Finally, the power-sharing elements of the Zimbabwe constitution signed at

---

8   Afghanistan (1987), Azerbaijan (1995), Bangladesh (1972), Bosnia-Herzegovina (1995), Cambodia (1993), Cameroon (1960), Chad (1989), Chad (1996), Chile (1981), China (1954), Colombia (1991), Congo (1964), Costa Rica (1949), Djibouti (1992), East Timor (2002), Ethiopia (1987), Ethiopia (1995), Georgia (1995), Guatemala (1986), Iraq (2005), Liberia (1986), Malaya (1957), Mali (1992), Namibia (1990), Nicaragua (1987), Peru (1993), Philippines (1973), Philippines (1987), Portugal (1976), Romania (1991), Russia (1993), Rwanda (2004), Tunisia (1959), Uganda (1995), Zimbabwe (1979).

9   Azerbaijan (1995), Cambodia (1993), Chad (1989), Chad (1996), China (1954), Congo (1964), Djibouti (1992), Georgia (1995), Nicaragua (1987), Peru (1993), Philippines (1973), Russia (1993), Rwanda (2004).

10   Bangladesh (1972), Cameroon (1960), East Timor (2002), Malaya (1957), Namibia (1990), Tunisia (1959).

11   Chile (1981), Costa Rica (1949), Ethiopia (1995), Liberia (1986), Mali (1992), Romania (1991).

12   Colombia (1991), Ethiopia (1987), Guatemala (1986), Philippines (1987), Portugal (1976), Uganda (1995).

Lancaster House in London in 1979, which gave the white community 20 per cent of seats, were abandoned in 1987 by a constitutional amendment as President Robert Mugabe began to consolidate power in his own hands. The fates of these three countries after the passage of the constitution would appear to confirm Widner's finding that the use of interim arrangements in conflict resolution cases may be preferable to drafting a new constitution at that point in time (Widner 2008, see Chapter 1). The Bosnian case in particular shows that an instrument that may be effective for conflict-resolution in the short term may undermine state-building in the long term.

## Three Conflict Resolution Cases

Clearly it is hard to reach consensus in the aftermath of a violent conflict. Rustow argued that while it may take a 'hot family feud' to build the sort of consensus needed to establish a democracy, this 'feud' must stop short of 'implacable hostility' if a lasting democratic peace is to be secured (Rustow 1970: 363). However, there are a small number of borderline cases in which a constitutional settlement marked the end of a (relatively) low-level violent conflict and ushered in a (minimally) democratic peace. In the next section we will briefly look at the constitution-making process in three such cases: Switzerland (1848), India (1950) and South Africa (1997). The first two cases occurred too early to be represented in the UCDP/PRIO Armed Conflict Dataset (the constitution-making process in India *began* before 1950). The third case (South Africa) was originally included as a conflict case for the years 1989–1993 (inclusive) in the dataset but was subsequently dropped. Nevertheless, in our view the conflict between supporters of the African National Congress (ANC) and supporters of the mainly Zulu Inkatha Freedom Party (which enjoyed the covert backing of elements within the white-led government) was sufficiently intense to classify it as a violent conflict.

### Switzerland

In his seminal study of the relationship between contentious politics and democratization, Charles Tilly (2003) notes that contrary to the stereotypical representations of Switzerland as a civil political backwater, during the first half of the nineteenth century it was the scene of bitter division and armed conflict. Indeed, the period 1830–1848, according to Tilly (2003: 168), offers a microcosm of the conflicts over democratization in what is 'Europe's oldest continuously functioning democratic regime'. Although framed largely in terms of religious conflict, the Swiss battle was ultimately one about the organization of the state. It is because of this that the constitutional settlement of 1848 offers a neat illustration of the interactions between the three process – violent conflict, constitution-making, and democratization – that form the core of this chapter.

The old Swiss constitutional order was a remarkably loose patchwork of overlapping jurisdictions in which the constituent units, the cantons, operated largely as sovereign powers. The Diet, the highest Executive organ of the confederation, was little more than a meeting point for strictly instructed Ambassadors representing the Cantons (Tilly 2003: 170). In the absence of a central government a rotating secretariat existed and decided on most issues on the basis of unanimity. That constitutional order was temporarily suspended following the French Revolution and Napoleon's subsequent occupation of Switzerland and the founding of the Helvetic Republic. Infused with the revolutionary ideas of its neighbour, the Helvetic Republic espoused liberal-democratic principles, representative democracy, secular education and equality of rights which, not surprisingly, clashed with the traditional ideals of the conservative Catholic cantons of central Switzerland (Dardanelli 2011: 144). Although it was soon to collapse and be replaced by the Federal Pact of 1815, the Helvetic Republic left an important political legacy.

Following the French defeat, the Federal Pact of 1815 restored much of the old constitutional order, and in particular the sovereign power of the cantons. However, there was one important restriction on cantonal sovereignty which prohibited internal alliances between cantons – when this provision was later violated it would become a trigger for outright civil war (Steinberg 1996: 42). Despite the relative briefness of the Helvetic Republic, the period of limited unitary government founded on liberal-democratic principles had an important impact on an increasingly vocal group of radicals calling for constitutional reforms. Their ideas chimed with the liberal movement of the times, which according to Steinberg (1996) was often no more than intense anti-clericalism. Between the 1830s and 1840s religious tension between liberalism and religion frequently triggered armed clashes across Europe and Switzerland was no exception. Initially, the Swiss liberal-radicals pursued their goals principally at the cantonal level. As this period of so-called 'Regeneration' between 1830–1848 gathered momentum a series of constitutional transformations providing for citizen equality, universal male suffrage, clearer limits on government, and popular constitutional ratification were implemented at the cantonal level by the 'regenerated' cantons (Dardanelli 2011: 146; see also Chapter 7 in this volume).

With the increase in number and relative power of the radical led cantons in the Diet, and their increasingly vocal demands for constitutional reform at the federal level, the stage for confrontation was set. The liberal-radical wing was calling for a constitutional transformation which effectively entailed the creation of a federal state based on liberal-democratic principles and with a central capacity to act in the economic and defence spheres. As the tension built up, with frequent local clashes, the conservative cantons signed a secret defensive alliance known as the *Sonderbund*. Once the defensive alliance was discovered the radical cantons pushed for it to be dissolved. Not long afterwards, and following a religious dispute over the expulsion of Jesuits that acted as a trigger, a short civil war erupted in the winter of late 1847.

Unlike its American counterpart little more than a decade later, the Swiss civil war was relatively bloodless with less than 100 battle deaths. As in the US, the conflict was precipitated by deep divisions over the constitutional power of central government to restrict practices at the constituent level. In both cases the clash was over opposing views of the state and how best to divide sovereignty between the two layers of government – that of the centre and the constituent units. As in the US too, it was the forces in favour of a more 'progressive' central government that triumphed over their conservative/secessionist opponents. Interestingly, the Swiss resolved their conflict through a constitutional settlement that borrowed much in terms of its content from the 1787 US federal constitution.

As noted earlier in this chapter, it is common for victors in a conflict setting where one side prevails over the other to want to alter constitutional 'rules of the game' in their favour. The victorious Swiss radicals were no different in this regard. In the early months of 1848 they quickly went about setting up a constitutional commission charged with reforming the 1815 treaty. In terms of the mode of representation the territorial principle was to be respected whereby the delegates were drawn from the cantons and represented the latter. Any other model would have been anathema to the Swiss tradition. In terms of style, there was little scope for public input into the constitutional negotiations. The negotiations took place behind closed doors with the focus directed at achieving difficult compromises rather than opening up philosophical debates. The pragmatic compromises among both losers and victors was a constitutional bargain that created a federal state, albeit one with a rather limited central government.

Although it was endorsed by the Diet in June 1848, the new constitution would need to be legitimated by the cantons themselves through a ratification process consisting of popular votes.[13] At this point, a curious outcome emerged. Nearly a third of the cantons, i.e. most of the conservative cantons on the 'losing' side, rejected the new constitution through popular votes. Under the existing rules governing constitutional change, this ought to have been enough to torpedo the new constitution. Yet it did not. The Diet was reconvened in September 1848 and in a strictly speaking non-legal revolutionary act promulgated the new constitution based on a majority vote. The losers ultimately accepted the outcome and even participated in the subsequent elections to the new federal parliament (Dardanelli 2011: 149).

Despite the fact that some observers were surprised by the compromises on the part of 'passionately committed nineteenth-century liberals, who had just won a short war, to share victory with what they must have seen as bigoted, backward Catholic communities' (Steinberg 1996: 49) the fact remains that a constitutional settlement was implemented against the wishes of a significant minority of cantons. No doubt it was the nature of the constitutional product itself, a federal state with a comparatively weak central government and strong safeguards against future encroachment by the centre, that made the settlement ultimately more palatable

---

13   The majority of cantons held constitutional referendums.

to the losing side. Indeed, the losers soon found ways to constitutionally block the accretion of powers by the centre. In doing so, the transformation of violent confrontation into constitutional obstruction changed the terms of the catholic vs. liberal-protestant hostilities and channelled them into the political domain.

For Tilly, Swiss democratization, in contrast to its major European neighbours, followed a weak-state path of democratization. Confrontation, conquest, and a constitutional settlement in which each side gave up advantages to remain in a larger union are what prevented Switzerland from splitting into two or more clusters of cantons – Switzerland survived as direct result of its war settlement (Tilly 2003: 197). The institutions of federalism and additional layers of direct democracy such as the mandatory constitutional referendum on the further transfer of powers to the centre allowed for religious confrontation to be transformed into religious accommodation. Future conflicts would be henceforth channelled through constitutional politics over the appropriate locus of authority among territorial levels that is so characteristic of federal systems.

*India*

The Indian Constituent Assembly had its first sitting on 9 December 1946, eight months before India achieved independence. It consisted of members selected indirectly from provincial assemblies that were elected by the people, albeit mainly on the basis of a limited franchise. The constitution was adopted by the Constituent Assembly on 26 November 1949 and entered into force on 26 January 1950. During the period in which the Assembly sat, communal violence began in Bombay and soon spread to other parts of British India. Independence on 15 August 1947 led to the birth of two states, rather than one: the Dominion of India and the Dominion of Pakistan.

Despite the dominance of the Indian Congress Party in the Constituent Assembly, there were three main issues that provoked real debate. The first involved the nature of the state: federal or unitary. The case for federalism had been paramount when the Constituent Assembly first sat, conditioned as it was by the need for autonomy of the Muslim regions. However, with partition in 1947 and the separation of the Dominion of Pakistan, the logic of applying federal rules to accommodate the Muslim minority was much weaker. Another motive for establishing a federal system was to accommodate the rulers or Maharajas of the princely states, which had become nominally sovereign when the Dominion of India was established in August 1947. However, by the middle of 1948 even the most powerful Maharajas had been co-opted or coerced into ceding their autonomous power and merging their territories with other provinces into much larger states. Some members of the Constituent Assembly, including members of the Congress Party, defended a more communitarian Hinduist legacy and a more decentralized federation, while others advocated a more centralist approach. Dalits, who were represented by the influential chairman of the Drafting Committee in the Constituent Assembly, Bhimrao Ramji Ambedkar, favoured a more unitary state because decentralization risked entrenching old hierarchical practices in the provinces (Pylee 2007).

The second critical issue was the position of minorities in the new state. Before the split with Pakistan, the key concern was how to accommodate two groups, Hindus and Muslims, but in the Dominion of India Muslims constituted a minority of around 10 per cent of the population. Despite the fact that overall, the Congress Party opposed special provisions for minorities, the influence exerted by Dr Ambedkar and other influential minority leaders led to a compromise. The new Constitution guaranteed cultural autonomy to its religious minorities, including the freedom to manage their religious affairs independently, and a proportional share of the state budget in religious issues (Harel-Shalev 2009: 1263). Special provisions were also made in the constitution for 'scheduled tribes' (disadvantaged indigenous peoples) and 'scheduled castes' (mainly Dalits or 'untouchables') in the form of reserved seats in the lower house of the federal legislature, as well as in state legislative bodies.

The third and final issue was whether or not India would establish a democratic system based on universal franchise. Franchise had previously been limited to around 10 per cent of the population by the 1935 Government of India Act and it was by no means a foregone conclusion that the principles of universal suffrage would be enshrined in the new constitution in order to give the socially excluded majority the right to vote. It was largely due to the insistence of the Dalit leadership in the Constituent Assembly that universal suffrage was adopted (Avritzer 2005).

The constitution-making process in India effectively forged a consensus whereby it was accepted by all major players that the Indian state would have ultimate authority across the territory. The kind of 'reserved feudal domains' enjoyed by the princely states was abolished. Initially, there was a real possibility of state failure; it had been feared that the new Dominion would degenerate into a mass of squabbling fiefdoms and the separation of India and Pakistan would be just the beginning of a much more far-reaching unravelling of the incipient polity. At the same time, however, a federal system was established according to which states enjoyed significant autonomy, but this autonomy was limited by a) a provision that it could be withdrawn in the event of a national emergency and b) the safeguard that no state could secede. The consensus also enshrined the basic principles of democracy based on universal suffrage as well as extensive provisions for safeguarding the rights of minorities. The constitution was, of course, elaborated by members of various Indian political elites and could not, therefore be considered as an expression of consensus across all strata of society. The consensus did, however, form the basis for a general acceptance of the principles of democracy that still holds today.

*South Africa*

Most of the compromises made to reconcile the outgoing apartheid-era government with the principles of universal suffrage and minority rule were made during the drafting of the 1994 interim constitution, which formed the basis for the final 1997 constitution. The constitution-making process began against a backdrop of incipient inter-communal violence that at times appeared to be on the verge of escalating into civil war. Whilst the limited bombing campaign of the African National Congress (ANC) had targeted property, rather than human life, and was curtailed as soon as negotiations begun, far more worrying was the outbreaks of so-called 'black-on-black violence' between supporters of the ANC and supporters of the Zulu movement Inkatha in KwaZulu Natal. Often provoked by the South African police force, in the early 1990s the number of deaths resulting from this violence was estimated at 250 per month (Hamber 1999: 115).

In September 1992 President FW De Clerk and ANC leader Nelson Mandela committed themselves to create a democratically elected power-sharing government for an interim period of five years after elections. After several abortive attempts at negotiations, in April 1993 the Multi-Party Negotiating Process (MPNP) began and included representatives of almost all political players. Within the MPNP a 208-member, 26-party plenary body was established, but the key negotiating forum was the Negotiating Council, which consisted of two delegates per party. In November the Negotiating Council reached a comprehensive agreement, which formed the basis for the interim constitution. The radical Pan-African Congress and the far-right Freedom Alliance failed to agree, and Inkatha's leader, Mangosuthu Buthelezi, boycotted the negotiations. However, all other political forces signed up to the deal. The interim constitution was ratified on 22 December 1993, and implemented on 27 April 1994 when the first democratic parliament was elected.

According to the interim constitution, a founding election was to be held for a legislature that would appoint an executive and simultaneously act as a constituent assembly. It would be elected by proportional representation based on regional lists with no minimum threshold. All parties winning at least 20 per cent of seats were entitled to a deputy executive president and in the event that only one party won more than 20 per cent of seats, the second-placed party would be granted a deputy executive president, irrespective of its share of the vote. Moreover, all parties winning at least five per cent of seats would be entitled to a number of Cabinet posts proportional to their electoral strength. A quasi-federal system with a ninety-member senate (later to become the National Council of Provinces) was established, in which each of the nine provinces was represented by ten senators.

The interim constitution represented a compromise between the incumbent government and the ANC. The government was able to limit the power of the newly-elected president during the transition period by insisting on a power-sharing agreement. On the other hand, De Clerk was forced to drop his demand that the power-sharing arrangement be somehow made permanent. The final constitution that was approved by the newly-elected legislature in 1996 and entered into force the following year did not include the power-sharing provision but retained the basic parameters of the interim constitution, including the quasi-federal system and the electoral system of proportional representation with no minimum threshold.

As a result, despite the fact that the ANC has won all subsequent elections with between 50 and 70 per cent of the vote, the opposition Democratic Alliance has retained significant representation in parliament and controlled Western Cape province from 1994 until 2001 and again from 2009 until the present day.

Although the deal was primarily between the De Klerk government and the ANC, the more marginal forces also soon either became accommodated to the deal or disappeared. Inkatha initially pledged to boycott the 1994 elections, but agreed to take part when they realized they would not be able to stop them taking place. After the elections they formed an uneasy coalition with the ANC in the province of Kwa-Zulu Natal. The Pan-African Congress also participated in the elections despite its misgivings about the Interim Constitution, but garnered only just over 1 per cent of the vote. The pro-apartheid far right could not agree about whether to participate; some far-right groups took part in the elections, while others boycotted. These groupings henceforth virtually disappeared from the political scene. The success of the new order can be gleaned from a number of surveys carried out in South Africa; an Afrobarometer survey carried out in 2004 showed that 50 per cent of white respondents agreed or strongly agreed that the 'constitution expresses the values and hopes of the South African people', while just 24 per cent disagreed or strongly disagreed. The corresponding figures for black respondents were 57 per cent and 20 per cent.[14] This suggests that ten years after the election of the first democratic government the white population, notwithstanding the fact that they lost their dominant position, had been brought into the democratic consensus, confounding pessimistic predictions that the two groups were destined to live in conflict.

*Summary*

The three vignettes provided above show, first of all, that constitution-making can, under certain circumstances, help to defuse violent conflicts. It must be emphasized, however, that in all three cases, the violence was contained within certain limits and did not escalate into a long, protracted civil war. Moreover, in all three cases, the violence had already been contained to some extent by the time the constitution entered into force. The constitutional settlements did, however, appear to contain future violence as a sense of constitutional patriotism gradually took hold. It is especially noteworthy that, especially in the cases of Switzerland and South Africa, it was the perceived losers of that country's transformation (conservative Catholic communities in Switzerland and whites in South Africa) that gradually became accommodated to the new constitution and accepted it as their own. This illustrates a point that will recur often in this book – that for a constitutional settlement to endure and become accepted amongst the people it must first become institutionalized informally, to the extent that the general

---

14   http://www.afrobarometer.org/files/documents/summary_results/saf_r2-5_sor.pdf.

principles it enshrines must gradually become accepted as guiding principles in politics.


## Conclusions

This chapter set out with two main aims. First, it explored the relationship between two elements of the constitution-making process – the mode of representation and the mode of legitimation – on the stability of authoritarian regimes. Using the qualitative research methodology QCA, it identified two configurations that were particularly conducive to the persistence of authoritarianism. Of these the most relevant configuration was one in which the constitution-making process was carried out behind closed doors by the political elite. In most cases that belong to this configuration the final document was passed by a referendum.

Although the constitution-making process is important for the future development of the political regime, the type of political dynamic that was in place before the constitution-making process even began can have a massive influence on *both* the constitution-making process *and* its outcome in terms of democratization. On other occasions a new political dynamic may assert itself shortly after the constitution has been adopted, derailing the new constitutional order and forming a roadblock to further democratization. Even then, however, entrenched political instability may be an underlying cause. Overall, we can conclude that if democracy is not in the interests of the main political actors, almost *any* constitution-making process can lead to an entrenchment of, rather than a release from authoritarianism.

In terms of conflict resolution, we discovered that successful resolution of violent conflicts through constitution-making is rare. Far more frequently winners of conflicts draft new constitutions on their own terms and according to their own interests. This is because achieving a consensus, even over the most basic principles of statehood, and resolving the co-ordination dilemma across society is highly problematic in a deeply divided society (Rustow 1970; Weingast 1997). Probably, the best that can be hoped for is a more limited peace treaty that defers critical constitutional compromises to a later date, although this is not always possible. The few unusual cases in which constitution-making did form a part of a conflict resolution process – for example, Switzerland, India and South Africa – represent intermediate cases in which violence has not spiralled out of control to such an extent that achieving a consensus is impossible. Under such circumstances, Rustow's dynamic of a conflict leading to a compromise that underpins the gradual institutionalization of a democratic consensus can still apply. Transition to democracy almost always involves conflict; the key issue is what level of conflict makes compromise and consensus impossible.

# PART 2
# Case Studies

# Chapter 4
# Constitution-Making in West Africa: Keeping the President in Check

Jonathan Wheatley

The African continent provides a unique environment for examining the role of the constitution-making process in political transition during the so-called third wave of democratization,[1] first because so many constitution-making events occurred within a very short space of time (the early 1990s) and second because the outcomes of the constitution-making process are so varied. In Chapter 1 we identified the core puzzle of this book: namely, what is the impact of the constitution-making process on the post-constitution political environment in terms of a) constitutional stability, b) conflict and c) democracy? In this chapter, the focus will be on five West African countries that drafted a new constitution and began a process of political transition at more or less the same time – during the first three years of the 1990s. Our main focus will be on the impact of the constitution-making process on the stability of the new constitution; however, we will also explore the extent to which constitutional stability during the transition process facilitates the gradual establishment of democracy. Finally, we will look at the interrelationship between the constitution-making process and the dynamic of conflict, on the one hand, and consensus, on the other.

The five West African countries that form the focus of this study are Benin, Burkina Faso, Congo-Brazzaville, Ghana and Togo. These countries have been selected on the one hand because of their similarities in terms of background conditions: their location is geographically proximate, all countries experienced a period of authoritarianism and by 1990 had not held competitive elections for at least a decade. By the same token, all five countries embarked on political reform in 1990–1992 and all held founding multi-party elections between 1991 and 1993. The constitution-making events also occurred at more or less exactly the same time and as a result of a single global process (the end of the Cold war). All countries

---

1    The so called third wave of democratization refers to a classification used by Samuel Huntington (Huntington 1991). Huntington defines the first wave of democratization as an initial period of democratization that began in Western Europe and North America in the nineteenth century, the second wave refers to the democratization of a number of countries after the Second World War, while the third wave of democratization refers to more recent democratization events in Southern Europe, Latin America, post-communist Eastern Europe and Africa that began in 1974.

adopted a new constitution between 1990 and 1992, and in all the new constitution was approved by a referendum.

On the other hand, the five cases encompass a wide variation in terms of the nature of the constitution-making process, in terms of political dynamics, in terms of the long-term stability of the constitution and in terms of the development of democracy. The first two sets of differences are summarized in Table 4.1 (below). First, an open and inclusive constitution-making process could be observed in Benin and Congo-Brazzaville, in Ghana and Togo a relatively open process was limited by constraints from the executive branch of power, while in Burkina Faso the constitution-making body was appointed exclusively by the ruling party. This corresponded to the dynamics of the early transition period: in Burkina Faso, Ghana and Togo, the transition process was controlled by the incumbent president in what is commonly known as a 'top-down' mode of transition, while in Benin and Congo-Brazzaville a 'bottom-up' dynamic meant that the president lost control of the process. Moreover, the constitutions that were born also met very different fates; the constitutions of Benin and Ghana have changed very little since their adoption, while in the other three cases the constitution has been subject to a number of very significant amendments that have led to an increased concentration of power in the hands of the president. Finally, today Benin and Ghana qualify at least as minimal democracies, Burkina Faso and Togo can best be described as competitive authoritarian regimes (Levitsky and Way 2010) with few attributes of genuine democracy, while Congo-Brazzaville can only be characterized as a full-blown authoritarian regime. This chapter will attempt to explain why in certain cases the incumbent president and the executive have managed successfully to alter the constitution in their favour, while in other cases this did not occur. A number of explanations will be considered.

**Table 4.1    Constitution-making in five West African countries**

|  |  | Constitution-Making Process | | |
|---|---|---|---|---|
|  |  | Open and inclusive | Inclusive, but some restrictions on public input | Exclusive (elite-appointed body) |
| **Dominant Actor** | President |  | Togo<br>Ghana | Burkina Faso |
|  | Opposition | Congo-Brazzaville<br>Benin |  |  |

The core puzzle is the impact of the constitution-making process on the future of the constitutional order. A number of authors (Ghai 2006, Ginsburg, Elkins and Blount 2009) have argued that if the constitution-making process is open and transparent and if a large number of actors – both elite and societal – feel that they are participants in the process, the constitution that emerges is more likely to be accepted as a manifestation of the will of the people and will therefore not be changed willy-nilly to suit the interests of individual power brokers. Based on our earlier classification of constitution-making processes outlined in Chapter 1, we propose the following hypothesis:

> H1: The endurance of the constitution is conditioned by the manner in which the constitution came into being.

There then comes the question of what comes out of the constitution-making process. Some constitutions, by their very nature, are easier to amend than others. Almost all constitutions include a number of articles that stipulate how the constitutional text can be amended. One would expect that the simpler this procedure is and the less it requires approval from countervailing powers (e.g. the parliament, the Constitutional Court or the people through a referendum) the more likely it will be that the executive will successfully change the constitution for its own ends. This leads us to formulate a second hypothesis:

> H2: The endurance of the constitution is conditioned by the provisions of the constitutional text itself.

Third, the capacity of the executive to amend the constitution may depend on political factors that have little to do with either the constitutional text or the constitution-making process. Within the framework of many constitutions, amendments to the constitution require a super-majority in parliament (typically either two-thirds, three-quarters or four-fifths). A pro-government party may dominate the legislature to such an extent that it commands such a majority and can then effectively marginalize opposition forces, allowing it to alter the constitution with little resistance. Alternatively, a president or government that has hegemonic control over the political and economic arena can simply ignore the existing constitutional order, suspend the constitution and draft a new one that is more congruent with the interests of the executive. Such 'constitutional coups' have taken place in a number of contexts across the world, including Africa. Finally, if a referendum is required for constitutional change, the vote can be manipulated or even falsified to obtain the desired result. These political factors provide us with a third hypothesis:

> H3: The endurance of the constitution is conditioned by political factors, most notably the balance of power between the different forces and the capacity of a pro-presidential faction to achieve hegemonic control.

This third hypothesis leads us to consider a rather more fundamental question and one that is also central to this book; namely, under what circumstances does an imbalance of power lead to an unstable equilibrium in which that imbalance becomes further accentuated, leading to the domination of one actor over all others? This leads us to ask first whether or not there is a consensus amongst all players that power must be limited and then to enquire under what circumstances such a consensus can be established. Can the constitution-making process mark the building of such a consensus? This leads us to suggest a fourth hypothesis:

> H4: a) The endurance of the constitution is conditioned by a consensus amongst all major actors that power must be limited, and b) under certain circumstances the constitution-making process can itself help to forge such a consensus.

The remainder of this chapter will proceed as follows. First, a brief outline of each of the five cases will be provided in terms of the original constitution-making process in the early 1990s and the subsequent constitutional changes that have been made in each case. We will consider the first hypothesis (H1) by looking at the way the constitution was adopted in each case to begin with and exploring the effect this had on the way it was perceived and the readiness with which it was (or was not) amended. A slightly more detailed examination of the political dynamics in each case will be provided in order to shed light on H3, in other words, the role of the political configuration on the endurance of the constitution. The third section will turn to the relevant parts of the constitutional texts in each country in order to examine how easy it is legally to amend the constitution in each case and whether this has any relation to whether it was, in fact, amended. In this way it is hoped to investigate the validity of H2. Finally, the impact of constitution-making on democracy will be considered by examining the relationship between the constitution-making process, on the one hand, and the development of a democratic consensus on limited government, on the other.

## Constitutional Developments

In all five cases that are the focus of this study, internal (mainly economic) and international pressures had led, by the end of the 1980s, to a crisis of legitimacy in autocratic rule. During the early 1990s, all five countries agreed to introduce a multi-party system and all adopted a new constitution to enshrine such a system.

In three of the five cases (Benin, Congo-Brazzaville, and Togo), the constitution-writing process was initiated and directed by large inclusive bodies, known as 'national conferences' that drew from different sectors of society. Robinson points to 'the historical precedent of the Estates General' in 1789 France as 'a principle for generating strategy on regime change in Francophone Africa' (Robinson 1994: 576–7) and the model of the Estates-General in terms of its capacity to represent different social strata appears to have been a model for the national conferences of Benin, Congo-Brazzaville, and Togo. All these bodies were formed by a process of indirect selection (see Chapter 1) and included a large number of delegates (418 in Benin, 772 in Togo, 1,100 in Congo-Brazzaville) that included representatives of the government, political parties and organizations, associations, trade unions, students' groups and religious groups. All were presided over by a religious authority. The initiative came from the opposition and the president and his retinue agreed only with reluctance to the establishment of such a body. The first country to establish a National Conference was Benin (in February 1990) and in many ways the Beninois Conference represented an 'archetype' that subsequent conference in Congo-Brazzaville (in February-June 1991) and Togo (in July-August 1991) sought to emulate. Table 4.2 (below) shows the timing of the national conferences and the date the constitution was ratified in each case.

**Table 4.2    Formation of national conferences in West Africa**

| Country | National Conference | Ratification of Constitution |
| --- | --- | --- |
| Benin | February 19–28 1990 | December 1990 |
| Burkina Faso | n/a | June 1991 |
| Congo-Brazzaville | February 25–June 10 1991 | March 1992 |
| Ghana | August 1991–March 1992* | May 1992 |
| Togo | July–August 1991 | September 1992 |

*Note*: * The relevant body is usually described as a Consultative Assembly, rather than a National Conference.

However, within these three cases, there were significant differences in the extent to which the Conference was able to impose its authority. In both Benin and Congo-Brazzaville, the Conference gained the upper hand over the president, declared itself sovereign and appointed an interim government, effectively sidelining the president. The president and his party then lost the first competitive elections. In both cases, the process was characterized by an open mode of deliberation; in Benin, proceedings at the Conference were broadcast live on Benin radio, rebroadcast on television and a video recording of proceedings was sold widely (Robinson 1994: 576). In Congo-Brazzaville, the Conference aired publicly allegations of corruption levelled against the governing elite over three decades (Robinson 1994: 589). In Togo, on the other hand, the National Conference, despite declaring itself sovereign, never achieved de facto sovereignty and never gained the upper hand over Gnassingbe Eyadema, who continued to manipulate events from above. In fact, Eyadema had the interim prime minister, Kokou Koffigoh, kidnapped and coerced into submission (Heilbrunn 1993). The Conference did not run its full course and the delegation from the powerful Togolese army walked out (Nwajiaku 1994: 440). In the end, the constitution that eventually emerged was moulded to the will of the president, who remained in power until his death in 2005.

In Ghana, a body rather similar to a National Conference was established, but this time under the express instructions of President Jerry Rawlings, who expressed a readiness for the gradual introduction of multi-party rule. The Ghanaian Consultative Assembly, as it came to be called, consisted of 117 members elected by the district assemblies, 121 members elected from 62 known organizations and corporate groups and 22 members appointed by the government (Aubynn 2002: 81).[2] Its role was to discuss and debate constitutional proposals drawn up by a nine-member Committee of Experts and to produce a draft constitution.[3] The proceedings of the Consultative Assembly were made public, but the ruling Provisional National Defence Council (PNDC) under the leadership of President Jerry Rawlings attempted to manipulate its composition and also picked members of the Expert Committee that were involved most intensively in the drafting of the Constitution. Rawlings therefore remained in control of the process and remained president until his presidential mandate expired in 2000.

Finally, in Burkina Faso in 1990, no inclusive body was established; the ruling Popular Front held a National Congress, which formed a committee to draft a national constitution. This committee was therefore the result of elite appointment and its proceedings, despite receiving some publicity, were held mainly behind closed doors.

Overall, the constitution-making process can be described as open and inclusive with a high degree of public participation in Benin and Congo-Brazzaville, partly open, partly inclusive with limited public participation in Ghana and Togo, and exclusive in Burkina Faso. In the latter case, active public involvement was more or less restricted to ratifying the constitution ex post facto by means of a referendum.

However, the type of process does not seem to have a direct relationship with the extent to which the new constitution remained stable and endured in its current form. In three out of five cases, Burkina Faso, Congo-Brazzaville and Togo, important aspects of the constitution regarding the separation of powers have been radically changed to reinforce the invincibility of the country's president. In the other two cases, however, the constitution has remained the same, in principle, with no amendments whatsoever being made to the Beninois constitution and the Ghanaian constitution only experiencing relatively minor amendments. At first glance, therefore, the nature of the constitution-making process seems to have had little effect on the stability of the constitutional text. Before continuing the analysis, it is worth briefly outlining the main constitutional changes that have

---

2    According to one source, '[t]he Consultative Assembly also included hitherto non-political associations like butchers, hairdressers, fishermen, fishmongers, drinking and chop bar owners'. See http://www.afrimap.org/english/images/report/AfriMAP_Ghana_PolPart. pdf>, Accessed 8 March 2009.

3    Ibid.; Kwame Boafo-Arthur, Democracy and Stability in West Africa: The Ghanaian Experience, Claude Ake Memorial Papers No. 4, Department of Peace and Conflict Research, Uppsala University, & Nordic Africa Institute, Uppsala (2008).

been made in each case subsequent to the adoption of the constitution (except in the case of Benin, where no changes have occurred).

In Burkina Faso, the first major constitutional amendments following the adoption of the 1991 constitution were those of 1997 that abolished presidential term limits, effectively allowing the president to remain in his position for life, providing he was re-elected every seven years. However, a further constitutional amendment, passed in 2000, reversed the previous amendment by introducing two-term limits of five years each to the presidential mandate. President Blaise Compaore and his supporters argued that the new laws could not be applied retroactively, and so Compaore ran again in 2005 for a new 'first term' and again in 2010 for a 'second term'. The constitutional amendment was seen as a compromise after a series of confrontations between government and opposition. All amendments were adopted by parliament without a referendum. Overall, therefore, despite the concessions granted in the 2000 amendments, the constitution has been manipulated effectively to allow President Compaore to remain in power continuously over the twenty years since it was adopted.

In Congo-Brazzaville, the new constitutional order did not last long. In 1997 former dictator Denis Sassou-Nguesso, a northerner, defeated the forces of Pascal Lissouba, a southerner, with the help of Angolan troops and other forces. Sassou-Nguesso's new government then replaced the country's 1992 Constitution with a new, temporary Fundamental Act, which established a strong and highly centralized presidential system of government. A new constitution was elaborated in 2001 and approved by referendum on 20 January 2002 to replace the Fundamental Act of 1997. It extended the president's term from five to seven years and allowed him to appoint and dismiss ministers. It removed the position of prime minister, and provided for a new bicameral assembly made up of a house of representatives and a senate. The assembly was deprived of the power to remove the president from office.[4] The referendum was widely criticized as rigged by the authorities. The case of Congo-Brazzaville is an example of a president tearing up a constitution that had been elaborated by a relatively broad-based National Conference in 1991 and replacing it with one that was specifically tailored to meet his own political goals.

The only amendment made to Ghana's 1992 Constitution was that made in 1996, which did not fundamentally alter the division of competences between the various branches of power. The 1996 amendments contained certain provisions concerning dual citizenship, and procedural provisions concerning the legislature. One such amendment provided for the hiring of retired civil servants (who must normally retire at age 60) on a consultancy basis for tasks requiring specific expertise. Other amendments concerned vacancies in Parliament, the chairmanship of the Armed Forces Council and the composition of the National Media Commission.

In Togo, although the Togolese constitution has only been significantly amended twice (and on the second occasion the amendment was reversed), the

---

4   24 January 2002. <http://news.bbc.co.uk/2/hi/africa/1779007.stm>, accessed 20 August 2012.

aim of the amendments has been to augment the power of the president in order to benefit President Gnassingbe Eyadema and his son, Faure Gnassingbe. On 31 December 2002 Togo's parliament amended the constitution to allow President Gnassingbe Eyadema to serve another term. The vote changed Article 59 in the Togolese constitution that limited the president to two five-year terms, allowing him to stand for an unlimited number of five-year terms. In February 2005, following Eyadema's death, Togo's parliament hastily amended the constitution to put a legal veneer on the military's appointment of 39-year-old Faure Gnassingbe to replace his deceased father as president, avoiding the need for new elections until 2008. However, later the same month, in response to pressure from abroad, including from the Economic Community of West African States (ECOWAS), the parliament of Togo reversed amendments made earlier in the month to allow for presidential elections within 60 days, which were duly won by Faure Gnassingbe.


**Political Factors**

Possibly it was the political dynamic subsequent to the constitution-making process, rather than the process itself, that played the key role in determining constitutional stability. In Congo-Brazzaville this dynamic involved the return of the former dictator in a military coup and the subsequent consolidation of his power (see above). It also involved consolidation of power in the hands of Presidents Blaise Compaore and Gnassingbe Eyadema in Burkina Faso and Togo respectively, despite a nominally democratic system that allowed an opposition presence in parliament but used electoral fraud and intimidation to ensure that the opposition would not win either presidential or parliamentary elections. In Togo, Eyadema's death was followed by his son's ascent to the presidency (see above). In Ghana Jerry Rawlings won the first competitive elections in 1992 and again in 1996, but agreed to step down in 2000 in accordance with the constitution. His favoured successor from the ruling National Democratic Congress (NDC), John Atta Mills, lost the 2000 elections however, and the candidate of the opposition National Patriotic Party (NPP), John Kufour, was elected president. Kufour was re-elected in 2004, but stepped aside at the end of his constitutionally-mandated two terms in office had expired, and his rival Atta Mills was elected. In Benin, formed dictator Mathieu Kérékou made a comeback when he defeated incumbent president Nicéphore Soglo in the 1996 presidential elections and won again in 2001 after his main rival boycotted the second round of the presidential elections amid allegations of electoral fraud. However, he agreed to step down in 2006, as required by the Constitution, and the presidential elections were won by the banker Yayi Boni. In 2011 Boni was re-elected with a first-round victory in the presidential elections, the first time a candidate had won elections without a run-off since the Constitution entered into force. Table 4.3 shows the percentage of votes won in the first round of successive elections by the incumbent president in all five countries.

**Table 4.3    Vote won by incumbent in presidential elections**

| Country | Election Year | Incumbent President | % of vote |
|---|---|---|---|
| **Benin** | 1991 | Mathieu Kérékou | 27.19 |
| | 1996 | Nicéphore Soglo | 35.69 |
| | 2001 | Mathieu Kérékou* | 45.42 |
| | 2006 | Mathieu Kérékou | Did not stand |
| | 2011 | Yayi Boni* | 53.14 |
| **Burkina Faso** | 1991 | Blaise Compaoré* | 100.00 |
| | 1998 | Blaise Compaoré* | 87.52 |
| | 2005 | Blaise Compaoré* | 80.35 |
| | 2010 | Blaise Compaoré* | 80.15 |
| **Congo-Brazzaville** | 1992 | Denis Sassou-Nguesso | 16.75 |
| | 2002 | Denis Sassou-Nguesso* | 89.41 |
| | 2009 | Denis Sassou-Nguesso* | 78.61 |
| **Ghana** | 1992 | Jerry Rawlings* | 58.40 |
| | 1996 | Jerry Rawlings* | 57.37 |
| | 2000 | Jerry Rawlings | Did not stand |
| | 2004 | John Kufuor* | 52.45 |
| | 2008 | John Kufuor | Did not stand |
| | 2012 | John Mahama** | 50.70 |
| **Togo** | 1993 | Gnassingbé Eyadéma* | 96.42 |
| | 1998 | Gnassingbé Eyadéma* | 52.10 |
| | 2002 | Gnassingbé Eyadéma* | 57.80 |
| | 2005 | None ( Eyadéma had died) | - |
| | 2010 | Faure Gnassingbé* | 60.89 |

*Notes*: * The incumbent won the elections and remained in power. ** Became president just four-and-a-half months before the election, following the death of incumbent John Atta Mills.

The implication of this is that political factors, namely the consolidation of power around one leader or group, have played a key role in explaining the endurance (or lack thereof) of the constitutional order. President Blaise Compaore was able to consolidate political and economic power in his own hands in Burkina Faso, as was President Sassou-Nguesso in Congo-Brazzaville and President Eyadema in Togo. All these presidents then commanded a majority in the National Assembly and with the help of that majority (or, in the case of Congo-Brazzaville, with the help of a rigged referendum) were able to massage the constitution further in their favour to such an extent that their power was virtually unassailable.[5] Although President Jerry Rawlings of Ghana also had a handsome parliamentary majority during the 1990s,[6] the opposition NPP proved a united and stable force and powerful counterveiling institutions, such as a relatively independent Supreme Court (from the outset of the transition process) and Election Commission (a little later on), helped put a check on abuses of power by the executive (Boafo-Arthur 2008). After the defeat of Rawlings's NDC in the 2000 elections, Ghana was left with a relatively stable two-party system. In Benin, no leader was able to fully consolidate power, which meant that no leader had the capacity or the support amongst the political elites to manipulate the constitution in his favour. It is telling, in this respect, that the pro-presidential party in Benin has never enjoyed a majority in the parliament.[7]

## Constitutional Provisions for Amending the Constitution

Of course, one factor that we have not yet considered is the possibility that the ease with which presidents and their entourage were able to manipulate the constitution simply depended on the constitutional text itself, specifically the ease with which it could be amended. The constitutions of the five countries that are the focus of this chapter have adopted some rather different mechanisms for amending the text of the constitution, meaning that it is significantly easier to alter the constitution in some cases, compared with others. Let us now focus more closely on what mechanisms are required to amend the constitution in each of our five cases.

*Benin*

The initiative for the revision of the Constitution belongs both to the president of the Republic, based on a decision taken by the Council of Ministers, and to members of the National Assembly. In order to be taken into consideration, the draft or proposal for revision must be approved by three-quarters of all members of the National Assembly (Article 154). The revision shall be agreed to only after having been approved by referendum, unless the draft or the proposal involved is approved by a four-fifths majority of the Assembly members (Article 155). No procedure for revision may be instituted or continued if it undermines the integrity

---

5   At the time the crucial constitutional amendments were adopted (1997 in Burkina Faso and 2002 in Togo) the ruling parties of the two countries (the Congress for Democracy and Progress in Burkina Faso and the Rally of the Togolese People in Togo) commanded the support of at least four-fifths of parliament.

6   Approximately two-thirds of seats in 1996–2000.

7   Although in 2003, a pro-presidential *coalition* of parties won just over 60 per cent of seats.

of the territory. The republican form of government and the secularity of the state may also not be made the object of a revision (Article 156).

## Burkina Faso

According to Article 161 of the constitution of Burkina Faso, the initiative for amending the constitution belongs to the President, the majority of members of the National Assembly and a group of at least 30,000 voters by petition (although this latter provision has never been used). The draft of the revision is, in all cases, first submitted to the National Assembly for evaluation, and then (until the constitutional referendum of 2002) to the House of Representatives for advice. According to Article 3 of Law 002/97 of 27 January 1997, the National Assembly decides either to support or reject the proposed amendment by an absolute majority of all its members. The draft amendments can be adopted without recourse to referendum if they are approved by a super-majority of three-quarters of members of the National Assembly, otherwise it is passed if it is approved by referendum.

## Congo-Brazzaville

According to the constitution of Congo-Brazzaville, the initiative for the revising the Constitution belongs both to the president of the Republic and to members of parliament. No procedure for revision may be instituted or continued if it undermines the integrity of the territory. The republican form of government, the secularity of the state, the number of terms the President can remain in his/ her post and the rights set out in Chapters I and II (on the state and sovereignty and on fundamental rights) may not be subject to revision (Article 185 of the 2002 constitution, Article 178 of the 1992 constitution). According to the 1992 constitution (Article 178), any draft revision to the constitution had to be approved by a two-thirds majority of both chambers in joint session and by a nationwide referendum. According to the 2002 constitution, this procedure still applies if it is parliament's initiative to amend the constitution, but if it is the president's initiative, the draft revision is put directly to a referendum, after approval by the Constitutional Court only. If it is parliament's initiative it must also be approved by the Constitutional Court (Article 186).

## Ghana

The Ghanaian constitution distinguishes between so-called 'entrenched provisions' of the constitution that involve fundamental rights and the relationship between the various branches of power and 'non-entrenched provisions' that involve less fundamental constitutional principles. In order to amend any article of the constitution, the amendment must first be referred to the Council of State (an advisory body of prominent citizens) for advice, before it is submitted to parliament in the case of entrenched provisions (Article 290) and after the first reading by parliament (Article 291) in the case of non-entrenched provisions. In the case of entrenched provisions, amendments cannot be introduced into Parliament until at least six months after their publication in the official Gazette; in the case of non-entrenched provisions, the amendments must be published twice in the Gazette with the second publication being made at least three months after the first and at least 10 days must have passed since the second publication for the bill to be introduced into parliament. In the case of entrenched provisions, after the first reading in parliament, the amendments must be submitted to a nationwide referendum and approved by the people by a 75 per cent margin on a turnout of at least 40 per cent. Parliament will then pass the bill and the president shall assent to it (Article 290). In the case of non-entrenched provisions, the parliament must approve the amendment by a two-thirds majority of all members, and the amendments are then passed to the president for assent (Article 291).

*Togo*

The initiative to revise the Constitution belongs jointly to the president of the Republic upon the proposal of the prime minister and at least one fifth of the deputies in the National Assembly. The draft or proposed revision shall be considered adopted if approved by a majority of four fifths of the deputies in the National Assembly. Failing such majority, a draft or proposed revision that is adopted by a majority of two thirds of deputies in the National Assembly shall be submitted to referendum. The republican form of government and the secularity of the state may not be made the object of a revision.

*Summary*

The constitutions of Benin, Ghana, and Togo all enshrine rather arduous procedures for amending the constitution. In Benin and Ghana, where, for the most part, no one group has been able to obtain an overwhelming majority in parliament, this has corresponded to a low instance of constitutional amendment. However, in Togo the overwhelming parliamentary majority enjoyed by the pro-presidential Rally of the Togolese People allowed the 2002 amendments to the constitution, which removed all term limits for the president, to be passed by parliament without recourse to a referendum. This could be seen as an indication that political factors help to determine the probability that the constitution is manipulated. In some cases the means used to amend the constitution can only be described as extra-constitutional. For example, in Congo-Brazzaville, despite a constitutional article that limits the presidential mandate to two terms and another article that prevents that article from being amended (see above), President Sassou-Nguesso had, by 2012, been in charge of his country for 15 years and still had another four years of office remaining, given that the two-term limit for presidential mandates is now applied from 2002 (the year the current constitution entered into force and presidential elections were held under that constitution) and a single presidential term lasts seven years. This case shows that even when constitutional constraints on amending the constitutional text exist, they are not always observed.

## Consensus/Democracy

In three out of the five cases, Burkina Faso, Congo-Brazzaville and Togo, there have been repeated attempts by incumbent presidents to gerrymander the constitution in order to augment their own power. In none of these three countries has a full transition to democracy taken place and all regimes remain either authoritarian (as in the case of Congo-Brazzaville) or competitive-authoritarian (as in Burkina Faso and Togo).[8] In contrast, the cases in which the constitution has remained unchanged (Benin), or has been changed only superficially (Ghana), are at least minimal democracies. Amongst our admittedly small number of cases there therefore appears to be a strong correlation between the endurance of the constitution that was elaborated at the beginning of the transition process and the success of that process in terms of democratization.

The two cases in which democracy has become at least minimally consolidated appear to be those in which at least a basic consensus seems to be shared amongst the main political actors that government must somehow be limited and that a power grab by the president is somehow beyond the pale. The Ghanaian case is particularly noteworthy in this respect; President Jerry Rawlings stepped down voluntarily when his constitutional term expired in 2000 despite the fact that he was in a relatively strong position, enjoying a majority in parliament and having governed continuously since 1982. Moreover, despite often bitter feuds between the two main parties (the NDC and the NPP), which has at times threatened to spill over into violence, the two parties have been able to sit down and agree over the basic rules of the game. Both the NDC and the NPP participated in a joint parliamentary committee that contained ten members of the parliamentary majority and ten members of the parliamentary minority over shortcomings during local elections in 2010. The committee successfully came up with a set of joint recommendations. Similarly, in 2012, both parties agreed on rules (the Presidential Transition Bill) to smoothen the transfer of political power from one administration to the other after an opposition victory in elections,[9] and following

---

8   If we look at the sum of the Freedom House scores for political rights and civil liberties for the five countries, which can vary from 2 (most democratic) to 14 (least democratic), we see that Benin and Ghana have scored 4 or less in every year since 2005, Burkina Faso has remained with a score of 8 during the same period, while Congo-Brazzaville has scored 11. Togo's score has gradually improved since 2006, and has stood at 9 in the years since 2009. Source Freedom House at <www.freedomhouse.org>.

9   VIBEGhana.com, March 20, 2012, 'Presidential Transition Act, Hallmark of cross-party efforts – IEA' at <http://vibeghana.com/2012/03/20/presidential-transition-act-hallmark-of-cross-party-efforts-iea>, accessed 20 August 2012.

the death of President John Atta Mills in July 2012, a peaceful transfer of power to vice-president John Mahama was supported by both main parties, despite their differences.[10] Although in early 2010 Mills had established a Constitution Review Commission to suggest recommendations for constitutional change, the Commission was independent, consulted broadly with the public and did not seem to be guided by the wishes of the president. According to Asare and Prempeh 'no objection or voices of dissent have been heard from any political party or politician' about the consultation (Asare and Prempeh 2012). Amongst its recommendations is one that presidents of the Republic should pay tax on their salaries.[11]

It is not clear the extent to which the constitution-making process in Ghana was a catalyst for the development of some kind of consensus. Certainly the constitution has been used as a focal point around which the consensus has consolidated, and incorporates the basic rules of that consensus. However, we cannot exclude the possibility that it developed only gradually over a relatively long period of time and the constitution may have represented only the beginning of that development. Certainly, the beginning of the transition process was marked by a paucity of trust between President Jerry Rawlings and the opposition, with the latter boycotting the first competitive elections in 1992. Nevertheless, the NPP never challenged the legality of the Constitution and even used the Constitution as the legal basis with which to challenge a number of government decisions at the Supreme Court during the mid-1990s (Boafo-Arthur 2008). The fact that the Supreme Court found in the NPP's favour on a number of occasions indicated that the Constitution was beginning to function as it was supposed to and this provided it with more legitimacy in the eyes of all political players.

There is some evidence to suggest that the way in which the Benin constitution was elaborated has had some impact on its endurability and the emergence of consensus. In 2006, members of parliament passed, with the required four-fifths majority, a constitutional amendment that would extend the duration of their mandates from four to five years. However, the Constitutional Court overruled the proposed constitutional change, arguing that the constitutional clause that limits the parliamentary mandate to four years was 'the result of a national consensus arrived at by the Conference of the bone and sinew of the nation in February 1990' and that the proposed constitutional amendment amounted to an attempt at 'power confiscation' and therefore did not respect the values embodied in the constitution. This was despite the fact that the amendment did not violate the constitutional rules for amending the constitution, i.e. it did not attempt to alter the integrity of the territory, the republican form of government or the secular nature

---

10   'Ghana's John Dramani Mahama promises stability', BBC news website (25 July 2012) at <http://www.bbc.co.uk/news/world-africa-18980041>, accessed 20 August 2012.

11   GhanaWeb (20 December 2011), 'Professor Emeritus Fiadjoe made it clear that government must share the full contents of the Report with the people of Ghana in its entirety' at   <http://www.ghanaweb.com/GhanaHomePage/NewsArchive/artikel.php?ID=226043>, accessed 20 August 2012.

of the state (CGD 2008). The notion that the constitution of Benin represented a national consensus was clearly conditioned by the open and inclusive nature of the constitution-making process, both during the national conference and subsequently.

In the other three cases, such consensus was absent. Several authors contrast the National Conferences held in Benin and Togo in terms of the success (in the former case) or failure (in the latter case) to achieve consensus over constitutional principles. Heilbrunn argues that Benin's transition was assisted by 'reconciliation and consensus', while Togo's (non-) transition was characterized by 'dyarchy and discord', with the struggle for power becoming 'increasingly violent' (Heilbrunn 1993: 299). Seely looks at the content of speeches made at the National Conferences in Benin and Togo and concludes that whereas in Benin, the 'National Conference delegates strove to create a transition government and sketch the outlines of a constitution that could navigate a way out of the country's difficulties', in Togo it 'became a forum for denouncing Eyadéma's regime with relatively little substantive discussion about the new democratic system that was to be established' (Seely 2005: 367). Similarly, most commentators on the National Conference in Congo-Brazzaville focus on its role as a forum for denouncing the actions of Sassou-Nguesso's government, but it would seem that the Conference failed to achieve a lasting consensus. The Constitution failed its first test in late 1992 almost immediately after it entered into force, as newly elected President Pascal Lissouba faced opposition from the parliamentary majority led by former president Sassou-Nguesso. Lissouba ignored the Constitution by refusing to appoint a prime minister that had the support of parliament, dissolved the legislative body and called new elections (Magnusson and Clark 2005: 562). The conflict eventually culminated in a coup by Sassou-Nguesso in 1997 and a two-and-a-half year civil war. Consensus seems to have been more or less absent in Burkina Faso too, as the authorities ignored opposition calls for a National Conference and imposed a constitution without opposition consent.

When we talk of consent, we are talking here about consent amongst the most important political forces in the country, specifically, those that have 'spoiler' potential to subvert the constitutional order either by means of a 'presidential power grab' or (in the case of the opposition) by fostering instability or uprising. It is an open question whether or not this consensus extends to all sectors of society, especially in developing countries such as those in West Africa in which a rural peasantry may have few connections with the body politic.

Mass consensus around constitutional principles is hard to measure. Afrobarometer surveys ask for respondents' attitudes on a number of issues relating to the constitution and limited government, but they are only carried out in countries in which there is at least a semblance of democracy. From our sample of five countries, the 2008 Afrobarometer survey was carried out in three: Benin, Burkina Faso and Ghana. Three issue statements appeared to be relevant to the principle of constitutionalism and limitation of power:

1. Elections and Parliament are abolished so that the president can decide everything.
2. a) Since the President was elected to lead the country, he should not be bound by laws or court decisions that he thinks are wrong; b) The President must always obey the laws and the courts, even if he thinks they are wrong.
3. a) The Constitution should limit the president to serving a maximum of two terms in office; b) There should be no constitutional limit on how long the president can serve.

For question 1, we subtract the percentage of those who either agreed or agreed strongly with the statement from those who disagreed or disagreed strongly with it. For question 2, we subtract the percentage of those who agreed or agreed strongly with statement a) from those who agreed or agreed strongly with statement b). For question 3, we subtract the percentage of those who agreed or agreed strongly with statement b) from those who agreed or agreed strongly with statement a). In this way we obtain a measurement of agreement with the principle of constitutional restraint on executive power. The results are shown in Table 4.4 (below).

This would appear to show that Beninois citizens adhere most to the principles of limiting the power of the executive, followed closely by Ghana, with the population of Burkina Faso significantly more tolerant of unlimited presidential powers than the populations of the other two countries. This would suggest that some kind of cross-societal consent over the limitation of presidential power has been achieved in Benin and Ghana, but not in Burkina Faso.

**Table 4.4     Public Opinion in Benin, Burkina Faso and Ghana**

|  | **Benin** | **Burkina Faso** | **Ghana** |
|---|---|---|---|
| On abolition of elections and parliament | 74 | 54 | 73 |
| On the courts limiting the president's powers | 54 | 24 | 33 |
| On the two-term limit for the president | 53 | 16 | 52 |
| Average | 60 | 31 | 53 |

## Conclusion

In terms of whether constitutional stability is important for democratization, we can conclude tentatively that it is. None of our three countries that has amended its constitution in such a way as to benefit the president or the executive branch of government has experienced a transition to democracy. At best, they have remained fundamentally authoritarian with formal trappings of democracy (as in Burkina Faso and Togo). At worst, they have remained fully authoritarian systems (as in Congo-Brazzaville).

Another tentative conclusion that can be drawn from an analysis of these five African cases is that the constitutional text itself has a limited role to play in determining whether or not the constitution will endure. We see from the case of Congo-Brazzaville that even where there is an article in the constitution that states explicitly that the article that determines the number of presidential mandates and the length of each mandate cannot be amended, it is always possible for ambitious leaders to get around the rules, if necessary by annulling the old constitution and drafting a new one.

Often, it appears, it is political factors that determine whether or not the constitutional order is able to survive and become internalized both by political elites and social forces. We have seen how manipulation of the constitution is often used as a strategy for power consolidation from the side of the president and his entourage. At the same time, however, we observe one case (Ghana) when a relatively powerful president (Jerry Rawlings) forswears the opportunity to change the constitution to remain in power.

In terms of the legacy of the constitution-making process, a superficial view of the process suggests that its impact is limited. Benin and Congo-Brazzaville experienced almost identical constitution-making processes, but very different outcomes in terms of constitutional stability and democratization. However, if we look a little more closely, we see that the process may have been more significant in Benin than in Congo-Brazzaville. As noted above, the Constitutional Court of Benin cited as a reason for rejecting constitutional changes proposed by the country's parliament the notion that the proposed changes were contrary to the spirit of the 1990 National Conference which designed the Beninois constitutional framework. In contrast, the National Conference of Congo-Brazzaville, despite the fact that it was declared sovereign, was not seen as a defining moment in the transition process and the constitutional principles that it established were not respected by the most powerful political elites. Possibly this is because the constitution-making process was superseded by civil conflict and the constitution as a means for maintaining peace and stability was discredited long before it could be accepted as a set of guiding principles in political life.

Our exploration of these five West African cases appears to suggest that an open and inclusive process constitution-making may contribute to the establishment of a democratic consensus amongst the main political forces – and, over time, across society as a whole – but does not necessarily do so. It also appears necessary that the development of such a consensus continue to be fostered after the constitution is approved. This occurred in Ghana, where the opposition successfully challenged the authorities' actions as unconstitutional in the Supreme Court, but did not occur in Congo-Brazzaville, where any precarious consensus that did exist broke down almost as soon as the constitution entered into force. Clearly, an open constitution-making process is a useful first step; the case of Burkina Faso shows that a broad consensus is unlikely to emerge if the constitution is drawn up by the incumbent elite behind closed doors. At the same time, we should not exclude the possibility that even under these inauspicious circumstances consent could be formed through means other than constitution-making. The constitutions in all five countries are, *de jure*, rather democratic; it is how they are put into practice that is undemocratic. Over time, consent around constitutional *principles* is more important than the constitutional text itself and such consent could potentially be formed without going to the trouble of writing a new constitution.

# Chapter 5

# Transitions from Above:
# The Constitution-Making Process
# and the Consolidation of Democracy.
# The Cases of Spain, Brazil and Poland

Yanina Welp


A neglected aspect within the study of democratic transition and consolidation concerns the contexts in which constitutional formulae are adopted and maintained (Linz and Stepan 1996: 81). According to much of the theory, the origin, duration and extent of transition depends either on socio-economic conditions (namely economic and, concomitantly, human development and openness of the economy to world markets), or the balance of power between the *ancien regime*, the democratic opposition and civil society.[1] These paradigms often lead scholars to assume that the constitutional formula adopted is little more than a reflection of either socioeconomic (pre)conditions or the balance of power between diverse actors. As a result, they neglect to study the role (if any) that the constitution itself plays during the process of transition and consolidation of democracy.

On the other side of the coin, literature dedicated to analysing *constitution making* has focussed on the importance of the constitution-making process and in particular on the relationship between 'the optimal design of the constitution making process' (Elster 1995: 365) and a 'successful' constitution in terms of whether it is durable, supported by citizens and able to establish the desired framework of coexistence. Even though it cannot be said that there is agreement over the necessary characteristics for such 'success', authors have highlighted the importance of whether or not the constitution is drafted by a body or 'constituent assembly' that was created exclusively for the purpose of constitution-making (Weber 1986–1987), whether members of the body are elected by means of a proportional system that allows for the representation of different social actors (Elster 1995), whether deliberation and debate within the body is open to citizens

---

1  The debate on the nature and causes of transition remains ongoing. In the 1960s theories that gave greater weight to economic, social and cultural preconditions dominated (Lipset 1959). Later, theories that placed more emphasis on the strategies and choices of actors (O'Donnell and Schmitter 1986) and prioritized political factors over structural factors (Colomer 1994, Linz 1990, Alcántara Sáez 1992) gained greater importance.

and publicized, or whether the constitutional text agreed upon is ratified by citizens in a referendum (Widner 2007, Ginsburg et al. 2007, Ghai 2006). Following these arguments, one might expect that constitutions made with greater participation and openness and legitimized by the votes of citizens endure over time and become a set of rules with which citizens identify. Other authors have gone further by suggesting that the ideal context for a constitution-making process is that of a *tabula rasa* in which the various actors involved have no idea about the positions they will occupy in the future. This would allow for a more disinterested quest for the common good (Buchanan and Tullock 1962, Rawls 1971).

Giving weight to the context in which a constitution is elaborated, Elster identifies three factors that should be considered crucial to the process: the constraints under which the constitution-making body operates, the motivations of the individual actors involved and the way individual preferences are aggregated into collective choices (what Elster refers to as 'interest aggregation'). One of his conclusions is that, paradoxically, while a constitution should be the result of a rational debate carried out in a calm environment, normally the context in which a constitution is elaborated is far from that ideal scenario (Elster 1995: 394). In this sense, regime change is usually an extreme situation that is far from calm and far from the *tabula rasa* advocated by Rawls and Buchanan. Instead transition is a period of extreme uncertainty in terms of the future of the political system and of the individual actors involved (Schedler 2001). During this period we see threats and promises, pacts and deals made against the background of an information deficit, risk taking, and attempts to secure guarantees for the future (Colomer 1994: 251).

At the same time the mode of transition may further complicate the establishment of minimum conditions of democracy. Particular problems arise in transitions initiated 'from above', i.e. by incumbent elites. In such cases, the transition depends upon a number of factors; amongst these is the debate around what future role members of the *ancien regime* are to play once democracy is finally (re)established, as well as the efforts of these actors to maintain positions of power by seeking to avoid the judgement of a volatile electorate and to protect those amongst them against possible legal action for human rights violations. These demands tend to impinge upon the legal framework of the new democracy. In particular, decaying authoritarian regimes that still have sufficient power to steer the transition process – like those that are the focus of this chapter – prefer either to create new constitutions or, alternatively, to block attempts to reform those approved during authoritarian rule (as in Chile). Finally, if transition is led by a regime that has already broken with the (previous) legal order, the constitutional process has no rules that precede it and guide its development, except those produced by the same authoritarian government.

This chapter looks at how new constitutions were drafted in Spain, Brazil and Poland during the transition to democracy. My aim is to identify the extent to which the endogenous elements of constitution-making, i.e. the type of body tasked with drafting the constitution, the way in which the constitution-making body is elected, the style of deliberation within that body and the way in which the constitution is ratified, can explain the degree of legitimacy and durability of the constitution, and, in the longer term, its contribution to the consolidation of democracy (understood as the moment in which the window of uncertainty is closed and the possibility of a return to authoritarianism becomes negligible, Schedler 2001). The alternative hypothesis is that rather than being a cause, both the characteristics of the constitution-making process and its 'outcome' should instead be understood as a consequence of other variables, such as the balance of powers between actors. Moreover, given that democracy cannot be understood as a 'finished product', the constitution can continue to play a 'constituting' role even beyond the moment at which it enters into force.

The three cases chosen for analysis have all undergone negotiated transitions to democracy in which the former power-holders played a guiding role. In all three cases too, the authoritarian regime had built a complex and extensive institutional structure. However, there are also a number of significant differences: namely, the origin of the dictatorship (civil war in Spain, a military coup in Brazil and the Second World War in Poland), as well as the type and duration of the regime (significant personalization of the regime and a long duration in Spain, domination of a communist apparat and long duration in Poland, rule by a series of military leaders over a slightly shorter timeframe in Brazil).

This chapter is structured as follows. First, I provide a brief overview of the transition process in each case. Next, I compare the constitution-making process in each case as well as the outcomes in terms of the indicators identified above. I close the chapter with a brief conclusion.

## Spain: Rapid Transition and Consolidation of Democracy

Spain is considered to be a classic case of rapid transition and consolidation of democracy (Linz 1990, O'Donnell et al. 1986). In contrast with many other cases of transition to democracy, the regime had not suffered a defeat in war, nor was the country in the grip of a severe economic crisis. Instead, the death of General Francisco Franco on 22 November 1975 brought his successors into contact with a Europe that no longer found dictatorship acceptable. Pressure from outside therefore played a key role in determining internal policy (Alcántara Sáez 1992). At the same time, domestically the regime could not have remained in power without renewed repression and control. Although by the mid-1970s the opposition may not have quite had sufficient power to overthrow the dictatorship, it already represented a significant social force. For this reason the Spanish case is sometimes described as a case of regime initiated transition that occurred under pressure from society (Linz y Stepan 1996: 88).

The Franco regime had been organized through the National Movement (Movimiento Nacional), but this structure could not be considered as a ruling party due to the apolitical nature of the regime and the concentration of power around an individual, rather than a party. The church, the military, trade unions and other groups such as the chambers of agriculture together formed the basis of a corporate system (Alcántara Sáez 1992: 16). High levels of repression (with no tolerance for dissent) and the organization of the regime around the figure of Franco exacerbated the problem of succession. The Act of Succession (1947) allowed Franco to propose to the Cortes (the legislative body created by the regime) the name of the person to succeed him either as king or as regent. On 21 July 1969, the dictator had designated Juan Carlos of Bourbon as his successor with the title of Prince of Spain.[2]

After Franco's death Juan Carlos of Bourbon became head of state and played a key role by driving forward change while simultaneously representing continuity with the Francoist institutions. When the first head of government in the post-Franco period, Rodriguez Arias, showed himself to be incapable of making the expected institutional reforms, the king replaced him with Adolfo Suarez. Suarez also played a major role in shaping the transition. He was able to convince the Cortes to pass Law no. 425 on Political reform, which envisaged its own dissolution and the creation of a new bicameral legislature. The law, which also convened the first free elections and opened the door to the legalization of all political parties, was approved with 425 votes in favour and 59 against. It was put to a referendum on 15 December 1976 in the first free vote for decades, gaining the support of 94 per cent of voters on a turnout of 77 per cent.[3] After the referendum the process of dismantling authoritarian structures accelerated. In December, Suarez met with the leaders of the opposition, in April 1977 the Communist Party was legalized and in June the same year the first open and competitive elections were held for a parliament that also served as a constituent assembly (see below). A year later a new constitution was approved and in March 1979 fresh elections were held within the framework of the new fundamental law. In October 1982, the Spanish Socialist Workers Party (Partido Socialista Obrero Español, PSOE) won the next general elections, bringing the transition period to an end with another change of government.[4]

## Brazil: The Slow March Back to the Barracks

The military regime that came to power in 1964 approved a new constitution in 1967, which it reformed in 1969, indicating its desire to break with the tradition of

---

2 This decision changed the order of succession that had given priority to Juan of Borbon (the father of Juan Carlos). The 1947 law had given Franco the power to make this decision. On 22 July 1969 Juan Carlos swore 'allegiance to the principles of the National Movement and other Fundamental Laws of the Kingdom.'

3 Data from the Interior Ministry, www.infoelectoral.mir.es.

4 On 23 February 1981 there was an attempted military uprising led by General Tejero. The broadcasting of the event through the media and the subsequent intervention of the king have bestowed great importance to it even though support for the coup attempt was low and Tejero was jailed.

short-lived military interventions and instead to consolidate power (Castro 2000). In these early years the military dissolved existing parties, introduced indirect presidential elections – through an electoral college – and created an artificial two-party system. The National Renewal Alliance Party (Aliança Renovadora Nacional, ARENA) backed the military government, while the Brazilian Democratic Movement (Movimento Democrático Brasileiro, MDB) was formed as an official opposition. At the end of the 1960s, as protests grew the regime responded by strengthening its capacity for repression (Castro 2000: 10).

In 1974, General Ernesto Geisel, who was seen as a moderate in a military that was ever more split between hardliners and moderates, was nominated president. In his own words, Geisel opted for a 'soft, gradual, safe' opening that began a process that can better be described as liberalization than democratization (Alves 1988, Castro 2000). At the end of the decade Geisel was succeeded by Joao Baptista de Figuereido (1979–1985). In the indirect elections of 1978 Figuereido, leader of ARENA, defeated Euler Bentes Monteiro (MDB) by 355 votes to 266.

As a result of the process of 'opening', in 1979 the two-party system was abolished and new parties appeared.[5] In 1982, the elections were relatively free and competitive, although the electoral rules were skewed to benefit the Democratic Social Party (Partido Democrático Social, PDS), successor party to ARENA. In 1983, the parliamentarian Dante Oliveira (MDB) proposed an amendment to the constitution that would abolish the system of indirect presidential elections. In April 1984 the proposal failed to achieve the necessary two-thirds majority in the Chamber of Deputies and this provoked widespread public protests under the slogan *Diretas Ja!* (Direct Elections Now). It is estimated that up to ten million people took to the streets during this period. Opposition elites from the centre-right were as surprised as the military by this reaction and an intense period of negotiations began in which citizens were no more than bystanders. The change in strategy was significant: Tancredo Neves (MDB) was promoted as the only leader capable of reanimating the transition. The PDS, the party that most had hitherto supported the civil-military coalition in power, split and many of its members, including José Sarney, joined the opposition (Alves 1988: 52).

On 15 January 1985, towards the end of Figuereido's term in office, the next (indirect) presidential elections were held as scheduled. The Electoral College (the composition of which had been approved by the National Congress in June 1982) gave its support to Tancredo Neves as president and José Sarney as vice-president.

---

5   The Democratic Social Party (Partido Democrático Social, PDS) and the Brazilian Democratic Movement Party (Partido do Movimento Democrático Brasileiro, PMDB) were formed as successor parties to ARENA and the MDB, respectively. The centrist Popular party (Partido Popular, PP) was also created and brought together parliamentarians from both main parties. The only party from before the authoritarian regime that was re-established was the Brazilian Labour Party (Partido Trabalhista Brasileiro, PTB). On the left the Democratic Labour Party (Partido Democrático Trabalhista, PDT) and the Workers Party (Partido de los Trabajadores, PT) appeared (Fleischer 1995).

Secret negotiations held between Neves and the military prior to the elections established a framework for transition. Among other agreements relating to the constitution they agreed that no member of the old regime would be tried for human rights abuses, as had occurred in the earlier transition in Argentina.

On the eve of his inauguration Neves fell gravely ill and later died. He was succeeded by his vice-president, who was opposed by those who wished to deepen the democratization process because he belonged to a party that had supported the military coup and supported the indirect election of the president.[6] Shortly before Sarney took office, the still acting president General Figueiredo, who was considered an ally of the military, signed a presidential decree transferring powers relating to the Armed Forces from the president to the Armed Forces themselves (Zaverucha 1998: 107). The fact once again highlighted the limited and controlled nature of the transition.


## Poland: Conflict and Uncertainty

During the communist era, some kind of de facto pluralism was maintained in Poland. The Catholic Church enjoyed relative autonomy that gave it the ideological and organizational capacity to resist full incorporation into the structures of the atheist regime. For example, in 1956 Wladyslaw Gomulka (head of government between 1945 and 1948 and again between 1956 and 1970) allowed the teaching of religion in state schools (Linz and Stepan 1996: 261).

In 1980, the Solidarity union was legalized, making it the first independent trade union to be recognized in communist eastern Europe. It secured from the government momentous changes such as reform of the *nomenklatura* and ensuring appointments in factories were made on the basis of qualification, rather than party membership. However, the economic crisis and the growing mobilization of citizens persuaded General Wojciech Jaruzelski (communist leader from 1981 to 1989) to declare martial law on 13 December 1981 and to outlaw the union shortly afterwards.

Society was divided between intellectuals and movements organized around Solidarity and the Catholic Church on the one hand, and a hierarchical military and security apparatus, on the other. By 1987–1988 the regime faced increasing opposition as the crisis persisted. Jaruzelski then proposed a package of economic reforms, which he submitted to a referendum, but his proposal did not receive the required majority. Solidarity launched a series of strikes until the interior minister, General Kiszczak, invited its leader, Lech Walesa, to begin exploratory talks. Walesa agreed in a letter dated 21 July 1988.

---

6    This did not pass without conflict, since Sarney, an oligarch who had supported the military before the alliance with democratic forces, was rejected by many members of the MDB.

The government wanted broad support for its economic policies, while Solidarity wanted the legal recognition that only the government could provide. Following the Round Table negotiations of February – April 1989, the first competitive elections in eastern Europe in more than 40 years took place on 4 June 1989. All members of the upper house or Senate, but only 35 per cent (161 out of 460) of the lower house or Sejm, were directly elected, with the remaining 299 Sejm members nominated by the regime. It had been agreed that the president would be indirectly elected by both houses, virtually guaranteeing Jaruzelski the presidency, and the constitution was amended accordingly. However Solidarity won all 161 elected seats in the Sejm and 99 out of 100 senate seats. Although Jaruzelski was elected president, he won by just one vote and could not form a government because his allies from the Democratic Party and the United Peasants' Party, both previously satellites of the Communist Party, withdrew their support. Poland thus obtained its first non-communist prime minister in decades when Solidarity member Tadeusz Mazowiecki was appointed to the post on 24 August 1989.[7]

Following a further amendment of the communist-era constitution in September 1990, the presidency became a directly elected office and a two-round presidential election was held in November and December that year. However, Solidarity had already split and Walesa and Mazowiecki stood against one another, further complicating the process of institutionalizing political parties. Walesa won in the second round with 74 per cent of the vote. The first fully competitive elections for both houses of parliament were held in October 1991 and this revealed an extremely fragmented party system. Twenty-nine parties gained seats in the Sejm and no party received more than 12.3 per cent of the vote. The four largest parties were extremely polarized and were unable to control even 50 per cent of seats (McQuaid, 1993).

During the following years the transition process continued despite the fact that it remained extremely difficult to form a consensus amongst the political elite as is aptly demonstrated by the long and arduous process of elaborating a new constitution (see below).

**Constitution-Making Processes**

Having described the overall transition process in the three countries, we can now look in more detail at the constitution-making processes. As I have already indicated, our interest is in identifying how (if at all) the type of constitution-making body, the way in which that body was selected, the style of deliberation

---

7    The Warsaw Voice Online, June 3 2009, at <http://www.warsawvoice.pl/WVpage/pages/article.php/20417/article>; POLAND Parliamentary Chamber: Sejm ELECTIONS HELD IN 1989, website of the Inter-Parliamentary Union, <http://www.ipu.org/parline-e/reports/arc/2255_89.htm>. Both accessed 2 February 2012.

and the mode of representation (see Table 5.1) may have influenced the outcome of the process in terms of the legitimacy and durability of the constitution and, in turn, the democratization process.

**Table 5.1    Characteristics of the constitution-making process in Spain, Brazil and Poland**

|  | Constitution-Making Body | Election of Representatives | Style of Deliberation | Mode of Ratification |
|---|---|---|---|---|
| Spain | Mandated constituent legislature | Direct | Partly Closed | Referendum |
| Brazil | Mandated constituent legislature | Direct | Partly Open | Promulgated by the ANC itself |
| Poland | Parliamentary Committee | Committee selected from both houses of parliament | Closed | Referendum |

*The Constitution-Making Body and the Election of its Representatives*

First of all, we must note that in none of the three cases analysed were there any predetermined rules governing the procedure to draft and ratify a new constitution. Given the background of an authoritarian regime and the concomitant suspension of the law, the institutional framework had to be built on a new basis, to be agreed upon (or imposed) by the actors involved.

In Spain the election of a constituent assembly occurred alongside the legalization of political parties and the restoration of basic freedoms. The assembly took the form of a directly elected bicameral parliament or Congress, elected on 15 June 1977, which was specially entrusted with drafting the constitution, although subsequently it also fulfilled other legislative functions. Soon afterwards, in October 1977, Suarez held a series of meetings that would subsequently become known as the Pacts of Moncloa. The objective of the Pacts was to provide stability to the transition process and to adopt an economic policy that could contain rampant inflation. Suarez brought together those political parties that had obtained parliamentary representation, as well as employers' associations and trade unions (although only the Workers' Commissions participated, as the Unión General de Trabajadores and the Central Nacional del Trabajo refused to take part in negotiations). The Pacts of Moncloa were approved by Congress on 25 October 1977 with only one vote against in the Chamber of Deputies and three votes against in the Senate.[8]

---

8    Boletin Oficial de las Cortes, 3 November 1977.

In Brazil, secret negotiations held between Neves and the military leadership (see above) had established a framework for the transition and for a new constitution. In these negotiations the military had vetoed the convocation of a constituent assembly, a demand of the ever more active citizens' movement, because it feared that such a body would be beyond its control. Instead they proposed a constituent assembly made up of members of parliament. In November 1985, President Sarney sent Congress a proposal for a constitutional amendment that would allow the convocation of a National Constituent Assembly (Asamblea Nacional Constituyente, ANC) formed by the two chambers of parliament and vested with special powers to draft a constitution. Most members of this parliament were directly elected on 15 November 1986, although the body also included 23 senators elected in 1982 (with a mandate until 1991). The PMDB (successor to the MDB) won 53 per cent of seats in the Chamber of Deputies.

In Poland there was no discussion about the characteristics of the constitution-making body. The various proposals discussed during the 1990s came from groups and individuals who looked to parliament as the body responsible for making a final decision. Soon after becoming president, Walesa sent to the Sejm his proposal for a constitution, which would increase the powers of the presidency at the expense of the prime minister and would grant the former the right to remove the latter as well as all the cabinet. The Sejm rejected this proposal and this led to a period of instability and conflict, which was partly settled in August 1992, when an agreement was reached to approve a 'little constitution', which added 78 new articles to another 62 from the 1952 constitution.[9] Inconsistencies in the text, combined with political tension between President Walesa and the Sejm, meant that the practical application of the Constitution was accompanied by constant bickering and arguments before the Constitutional Court (Chrusciak 2007) and highlighted the need to draft an entirely new constitution. The process of drafting the new constitution only reached an active phase during the period January 1995 to June 1996, when a joint committee from both houses of parliament (the Sejm and the Senate) drafted a new text, which it then passed on to an editing committee consisting of experts. The editing committee then passed the draft back to the joint committee for final changes. The drafting process was therefore carried out by a parliamentary committee with the active participation of unelected experts.

### The Mode of Deliberation

In Spain the political parties with parliamentary representation acted as channels of information between the discussions held at Moncloa and civil society and this set the scene for the constitution-making process. The institutional framework chosen

---

9   This text included significant changes such as a tripartite division of powers, a form of regulation of relations between the executive and legislative branches typical of parliamentary systems of government (with a vote of no confidence) and increased autonomy of the Prime Minister and the Cabinet (Chrusciak 2007).

allowed for the representation of all key actors and an inclusive balance of forces, but at the same time it largely relegated civil society to the status of observers in a process that was led and steered by parties.[10] Both parliamentary deputies and the Spanish government were involved in long conversations both privately and in public about defining the constitution and future political institutions. One of the most difficult issues to resolve was the territorial-administrative arrangement of the country and the recognition of the historic nationalisms, which had at various times demanded self-determination for their territories. Catalan and Basque nationalisms, in particular, sought to create a new decentralized territorial organization, but the violence of the armed Basque organization ETA (Euskadi and Freedom) strengthened opposition from the military, who equated regional nationalism with terrorism.[11] For some the territorial conflict had the potential to escalate into civil war. Both for historical reasons and because of the context (the presence of ETA) the issue deeply divided the different groups, so it is especially remarkable that consensus was reached on the creation of a new decentralized power structure, based on 17 regions, and an unprecedented transfer of power to the peripheral nations.

In Brazil, both upper and lower chambers of the ANC sat as a unicameral body for constitutional matters, passing decisions by absolute majority. However, despite the agreements reached with the military before its convocation, the process was open to the participation of citizens and civil society associations. This was unprecedented in Brazil and was something of a novelty in the region as a whole. There were three ways of participating: suggestions by citizens were accepted (equivalent of the right of petition)[12]; there were around 400 citizens' meetings at local level that generated about 2,400 suggestions; finally, once the first draft of the constitutional text was presented, associations that were legally registered could make new suggestions if they gathered 30,000 signatures[13] (Rauschenbach 2011). However, the final decisions were made in parliament. Eight commissions and various sub-commissions worked on the different topics that were to be included in the constitution. A systemization committee was created

---

10   After the elections of June 1977 power was distributed among various forces, including: Suarez's centre-right Union of the Democratic Centre (47.4 per cent of seats); the right wing Popular Alliance (4.6); the left-leaning Spanish Socialist Workers Party (33.7) and the Communist Party of Spain (5.4). Regionalist parties were represented by Democratic Pact for Catalunya (3.1), and the Basque Nationalist Party (2.3). Source: Election Resources on the Internet: <http://www.infoelectoral.mir.es>, accessed 11 September 2012.

11   In the period 1978–1983 37 members of the armed forces were killed by ETA (Linz and Stepan 1996: 99).

12   72,719 were accepted and registered in a computer support system for the constituent assembly and can still be found at http://www.senado.gov.br/sf/legislacao/baseshist/.

13   122 associations gathered about twelve million signatures and 83 met the formal prerequisites for presentation to Congress, making Brazil an archetype for the popular initiative (Rauschenbach 2011).

to gather together the parts. The influence of progressive views was evident in the decentralized committee meetings (Gomes 2006). This produced successive versions of the constitution that were rejected by the parliament; the centre-right insisted on changes that amended key aspects of these texts (Gomes 2006, Praça 2012). The end result was the so-called 'Citizens Constitution', which contained a set of articles that left the military with significant powers (Zaverucha 1998: 114).

In Poland tensions between the different actors, exacerbated by divisions within the democratic opposition, made it difficult to obtain the necessary agreements to adopt a constitution, leading to a deadlock which lasted from 1989 to 1997. Poplawska (2008) notes that there was little or no public participation in the constitution-making process.[14] In January 1997 it was the joint committee from the Sejm and the Senate that finalized the draft of the constitution (237 articles in 13 chapters) and sent it to the National Assembly, where it was eventually approved (in April) with 451 votes in favour, 40 against and 6 abstentions. Both the discussions in the committee and in the whole assembly were closed and dominated by partisan political actors. Once in parliament, parties made numerous calls for reform that slowed down the adoption of the final text. In March, the president also added his own amendments.

*The Ratification Process*

The Spanish Constitution was submitted to a referendum on 6 December 1978, when it was approved by 91.8 per cent of those casting a valid ballot on a turnout of 67.1 per cent. It was also approved in those territories in which peripheral nationalism was strong. In Catalonia 95.1 per cent approved the constitution on a turnout of 67.9 per cent, while in the Basque Country it was approved by 74.6 per cent, although on a much lower turnout (44.7 per cent).

The Constitution of Brazil was promulgated on 5 October 1988 by the ANC itself without any mechanism for citizen ratification.

In Poland the constitution was ratified by a referendum held on 25 May 1997 and was approved by 53.5 per cent of those casting a valid ballot. However less than half of the electorate (42.9 per cent) turned out to vote. Various actors campaigned for a 'no' vote including Solidarity (now in opposition), former president Walesa and the Catholic Church. Opposition groups not only questioned the legitimacy of the new constitution, but petitioned the Supreme Court to annul the referendum. However, the Court approved the referendum results and the constitution entered into force on 17 October 1997 (Osiatyński 1997).

---

14   In 1990 and 1991 constitutional drafts were accepted. In general, the authors of these proposals were experts in the field of state law. Drafts from the public or civic organizations were admitted for consideration by the National Assembly in 1994 on the strict condition that they were supported by at least 500,000 of those entitled to vote in a general election. This condition was fulfilled by a draft from Solidarity (Poplawska 2008: 282). None of these proposals achieved consensus.

## The Constitution: Durability, Legitimacy and its Contribution to the Consolidation of Democracy

Democracy is considered to have been consolidated in all three countries, although the transition and consolidation processes were faster in Spain and Poland than in Brazil. Table 5.2 shows a similar trajectory in terms of the Freedom House scores for political rights and civil liberties (both of which have the potential to vary between 1 (most democratic) and 7 (least democratic). Spain and Poland have maintained the most democratic scores possible since 2002 and 2004 respectively, while Brazil has never quite achieved this.

**Table 5.2    Freedom House rankings: Political rights (PR) and civil liberties (CL)**

| Country | Constitution enacted | 1975 | | 1980 | | 1985 | | 1990 | | 1995 | | 2000 | | 2005 | | 2010 | |
|---|---|---|---|---|---|---|---|---|---|---|---|---|---|---|---|---|---|
| | | PR | CL | PR | CL | PR | CL | PR | CL | PR | CL | PR | CL | PR | CL | PR | CL |
| **Brazil** | 1988 | 4 | 5 | 4 | 3 | 3 | 2 | 2 | 3 | 2 | 4 | 3 | 3 | 2 | 2 | 2 | 2 |
| **Poland** | 1978 | 6 | 6 | 6 | 4 | 6 | 5 | 2 | 2 | 1 | 2 | 1 | 2 | 1 | 1 | 1 | 1 |
| **Spain** | 1997 | 5 | 5 | 2 | 3 | 1 | 2 | 1 | 1 | 1 | 2 | 1 | 2 | 1 | 1 | 1 | 1 |

*Source*: Freedom House.

One difference that can be observed between Brazil and Poland in terms of the difficulties each country faced in consolidating democracy is that in the first case the civil-military coalition that had led the dictatorship retained significant 'reserved domains' of power throughout the first years of the transition. In Poland, on the other hand, the constraints imposed by the former regime were overcome very quickly (by 1991), but the main challenge was the fragmentation of the party system and conflicts within and amongst the new democratic forces.

In Spain, the constitution has only been amended twice since its adoption and these amendments have not affected the separation of powers in the domestic arena.[15] Although successive opinion polls indicate that most of the population supports the constitutional framework, these same polls show that this apparent legitimacy does not stem from an in-depth knowledge of the text itself. A 2004 study showed that

---

15    The first time was in 1992, when Article 13.2 was amended to allow citizens from other EU countries to vote and stand as candidates in local elections in order to conform to the Maastricht Treaty. In 2011, Article 135 was amended to promote financial stability by setting a legal limit to the deficit.

most Spaniards confessed to knowing very little or almost nothing of the content of the constitution.[16]

In Brazil, many of the articles of the constitution that were passed by the military regime in 1967 and amended in 1969 remained untouched in the 1988 Constitution. These included articles that regulated the armed forces, the police and the judicial system. Moreover, the president retained the power to ignore the wishes of Congress and declare a state of emergency if the armed forces demanded it (something the president was not empowered to do without the backing of the armed forces if Congress did not approve). A number of authors argue that the possibility of members of the military being judged in civilian courts was negligible (Zaverucha 1998: 114). However, between March 1992 and March 2012 the constitution was amended on 60 occasions, on many such occasions significantly.[17] Among the amendments, one allowed the president to be re-elected for a second term, but another shortened the term from five to four years. Another empowered the Senate to prosecute crimes committed by the armed forces, and others were designed to enhance the protection of human rights. Other amendments related to the economy and tended to reduce restrictions on foreign capital and ease the state monopoly in certain sectors.

In Poland a large number of groups rejected the constitution and have even made claims against it in court. Those who opposed it did so both because of its content and because of the way it was ratified, arguing that a constitution that was approved by only 25 per cent of the electorate (as a result of the low turnout) was not legitimate. However, while this discontent rumbled on, democracy continued to consolidate within society and the party system gradually became more stable. The constitution has rarely been amended and then only superficially: once to make it compatible with European law in 2006 (to accommodate for the European Arrest Warrant), and again in 2009 to change the electoral law to prevent those who have been sentenced to prison from being elected to the Sejm and the Senate. Thus, despite its questionable legitimacy, the Polish constitution has proved remarkably durable.

In Spain, consensus over the desirability of democracy is almost universal, despite the often sharp polarization between Left and Right. A Eurobarometer Survey carried out in 1997 revealed that 78 per cent of Spaniards thought that democracy was the best political system, while just 6 per cent believed that in certain situations dictatorship can be preferable (Lagos 2003: 474). This is similar to results from other Western European countries. Earlier data is rather more sparse, although results from a 1985 survey compiled by Larry Diamond show broadly similar results; 70 per cent of respondents indicated that democracy is always

---

16 Study 2410 by the *Centro de Investigaciones Sociológicas*. 9 per cent of respondents claimed to know the constitution 'well', 31 per cent 'more or less', 32 per cent 'very little' and 28 per cent 'almost not at all'.

17 A full list of amendments is available on the government's own database http://www.planalto.gov.br.

preferable, while just 10 per cent held the view that sometimes authoritarianism is preferable (Diamond 2001). This appears to show that a reasonably robust democratic consensus was achieved relatively early in Spain.

In Brazil, support for democracy has been lower than in Spain, which possibly reflects that economic crisis that bedevilled the country throughout the 1980s and 1990s. A Latinobarómetro survey carried out in 1995 showed that just 48.0 per cent of Brazilians thought democracy is better than any other form of government, while 24.7 per cent considered that sometimes authoritarianism is better. There is also more significant support for a strong leader than in either Spain or Poland (see below). However, support for democracy in Brazil seems to have gradually consolidated during the first decade of this century; while those who perceived democracy to be preferable had fallen to just 41.7 per cent by 2000, according to the Latinobarómetro survey from that year, with 27.5 per cent considering that sometimes authoritarianism is better, by 2010 the respective figures stood at 60.9 per cent and 21.7 per cent.[18]

In Poland, support for democracy nine years after the fall of communism was greater than in Brazil, but less than in Spain. According to a New Democracies Barometer carried out in 1998, 69 per cent of respondents thought that democracy was preferable, compared with 16 per cent who considered that under certain circumstances authoritarianism was preferable (Lagos 2003: 474). At the same time, despite the fact that Poland could not agree on a constitution, there did appear to be more support for the *principles of constitutionalism*. According to a World Values Survey carried out in 2005, 30.5 per cent of Poles thought that having a strong leader was either 'fairly good' or 'very good', while 69.5 per cent thought it either 'fairly bad' or 'very bad'. In Spain (2007), the respective figures were 32.7 per cent and 67.3 per cent, while in Brazil (2006) they were 64.1 per cent and 35.9 per cent (i.e. with a majority preferring a strong leader).[19] Most Poles therefore appeared to support the principle of limited government and would oppose a 'power grab' by the executive.

Thus, despite the differences between the three cases, in all cases we observe the consolidation of democracy and the legitimization of the constitution, or at least the gradual adherence to principles of constitutionalism. The pace at which this occurs varies somewhat between the cases; in Spain it is rapid, in Poland, slower, and in Brazil, slower still.

At first glance the issue of the durability of the constitution appears a simple one; the constitution remains in force in all three cases. However, if we look in greater depth, we are faced with the following dilemma: Is the Spanish constitution more durable than the Brazilian constitution because it has only been amended (superficially) twice, while the latter has been amended extensively? And if it is, does this mean that it is more legitimate? Or is the legitimacy of a constitution

---

18   Source: Latinobarómetro at http://www.latinobarometro.org.

19   Compiled by the author from the World Values Survey website: www. worldvaluessurvey.org.

instead associated with the way it is implemented and in particular to its functioning as a framework of basic principles that not only prevents authoritarian regression, but also evolves over time by expanding democratic rights and institutional guarantees for the better functioning of democracy?

## Conclusions

In a process of transition to democracy, the constitution represents the institutional structure on which a new political system is built. While the old actors in power try to secure concessions and safeguards, the delayed demands of actors hitherto excluded from political life are also heard. The constitution becomes a cherished spot from which one can embark on a search for consensus on the one hand, and/ or attempt to gain or retain power on the other.

But the 'success' of a constitution does not appear to be directly influenced by endogenous variables. All constitutions described in this chapter have proved relatively 'successful' in terms of the future consolidation of democracy, despite significant differences in the constitution-making process in terms of the mode of representation, style of deliberation and mode of ratification The speed and force with which democracy became consolidated in Spain seems to be based on a shared perception that there were not many alternatives. During the drafting of the constitution, consensus building, especially over such controversial issues as the territorial organization of the country, was central to raising levels of legitimacy. The role of the King and later Suarez, as well as the newly-legalized parties, in acting as channels of communication between different actors and the population seem to have compensated for the lack of openness in a process in which the population was an observer, but unable to intervene directly, except in the end, by referendum, when the constitution was ratified.

In the context of this book, the Brazilian case is particularly relevant because it shows both the influence and the limits of the procedures adopted for the drafting of the constitution. Some authors have noted that the structure of decentralized commissions explains why the first versions of the constitution were of a clearly progressive bent. The rejection by the centre-right sectors blocked these early proposals and, after a long process of discussion, this resulted in the adoption of a constitution closer to the interests of these sectors. In turn, the broad public participation process ensured its legitimacy (especially for the recognition of social rights), but at the same time failed to prevent the ring-fencing of authoritarian enclaves. The Brazilian constitution-making experience also suggests that the constitution can last despite extensive amendments and, moreover, that these amendments can actually facilitate the generation of consensus and, in turn, the consolidation of democracy. In short, a further expansion of the constitution-making process in the years after the transition can promote a gradual process of consensus-building and democratization.

The Polish case shows how difficult it can be to achieve consensus on the constitutional text. After the transition process began in 1988 (with the call by General Kiszczak to the leader of Solidarity to begin talks), it was only in 1997 that the final constitutional text was approved after the failed attempt of the 'little constitution' in 1992. The 1997 constitution was itself later challenged by core actors in the political system. Nevertheless, at a more fundamental level Polish elites and society may have reached at least a minimal consensus on the principles of democracy and the limits of government rather earlier, as the Round Table discussions and the semi-competitive 1989 elections showed minimal public support for the existing authoritarian system. Seen in this way, the details of the constitution that was eventually ratified in 1997 were little more than an irrelevant after-show to which the public paid little heed.

In short, the constitutional formula adopted with transition is highly conditioned by the strategies and choices of actors. We see neither a *tabula rasa* nor ideal models of constitution-making; what instead drives the process is a combined calculation of the costs and benefits that each group would accrue as well as the vision of each for society. In turn, against the backdrop of the inevitable uncertainty of a transition process, it is time that is the key variable. In Spain, an initial consensus led to a rapid transition that kept the players from changing their strategies in response to changes in their positions and strengths and allowed a rapid elaboration of the constitution. In Brazil the constitutional process was tied up with a rather protracted transition dynamic while in Poland the transition occurred relatively independently of the inability of the actors – observed for nearly a decade – to agree on a new fundamental law.

This chapter highlights the contrast between the constitution as a text and the principles of constitutionalism. In Spain both were settled at more or less the same time. In Brazil, where the constitution was itself a work in progress, the 1988 constitution marked only the beginning of a process of generating a consensus over basic constitutional principles. Finally, in Poland it appears that there was some agreement on the basic principles of democracy and limited government well before the constitution was set in ink.

Chapter 6

# Legality and Legitimacy: Constituent Power in Venezuela, Bolivia and Ecuador

Nina Massüger Sánchez Sandoval and Yanina Welp

## Introduction

In the last 35 years all countries in Latin America have replaced or reformed their constitutions. Most of these processes were carried out with scant regard for the law. Rather it may be said that often they were the result of actions that were bestowed ex post facto with political legitimation through constitutional change (Brewer-Carías 2004). Shifts in the rules of the game that favour the promoters of change and the legal controversies that such processes engender are by no means a novelty. However, three recent experiences have attracted special attention from both local and international researchers. These are the constitution-making processes that have occurred in Venezuela (1999), Bolivia (2006–2009) and Ecuador (2007–2008). There are a number of reasons that explain the interest in these cases, most notably the fact that the three countries have experienced a political revolution through the elaboration of new constitutions that emanated from a constituent power embodied in a constituent assembly. Furthermore, the three cases share in common both that the parties or movements that pioneered the changes had recently assumed political power and that inequality, social crisis, corruption and the discrediting of party politics were all evident. Such a generalization may hide certain relevant differences, but reveals a common underlying theme: the insertion of a political conflict into the constitutional process, a conflict between, on the one hand, the elites that had hitherto controlled access to power, and, on the other, an emerging group that promoted far-reaching institutional changes with the support of previously excluded social sectors.

In all three cases the opposition (made up of the former elites) maintained a strong presence in other institutions, especially in parliament, and championed – at least in their rhetoric – the defence of the existing juridical and institutional order, while the new government based its legitimizing discourse on citizens' support. The cornerstone of the debate was therefore between the original constituent power, which drew its legitimacy from citizens' support, and derived constituent power, which relied on a number of existing institutions and enjoyed very low levels of legitimacy.[1] How could such a conflict between democratic legitimacy and legality be resolved? Would it be possible to find a way to respect both criteria or was it inevitable that one would prevail over the other? To what extent could these processes lead to a 'break' or 'rupture' in the institutional framework? To what extent would these countries' constitutions be forged by an inclusive process based on consensus?

To address these questions, we analyse the three constitution-making processes by taking into account both the legal and the political aspects. For each case we consider first the origins of the process, then the operation of the constituent assembly, and finally we examine the outcome. In the final part of this chapter, we present our conclusions.

## Venezuela: The Bolivarian Revolution and the constitutional project

In Venezuela, demand for a new constitution had been evident long before Hugo Chávez assumed the presidency. In 1958, after the coup against Marcos Pérez Jiménez, a power-sharing agreement – known as the Punto Fijo Pact – was sealed between the main political parties (excluding the communists). In the short term the Pact helped establish democracy, but in the long term turned electoral politics into little more than a farce that gave a fig-leaf of legitimacy to a system in which power was effectively divided up between the principal parties. From the end of the 1980s, social conflict, marked by civil protests and military uprisings, broke out. In response, the Congress established in 1989 the Bicameral Commission for the Revision of the Constitution to explore the possibility of constitutional change. In March 1992, a few days after the uprising by Hugo Chávez's Revolutionary Bolivarian Movement 200 (MBR-200), the Commission presented Congress with its proposals on initiating a fairly far-reaching reform. However, the two most important parties, Democratic Action (Acción Democrática, AD) and the Political Electoral Independent Organization Committee (Comité de Organización Política Electoral Independiente, COPEI) decided to suspend the debate.

MBR-200 would later form the basis for the establishment of the Fifth Republic Movement (Movimiento V República, MVR), which catapulted Hugo Chávez to the presidency in the elections of 6 December 1998. The main promises of Chávez's campaign were the transformation of the state: a new fundamental law was to be elaborated by a constituent assembly (Asamblea Constituyente, AC) which was to be convened by the people through a consultative referendum envisaged by Article 181 of the Organic Law of Suffrage and Political Participation (LOSPP). However, the 1961 Constitution (Articles 245–9) had enshrined a different procedure for its

---

1   Derived constituent power is subject to the limits set by the Constitution or existing legal framework and is exercised by the authorities defined by the existing constitutional order; original constituent power goes beyond these limits and is exercised by a body that does not derive its powers from the existing constitution.

own reform, or, in other words, the exercise of derived constituent power: namely, that it had to be conducted by the Congress and then ratified by the people in a constitutional referendum. In October 1998, as a reaction to the plans of the possible future president, an appeal was filed with the Supreme Court of Justice (CSJ) requesting that the Court resolve the questions of: 1) whether Article 181 of LOSPP permitted a referendum on convening a National Constituent Assembly (ANC) and, if it did, 2) whether it would authorize the immediate establishment of an Assembly, or whether it would first require a reform of the Constitution. This, and another similar appeal, reflected the debate between those who demanded more weight for the democratic principle, equating it with popular sovereignty or the original constituent power and thus interpreting Article 4 of the Constitution as allowing the people to exercise sovereignty directly, and those who defended the supremacy of the Constitution (interpreting Article 4 as conclusively delegating the exercise of sovereignty to the powers that be).[2]

On January 19, 1999, the CSJ declared that a popular consultation on convening an AC based on the LOSPP was lawful, but did not pronounce upon the second, possibly more essential question about the procedure for convening it. The content of certain passages, together with a general lack of precision in the rulings led a large part of society, especially the press, to interpret them as meaning that it was viable to convene the ANC by means of a consultative referendum (Brewer-Carías 2002: 197). Accordingly, Chávez called the referendum by Decree No. 3 of 2 February 1999, which fixed the questions to be voted upon.

The wording of the referendum, endorsed by the National Electoral Council (CNE) by Resolution no. 990217-32, opened up a new debate. While in the first question the people were asked to accept or reject the creation of the ANC, the second question was formulated in such a way that, if approved by the citizens, it would have granted discretionary power to Chávez to manage the reform process.[3] On 18 March 1999, after more than a dozen unsuccessful appeals for annulment, the Supreme Court of Justice issued ruling n° 271 that forced the CNE to rephrase the latter.[4] The final version of the second question read: *'Do you agree with the conditions proposed by the National Executive for the Convening of the National Constituent Assembly, reviewed and modified in part by the National Electoral Council meeting held on 03.24.99, and published in full in the Official Gazette*

---

2   Article 4 of the 1961 Constitution states: 'Sovereignty rests with the people, who exercise it by the suffrage, through the organs of public power'.

3   The question read: 'Do you authorize the president to set, by means of an act of government and heeding the opinion of the political, social and economic sectors of society, the terms of reference of the electoral process according to which the members of the ANC are to be elected?'

4   A first version of the presidential proposal for the 'basic rules' for convening the AC had already been issued on 10 March (G.O. no. 36,358, 10 March 1999). It was amended twice, first by the President (cf. G.O. no. 36,660, 12 March 1999) and then again by the CNE (G.C. 36,669, 25 March 1999).

*of the Republic of Venezuela, No 36,669 dated 03/25/99?'* The consultative referendum held on 25 April 1999 enabled the ANC to be convened: With a low turnout (37.6 per cent), the two questions were approved by more than 80 per cent of the voters.

*The National Constituent Assembly*

The above-mentioned 'basic rules' (*bases* in Spanish) for convening the ANC regulated both the procedures for holding the election of its members as well as its nature, functions and term of office. According to them, the ANC would vest itself with its own rules of operation. As it embodied popular sovereignty it was considered to be a source of original constituent power. However, it would be bound by the values and principles of the historic Venezuelan republic, by international treaties, by the progressive nature of fundamental rights and by respect for democratic guarantees. On 13 April, the Supreme Court ruled that to denominate the ANC as an 'original power' was not appropriate because it was the 1961 Constitution that allowed the ANC to act.

The system to elect the ANC determined that there would be a total of 131 assembly members, 104 elected from 24 regional constituencies (the 23 states and the Federal District of Caracas), 24 from a single national constituency (with ten votes for each voter) and three representatives of the indigenous peoples. The election was to be for individuals proposed on their own initiative, by political parties or by actors in civil society, with the endorsement of voters' signatures,[5] but not for parties; however, after a debate that once again ended with an intervention by the Supreme Court, candidates' party affiliation could be displayed next to their notice of nomination in the Electoral Gazette (Gaceta Electoral), but not on the ballot paper (ruling of 21 June 1999).

Elections to the ANC were held on 25 July 1999. During the campaign (24 June – 23 July) the candidates – including actors from traditional parties to the pro-Chávez Fifth Republic Movement (MVR) and Patriotic Pole (PP), as well as from social movements and NGOs – raised issues they wanted included in the new constitutional text. The proposals of the NGOs were especially focussed on the design of a more efficient model for the economy and recognition and respect for civil rights. The traditional parties proposed a range of issues but paid less attention to those related to social protection. The groups aligned with the Bolivarian Movement, meanwhile, emphasized the reform and restructuring of the state (Maingon et al. 2000: 111). At this point in time there were hundreds of forums, seminars and events, organized by various actors, that spread information about the AC and the issues it would be dealing with (Maingon et al. 2000: 114). In the end the election gave a resounding victory to the government's allies (92.3 per

---

5   Twenty thousand signatures at national level. For the regional constituencies, the CNE ruled that the number of signatures required should be calculated by a formula based on the number of inhabitants resident in each one of the federal entities.

cent of the total number of seats), although the level of abstention (53.7 per cent) also left unanswered the question of what degree of consensus a reform process of this magnitude would generate. The result was not particularly surprising given that the majoritarian electoral system was clearly detrimental to the representation of minorities (Gómez Calcaño 2000, García Guadilla y Hurtado 2000).

Contrary to the aforementioned decisions of the Supreme Court and the public will expressed in the referendum of April, just days after opening, the ANC declared in its own by-laws that it was an 'original constituent power', and therefore empowered to limit or dissolve, by decree, the existing constituent powers (the legislative and judicial branches) , and that the 1961 Constitution would remain in force only in areas that did not conflict with the acts issued by it.

The first three months of the ANC's mandate were characterized by a participatory debate, whereas the second phase of the discussion of the draft constitution took place over a few days in late November. Within 120 days the ANC (which had a fixed term of 180 days) had finished its project of reforming the state and creating the Fifth Republic. Its low level of representativeness (caused by the electoral system), the large majority enjoyed by the pro-government coalition that allowed it to approve articles without any real discussion and the direct intervention of Chávez in revising the final text resulted in a text that was far from fulfilling the expectations that the process would be open to participation from various sectors (García Guadilla y Hurtado 2000: 24 and ff.). In the referendum of 15 December 1999, citizens approved the new Constitution with 72 per cent in favour (with the abstention rate inching up to 55 per cent). It is worth mentioning that, although the Constitution entered into force in 1999, the ANC continued functioning until the end of January 2000. Without putting the issue to a vote it established a 'regime of transition' which, among other things, allowed it to dissolve Congress and replace it with a commission composed of several members of the ANC itself and other unelected members. Moreover, it named the members of the newly-formed Supreme Tribunal of Justice (Tribunal Supremo de Justicia, TSJ) and the CNE. These actions obviously led to criticisms about the lack of consensus mechanisms to allow transition to a new regime and about the appointment of individuals close to the government to fill these key positions (Brewer-Carías 1999, Maingon et al. 2000).

*The Constitution of 1999*

There are many new features in the Venezuelan constitution of 1999, amongst which (in addition to a change in the name of the republic, which came to be called the Bolivarian Republic of Venezuela) the most notable were the inclusion of second and third generation rights (economic and social) and those of indigenous peoples. The text granted citizens a new role with the creation of institutions such as the attorney general, ombudsman and the treasury inspector's office as well as by expanding the list of political rights. It introduced new measures including the mandatory referendum (to amend or rewrite the constitution), the legislative initiative, the abrogative referendum and the possibility of popular recall for all elected officials.

Certain institutions were replaced or removed. The electoral body became an autonomous institution, accountable only to citizens. Congress became unicameral despite the fact that Venezuela remains a Federal State, while the Judicial Council was not included in the new constitution. Executive power was strengthened by various reforms. The mandate of the president was extended from five to six years and the president could be re-elected. The executive was given added competences at the expense of the legislature (for example, if the latter passes a motion of censure against the Vice-President three times during the same presidential term the president can dissolve it).

## Ecuador: A Transformative Neoconstitutionalism

In Ecuador, the convening of an AC in 2007 was preceded by a period of deep crisis that involved all aspects of political life and was marked by institutional fragility and instability, as evidenced by the fact that there were eight presidents between 1996 and 2006 and that in 2005 the Supreme Court did not work for almost a year. It also involved an economic crisis that was especially severe in the beginning of the first decade of the new century. These inauspicious circumstances were exacerbated by the tight control exerted by the so-called 'partidocracy' (*partidocracia*) in a country that was fragmented by regional divisions and an electoral system that promoted a weak executive power insofar as even a president obtaining an absolute majority of votes could seldom get a relative majority in Congress (Pérez Loose 2009: 242). There was also an indigenous movement that was organized and active.

In 2006 Rafael Correa ran as presidential candidate for PAIS Alliance (Alianza País). His coalition did not present candidates for the parliament as an expression of protest against the parties that had governed the country until that time. Like Chávez, during the election campaign Correa promised far-reaching reforms by means of an AC. Having won the elections and assumed the presidency he decreed the Supreme Electoral Tribunal (Tribunal Supremo Electoral, TSE) to hold a referendum on the basis of Article 104, section 2 of the 1998 constitution in order to decide on the establishment of an AC that would be granted 'full powers' and on its rules of operation (Executive Decree N°2 of 15 January 2007).

However, the 1998 Constitution did not envisage the use of an AC for its own reform but instead delegated this function either to the Congress or citizens (Article 280). It could thus be argued that the president's proposal amounted to an amendment to the procedure for revising the Constitution. The Constitution granted the President the power to call for a referendum on matters that, in his view, were of vital importance to the country, but this excluded constitutional reforms. These could be put to a referendum only if the Congress, upon the request of the President, deemed a reform bill as urgent or if within a year Congress had refused to discuss, approve or reject such a draft bill that had been submitted by the President (Article 283, relating to Article 104, section 1). The decree did not fulfil these conditions. However, the Congress, upon the request of the TSE, called for an urgent consultation, suggesting a number of amendments to be made to the statute governing the establishment of an AC, including the requirement that each candidate had the backing of one per cent of registered voters on the electoral roll of the respective constituency. In February 2007, the TSE, in contrast to a decision made in 2005,[6] ruled the referendum to be constitutional, ignoring the above-mentioned request of Congress.[7] The response from Congress was immediate: a majority of deputies decided to remove from office four of the seven members of the TSE. The next day the TSE adopted another unconstitutional resolution dismissing 57 deputies from the opposition parties and calling for them to be replaced by their 'surrogates'.[8] The TSE claimed that it was its prerogative to safeguard the electoral process and that the decision of the Congress was aimed at preventing a referendum that had already been called. After the police, by order of the President, prevented the dismissed members from accessing the Congress building, their substitutes took their posts and sided with the President against the parties from which they had been elected. Against a backdrop of growing polarization and conflict between institutions and groups, the referendum of 15 April 2007 gave resounding victory to the 'Yes' camp, with 81.7 per cent of votes in favour of electing a constituent assembly and a turnout of 71 per cent.

Shortly after the referendum, the Constitutional Court (Tribunal Constitucional, TC) declared unconstitutional the resolution according to which the TSE had dismissed the deputies. However, because of another police operation aimed at preventing the entry of the re-enfranchised deputies, the decision was never implemented. Congress (composed partly of the 'surrogates') then dismissed the TC, which remained vacant until 31 May 2007.

*The Constituent Assembly*

In the referendum of 15 April, citizens not only approved the convening of an AC but also a Statute that determined how it was to be elected and how it would operate.

---

6    Ex-President Alfredo Palacio had issued an executive order (No. 705 of October 26, 2005) calling for a referendum on the establishment of an AC. But on that occasion the TSE declared the decree inapplicable (Resolution of November 1, 2005), noting that the 1998 Constitution does not empower the President to convene an AC.

7    PLE-TSE-13-13-2-2007 of 13 February 2007, R.O. n° 26, supplement, 22 February 2007. It is Resolution PLE-TSE-2-1-3-2007 of 1 March that contains the final version (R.O. n ° 37, 9 March 2007).

8    According to the Ecuadorian electoral system, every elected deputy has a 'surrogate' from his or her own political party who would replace him/her in the event of his/her incapacitation.

In conformity with Article 1, Section 1 of the Statute, the AC was to be vested with 'full powers to transform the institutional framework of the State and to draft a new Constitution', a process that was required to conform to fundamental rights. It also stipulated that both the institutional transformation and the new constitution would enter into force only after having been accepted by the people by means of a referendum. However, it fell to the TC to clarify the meaning of this guideline. On 15 June, the TC stated that the attribution of 'full powers' to the AC did not grant it the power to assume the competences of constituted powers but that it would be limited to issuing the new constitutional text and while it was exercising its constitution-making powers the established constitutional order would remain in force.

The AC was to bring together 130 elected deputies, of whom one hundred would be elected by the provinces, 24 at national level and six by Ecuadorian citizens registered abroad. The electoral victory of Correa's supporters exceeded the most optimistic expectations. The PAIS Alliance not only won a large majority (80 out of the 130 seats, with high levels of participation) in the vote that was held on 30 September 2007, but also, for the first time in 27 years of civilian rule, the vote distribution did not reflect the historical territorial divisions.

Contrary to the decision of the TC, the AC, with its own particular interpretation of 'full powers', determined that its decisions were superior to any other legal norm and that it would therefore not be subject to control from or challenged by the existing constituted powers. It warned that judges and courts that brought any kind of action against its decisions would be dismissed and subject to prosecution accordingly. On 29 November 2007, the AC, affirming and guaranteeing the existence of the rule of law, confirmed the President and Vice President of the Republic in their posts. At the same time it assumed the powers and duties of the legislative branch of government, and declared members of the existing Congress elected on 15 October 2006 to be in recess. Finally, on 11 December it established that the existing legal system would remain in force with the exception of measures that contradicted those of the AC. All this happened not only in violation of the ruling of the TC, but also of the Statute approved by citizens in the referendum. It also explains why the Assembly devoted a part of its work to producing laws that are normally the remit of a regular legislature (such as a tax law, a law on the remuneration of public employees or draft laws on road traffic) (Pérez Loose 2009: 256ff; Conaghan 2008: 210).

In terms of the debate within the Assembly, one of the main fault lines was within the pro-government bloc between 'extractivists' (those who prioritize the extraction of natural resources) and 'environmentalists'. The environmentalist position was championed by Alberto Acosta, president of the Assembly and founder of PAIS Alliance, and also the Assembly member who had won most votes. The conflict centred on environmental limits to mining, the declaration of water as a fundamental human right and the need either to consult (the thesis of Correa) or obtain the consent (the thesis of Acosta) of populations and communities where the State intends to exploit the natural resources in the territories they occupy. Acosta enjoyed the support of Pachakutik (an influential left-wing party representing indigenous communities), which led to many of his proposals being included in the constitutional text. The relationship between Correa and Acosta deteriorated, as did the relationship between Correa and the indigenous movement. There were also defections from the ruling bloc as a result of tensions between progressive groups that promoted the incorporation of sexual and reproductive rights into the constitutional text and Correa, who made no secret of being a practicing Catholic.[9]

The AC was given eight months to draw up the new constitution. After seven months, only 57 articles had been adopted in their final form, which led Acosta to ask the President to extend the deadline by two months. Correa rejected the request, leading to the resignation of Acosta. With a new president of the AC, 387 articles were approved in three weeks (Souza Santos 2010: 113 and ff.). On 28 September 2008 almost 76 per cent of citizens with the right to vote came to the polling stations and approved the new Basic Law with 64 per cent of votes in favour.

*The 2008 Constitution*

In Ecuador, unlike Bolivia and Venezuela, the existing regulatory framework provided several mechanisms for citizens' participation and had also expanded the rights of indigenous communities. A number of authors agree that the 2008 Constitution, expanded these rights further, and also created a 'fourth power' of control by society (Ortiz Crespo 2008, Morales Viteri 2008). A controversial aspect of this change is that it gives equal priority to individuals who become involved through their own choice or are brought in by the executive as to those who have been elected by universal suffrage. For example, the Council for Citizens' Participation and Social Control, the members of which are either ordinary individuals selected by open competition or representative of citizens' organizations, assume functions previously carried out by the legislature (Basabe Serrano 2009: 388).

The new constitution also increased the capacity of the state to intervene in the economy, especially through the powers given to the National Secretariat for Planning and Development (Secretaría Nacional de Planificación y Desarrollo, SENPLADES). The state would also decide on the control of strategic sectors such as energy (in all its forms), telecommunications, non-renewable natural resources, transportation and refining of hydrocarbons, biodiversity and the gene pool, broadcasting frequencies, water resources, and others determined by law (Articles 313 and ff). Although rights linked to the protection of the land and to the environment were increased, the 'extractivist' vision prevailed insofar as the constitution established the need for consultation, rather than consent, before

---

9 For detailed analysis of the debates within the Assembly and the pro-government bloc, see Kingman 2008, Souza Santos 2010.

embarking on the exploitation of indigenous territory.[10] In terms of the division of powers, the president saw his powers increased at the expense of the other branches: the constitution created a national system of decentralized participatory planning to manage planning for development, consisting of various levels of government and open to citizen participation, but chaired by the president (Article 279); the executive branch was also henceforth responsible for drafting the state budget (Articles 292 to 296).[11]

## Bolivia: Towards a Multinational State

In Bolivia, the proposal for an AC was placed on the agenda of the social movements in the early 1990s, but gained pace in the early 2000s, notwithstanding a lack of responsiveness on the part of the traditional political parties, who felt under attack from this demand. It is worth mentioning that in 2001 the Constitutional Court, in consultation with the President of Congress, declared unconstitutional a bill calling for an AC.[12] Nevertheless, in 2002, the indigenous people of the lowlands mobilized for an AC in the march of Santa Cruz, but received no immediate response.

The critical moment came in 2003 when the 'gas war' triggered the fall of President Gonzalo Sánchez de Lozada (2002–2003) due to the popular outrage provoked by his decision to export oil to the United States via Chile.[13] The crisis was resolved by holding a referendum on energy policy. As the referendum was not regulated, it was first necessary to reform the 1967 Constitution. One of the most important changes introduced in 2004, was an amendment to Article 4 which provided for instruments of direct democracy such as the citizens' legislative initiative and the referendum. This background fuelled expectations for political renewal and helped bring new social forces to power. The electoral victory of Evo Morales in 2005 was unprecedented as it was the first time since 1978 that a candidate – of indigenous origin – had obtained sufficient support to reach the presidency without the necessity of an intervention from Congress and the establishment of inter-party pacts and negotiations.

The idea of adopting a new constitution was not new, as the constitutional history of the country shows; the novelty was that it had become the demand

---

10   In January 2009 the Mining Act was approved without consultation, creating one of the first serious conflicts faced by the government after the adoption of the Constitution. CONAIE filed appeals against the law asking for it to be declared unconstitutional.

11   For an overview of opinions on the 2008 Constitution written directly by constituents and other stakeholders, see Acosta et al. (2008).

12   Constitutional Declaration no. 0112001 of 17 January 2001.

13   This can be explained by the often fraught relationship between Bolivia and Chile, which dates back to the Pacific War (1879–1884) in which Bolivia lost its access to the sea. The Nineteenth century war is still a cause of tension between the two countries.

of a social force that coalesced around groups that had organized in the 1990s (Lazarte 2008). One could even argue, as de la Fuente Jeria (2010) has, that the establishment of an AC was not a central plank in the strategy of MAS,[14] the left-wing social movement of Evo Morales (which had remained on the margins during the indigenous march of 2002), but that the issue was imposed by the broad mobilization and expectations of renewal generated from the bottom up.

Since the Constitution provided for the convening of an AC for its own reform, the debate focussed on the the powers that the assembly could assume rather than on the (un)constitutionality of its establishment. Some assumed that the AC would merely be vested with derived powers given that its legal basis was determined by the state constitution and the law relating to its convocation; others, taking as a starting point the crisis and social mobilization of 2003, held that it must take on an original, plenipotentiary character with unlimited powers (MAS 2006, Cordero Carraffa 2005). The Convocation Law of the Constituent Assembly (Law 3364) resolved this controversy until the first debates of the AC, stipulating that the goal of the assembly was to draft a new constitutional text and that the AC would not depend on or be subject to the constituted powers but at the same time would not interfere in their work. In addition to the electoral process, the law determined the majority required to pass the new constitution (two thirds of members present) and ruled that it must be ratified by the people. Given the complex electoral system (see below) it was impossible for a single party or electoral bloc to win more than about 62 per cent of seats, virtually ensuring that diverging interests would be represented in the AC.

The election of assembly members was set for 2 July 2006. On the same day, voting took place on a referendum on departmental autonomy, which had been initiated by the Santa Cruz Civic Committee (Comité Cívico Pro Santa Cruz). The referendum was not only about long-neglected demands for decentralization, but also the country's division between rich departments (in the east) and poor (in the west).[15] The results would be binding for the AC, and those departments in which the 'yes' vote won would acquire the appropriate level of autonomy as soon as the new constitution entered into force (Article 2 of the Convocation Law 3365).

Morales had begun by supporting the autonomy demand, but later he and his party campaigned for a 'no' vote. The popularity of the demand for autonomy and the fact that the two votes were held simultaneously explains why, contrary to its expectations, MAS obtained only 51 per cent of the vote in the election for assembly members and 137 out of 255 seats. The growing polarization and the

---

14    Movement for Socialism-Political Instrument for the Sovereignty of the Peoples (Spanish: Movimiento al Socialismo-Instrumento Político por la Soberanía de los Pueblos), abbreviated MAS-IPSP, or MAS.

15    In February 2005, the Committee delivered 454,635 signatures to the National Electoral Court (CNE). On April 5 the Court certified that the number of valid signatures were greater than the minimum required and requested Congress to authorize the referendum (Salazar Elena 2009).

great difficulty in arriving at a consensus was a major problem that would cast a shadow over the work of the AC.

*The Constituent Assembly*

The election of the AC was marked by a high (84.5 per cent) turnout in a country in which a majority of the population identifies itself as indigenous and 36 nationalities co-exist. However, the issue of recognizing indigenous communities and the subsequent establishment of a multinational state had not yet been settled and, together with the long-delayed issues of autonomy and the location of the capital, this was one of the key areas that the AC would have to deal with. This is evident from the proposals and projects for a new constitution presented during the campaign by the political organizations MAS and PODEMOS,[16] and by the (indigenous) social movements (Lazarte 2008, Mayorga 2010).[17]

210 of the 255 assembly members were elected from 70 constituencies, each of which elected three candidates: two from the first placed party or alliance and one from the second placed entity. The remaining 45 members were elected from the nine departments, five from each department with the winning party or group taking two seats and the second, third and fourth-placed entities each taking one seat. In terms of candidate selection, parties assumed a predominant role, even though the Convocation Law provided that parties, citizens' groups and indigenous peoples all had the right to nominate candidates. In the eastern regions, corporate interests represented by the conservative bloc PODEMOS dominated (de la Fuente Jeria 2010). In the rest of the country, candidates from the right were members of their respective parties, while candidates for MAS were determined by negotiations within the movement itself and associated social, rural, farmers and indigenous organizations. Another fourteen political entities, including minor parties and citizens' groups, nominated candidates, typically the leaders of the respective organization.

MAS obtained 137 seats, while PODEMOS won 60. The remaining seats were distributed amongst another 14 organizations. The Constituent Assembly began its sessions with a heated debate on the general rules and, in particular, on the majority required for approving the new constitution. Finally, in February 2007, when half the time allowed for drafting the constitution had elapsed, an agreement

---

16   Podemos (Social and Democratic Power, in Spanish Poder democrático y Social) is a right-leaning pro-business party established in 2005. It is the successor of Nationalist Democratic Action, a right-wing party that was founded by former dictator Hugo Banzer in 1979.

17   The National Assembly of Indigenous, Native, Farmers and Settlers Organizations of Bolivia (of which the coca-growing peasant federations aligned with MAS do not form a part) participated in the process with a proposal submitted to the Constituent Assembly (Assembly 2006). The MAS presented its proposal and PODEMOS presented its draft constitution.

was reached: the full constitutional text would need to be adopted by an absolute majority, while individual articles would be approved by two-thirds of all members present. The change in the rules (from the Convocation Law, which had insisted on a two-thirds majority for the full text, see above) implied that the AC was not subject to existing law.

Once the Assembly was up and running, the participation of different social groups in its vicinity was intense; these included women's groups and unions close to assembly members from social movements. The Catholic Church, the police, the armed forces and the miners joined in from the corporate level. International cooperation was manifest through institutions such as the UNDP, GTZ, the Konrad Adenauer Foundation, and others. However, a number of authors criticize the lack of debate within the Assembly and the overt racism that was evident in the way individuals were barred on grounds of dress and comportment and in the way those identified as indigenous were barred from restaurants and hotels near where the Assembly was meeting (de la Fuente Jeria 2010, Souza Santos 2010). Regional meetings helped offset the absence of debate in the Assembly. These meetings were designed as a journey through the country by the 255 assembly members and support staff to listen and make proposals. This was one of the few occasions when Assembly members could work independently and in a more cooperative manner. However, they had little impact on the final text (de la Fuente Jeria 2010: 20), helped to reinforce territorial cleavages (Souza Santos 2010: 105) and further delayed the progress of work. Since by the early summer of 2007 it was obvious that the AC was not going to approve the new constitution within the one-year deadline that had been established by the Convocation Law, it decided on its own initiative to extend the deadline until mid-December.[18] On 31 July, Congress sanctioned the extension and the amendment of the internal rules of the AC, demonstrating both the derived nature of the latter's powers and its own capacity to intervene in its internal regulatory powers (Law 3728).

Finally, although it was established that the assembly would act independently and with few constraints, it was locked in a relationship of strong dependency on the party machines (De la Fuente Jeria 2010: 10). In August the old demand of moving the capital from La Paz to Sucre re-emerged with force. The issue divided forces aligned with MAS, which refused to introduce it into the Assembly, and this provoked a violent reaction from the people of Sucre (hitherto largely supportive of MAS), which had been hosting the AC. The violence led the AC to move its meetings to a Military School on the outskirts of the city of Sucre. However, it was not possible to approve the whole text there. The location was moved once again, this time to Oruro. Finally, in December, the constitution was approved in a session that lasted for seventeen hours and in which only assembly members from MAS were present. The other members had not been informed about the session. Later, the Constitution was subject to revision by the executive

---

18   Resolution AC/PLEN/RES/0010/2007 of 2 July 2007, analysed by Gamboa Rocabado (2009).

and by congressional commissions, which changed 144 articles behind closed doors, without either the consensus or mandate to do so.[19] After a year marked by conflicts over the issue of autonomy and a recall referendum in which Morales was re-endorsed as president by a majority of citizens, the Constitution was ratified by referendum on 25 January 2009.

*The Constitution of 2009*

The new constitution defines the state as a Unitary Social State of Plurinational, Community-Based Law. Amongst its innovations is its definition of Bolivia as a multinational state, the full recognition of cultural diversity, the creation of indigenous autonomy and the defence of natural resources. In addition, it adds to the list of fundamental rights and introduces social rights (many of which are difficult to put into practice). It incorporates mechanisms of direct and participatory democracy. It retains a bicameral legislature, despite the fact that the country conserves a unitary state structure. The system for electing a president was changed, with the incorporation of a second round of voting (thereby eliminating the need for the Congress to elect a winner as previously). Another significant innovation is the popular election of the members of the Supreme Court (Tribunal Supremo de Justicia).

Most of the changes introduced after the closure of the AC served to limit the transformatory power of the Constitution. For example, agrarian reform was limited by not making the law on the maximum size of land holdings apply retroactively. Similarly communitarian justice was restricted to indigenous people in their own territories and amongst one another (Souza Santos 2010: 109).

**Analysis and Conclusions**

As has been shown, there are parallels between the cases studied here, not only before the constitution-making processes but also in the course of them. These include the use of the referendum as a legal mechanism enabling the convening of the AC in Ecuador and Venezuela, and the prominent role of institutions such as the TSE (in Ecuador) and the Supreme Court (in Venezuela) in legitimizing the AC. In contrast, in Bolivia the AC had been introduced as an institution by the 2004 reforms to the 1967 Constitution, so there was no dispute about the admissibility of convoking it. In all three cases the president played a key role by leading the campaign for a new constitution. In each case the opposition consisted of those who had held power previously, and there was a high degree of polarization and conflict between the two sides. Despite the fact that this conflict went beyond the limits of legality and peaceful debate, in all three cases it was resolved by reconfiguring the institutions but without total institutional breakdown.

---

19    For details, see Souza Santos (2010: 109) and ff. See also Lazarte (2008).

If in formal terms these constitutional processes can be considered as amongst the most democratic of those analysed in the book (the new constitution was ratified by referendum, the constitution-making body was directly elected by citizens and in two of the three cases the decision to elect a constituent assembly was also decided by referendum), at the same time they were all marked by violations of the law – and on occasions they even infringed the regulations that were established ad hoc to manage the constitution-making process itself.

In Venezuela and Ecuador, the legal dilemma at the core of the constitution-making process was that convening an AC was not regulated by the constitutions in force at that time (1961 and 1998). With a parliament dominated by an opposition majority – in Ecuador the PAIS Alliance had not event fielded candidates in the parliamentary elections – Chávez and Correa relied on the 'popular will' expressed in the polls to carry out the reform by overstepping the existing legal framework, but legitimized by the CSJ in the case of Venezuela and by the TSE in Ecuador. The legal contradiction is clear: How is it possible to appeal to original constituent power, when there is already a functioning legal and constitutional framework. In legal terms, if the constitution and other institutions of the political regime are operating, the will of the people is not sovereign insofar as it is also subject to the legal order. In Bolivia citizens were not consulted about convening an AC (which was permitted according to the existing constitution), but at the same time, like the other two cases, the executive appealed to the will of citizens to set in motion a constituent assembly with unlimited powers.

In theory, the assembly could not be sovereign. It is the people that transfer the exercise of (parts of their) sovereignty to their representatives. For this reason the assembly must respect the framework that the people established. In Venezuela and Ecuador, the framework was built around controversial statutes proposed by the presidency. Yet in both cases, the Assembly declared itself sovereign, dissolved Congress and the Supreme Court, enacted laws, and, eventually, worked even after the deadline established and ratified by the people in a referendum had expired. In Bolivia, the difficulty of building consensus in a context of growing polarization (exacerbated by divisions amongst MAS supporters about departmental autonomy and the location of the capital) as well as the requirement that decisions be taken by a two-thirds majority of the members present prolonged the time it took before the AC even started to function. In the end, the debate on its internal rules was settled by Congress, which at the same time also granted the extension of the deadline that had become necessary due to the delays. The violence unleashed by the conflict over the location of the capital resulted in a constitutional text that was approved in a session in which only assembly members close to MAS participated. This text was later altered by authorities that had no jurisdiction to make substantive changes.

In terms of the content of the new constitutions, in all cases we observe a considerable increase in so-called second and third generation rights. The articles of the three constitutions include new notions of cultural and ethnic recognition, a wide range of participatory institutions and environmental protection. At the same time, we see an expansion of presidential powers, the creation of new institutions of control and a reduction in the powers of the legislature.

What we have seen throughout these pages is that in societies with deep social divisions observance of the law as well as the institutional framework are weak. This is reflected in the new constitutions which, despite their ratification by citizens through a referendum, embody a deeper political conflict born out of this deficiences. This does not relate specifically to Chávez, Correa or Morales, but is part of a long-running political game in which those who win the game change its rules in their favour. The defining feature in these cases is the support of citizens for a process of radical transformation. At the same time, we have seen how, once they had been initiated, the three constitution-making processes relegated citizens to the role of "observers" that were called upon mainly to give their blessing to decisions that were made both by force of numbers (without attempting to seek consensus) and in defiance of the rules agreed with public consent. Meanwhile, it was the presidents that had become the main protagonists.

Chapter 7

# Constituent Assemblies in Swiss Cantons

Ana Tornic and Nina Massüger Sánchez Sandoval

## I. Introduction

The first constituent assemblies in Swiss cantons were convened in the 1830s. More than 50 per cent of the over 100 total revisions of cantonal constitutions that have been conducted successfully so far have been brought about by such assemblies. In the intervening period, the political, economic and legal circumstances have changed in a substantial way. However, over one third of the most recent cantonal constitutions emanate from constituent assemblies.

Drawing from both legal provisions and empirical evidence, this article aims to analyse the use of constituent assemblies for constitution-making at the cantonal level over the last 180 years, and to figure out to what extent its importance has been subject to changes. Special attention will be paid to the relationship between constitution-making by constituent assemblies and the use of direct democracy. After having defined the term 'constituent assembly' (II) and given a brief historical overview (III), the subsequent sections will be dedicated to a chronological analysis of the different 'waves' of constitution-making from 1830 until the present day (IV). The chapter will end with a brief conclusion (V).

## II. Definition

Despite the diversity of constitution-making bodies which have been engaged in the drafting processes in the Swiss cantons, one type particularly stands out: the constituent assembly (CA), which is directly elected by the people for the sole purpose of elaborating or totally revising[1] a cantonal constitution.[2] As an expression of the principle of popular sovereignty these assemblies were restricted to drafting the new constitutions and in almost all cases the ratification of the new charters was reserved to the citizens (constitutional referendum). The following

---

1   CAs can also be mandated with drafting a partial constitutional revision. This article only examines the elaboration of new constitutions and their total revisions, whereby total revision is to be understood in a formal sense. As the only exceptions the formal partial revisions in the Cantons of Ticino in 1891/92 and Schwyz in 1898, which are unanimously qualified as material total revisions, were included.

2   Cf. type no. 9 of the typology shown in Chapter 2.

types of constitution-making bodies, which only differ slightly from the definition above, were also taken into account: (1) indirectly elected CAs, whose members were nominated by, to this purpose, directly elected electors;[3] (2) parliaments, which have been elected in view of drafting a new constitution;[4] (3) CAs, which appointed a number of their members themselves, and (4) the two cases (Fribourg 1831 and 1848) in which the drafts were not put to a referendum.

## III. Origins

The origins of CAs coincide with the creation of the first constitutions in the modern sense in the revolutionary processes of the late eighteenth century. For the first time CAs were established in the wake of the American declaration of independence in the former British colonies: In Massachusetts in 1778 the citizens did not only approve the convening of a CA but also the constitutional draft. Having accomplished its task, the assembly was dissolved – the people had the final say.

In Europe, the institution of the CA emerged for the first time in revolutionary France of the 1790s. Based on Sieyès' theory, constituent power was exercised by a representative assembly, which was institutionally separated from the legislative power. The participation of the citizens was limited to the election of their representatives which, in turn, exercised not only the constitution-making but also – without being authorised – the legislative power (Erb 1962: 46ff., Rüegg 1989: 58ff.).

In the Swiss cantons the people have played a fundamental role in the constitution-making processes since 1830. Accordingly, the nature of the CAs corresponded to a greater extent to the American model.

## IV. Constitution-Making by Constituent Assemblies in the Swiss Cantons

Since 1830, 112 new cantonal constitutions have entered into force.[5] 60 of these were elaborated by CAs. According to the number of constitutional revisions carried out per year, five 'waves' of constitution-making can be identified over the entire time period. While, roughly speaking, during the nineteenth century intensive constitution-making processes were conducted every ten years, total

---

3　This type is the equivalent on state-level to type no. 5 in Chapter 2, except that the electors, elected directly by the people in communal constituencies, represented their voters' interests.

4　Cf. type no. 8 of the typology in Chapter 2.

5　Six of these were in newly established cantons (Basel-Countryside 1832, Basel-Town 1833, Schwyz Outer Lands 1832, Schwyz 1833, Neuchâtel 1848 and Jura 1977).

revisions of cantonal constitutions in the twentieth century became more frequent again only as of 1960.

## The Liberal Movement of the 1830s

The first and most distinct wave of constitution-making coincided with the liberal phase of the regeneration[6] in the 1830s. Even though by that time the first liberal constitution had already entered into force in Switzerland, one can assume that it came about as a reaction of the outbreak of the French revolution in July 1830.[7] 23 cantonal constitutions entered into force between 1830 and 1839, of which eleven did so in the year 1831. While twelve constitutions were drafted by (predominantly) directly elected CAs, two were elaborated by indirectly elected CAs and three by newly elected parliaments.[8]

*Legal framework*   Pursuant to the Federal Treaty of 7 August 1815 the federation – a loose confederation and not yet a Federal State – had only minor competences. The cantons reciprocally guaranteed their constitutions. No formal requirements such as the holding of a referendum were stipulated for their adoption. At the cantonal level, the constitutions of the restoration period[9] made up the legal framework.

The elections in the cantons were predominantly indirect. As the general franchise was predicated on property and wealth, large segments of the population were excluded from political participation. In many places the electoral systems induced an over-representation of the urban regions with respect to the rural regions. Only in the Landsgemeinde cantons, where all the enfranchised citizens gather to deliberate and decide political issues, did citizens participate directly in government activities. Fundamental liberties were only guaranteed to a limited extent (Erb 1962: 65ff.). Only the constitutions of Fribourg, Schaffhausen and Vaud contained regulations with regard to their own revision, which had to be conducted by the legislative power (in Fribourg and Schaffhausen together with the executive power) and be approved by the people. Apart from that, the constitutions were assumed to be non-revisable.

*Events*   After the middle of the 1820s, a liberal opposition began to emerge in several cantons and made its effects felt even before the outbreak of the French

---

6   The regeneration period lasted from 1830 till 1848 and comprised the liberal renewal on the cantonal level and the conservative counter movement, as well as the subsequent radicalization of the regeneration movement.

7   Erb 1962: 72f.; Fazy 1890: 221; Feddersen 1867: 83; Kölz 1992: 215ff.; NZZ 1980: 68.

8   For an overview on all the constitution-making processes in the cantons between 1830 and today, see Appendix Table A7.1.

9   The restoration constitutions were enacted in 1814 after the withdrawal of the French troops. Returning to the political principles from before the occupation, they were based on privileges of the urban aristocracy and a dominating executive.

revolution of 1830. On 4 July 1830 the first liberal constitution in Switzerland was adopted by the people in the canton of Ticino. The events in France provided an additional impetus to the liberal movement, which succeeded in enacting new liberal constitutions in the cantons of Zurich, Berne, Lucerne, Fribourg, Solothurn, Basel, Schaffhausen, St. Gallen, Argovia, Thurgau and Vaud (Heusler 1920: 256f., 361, Kölz 1992: 210ff., 218).

Since at that time censorship had already been revoked in several cantons, liberal ideas, which were advocated initially by the middle class and by parts of the urban upper class (NZZ 1980: 68), could be spread among the population by means of leaflets and the press (Kölz 1992: 214, 218, Nabholz 1911: 17f., Scherer 1954: 13). The liberals demanded the enactment of new constitutions, which – by introducing the mandatory constitutional referendum – should realize the principle of popular sovereignty (Appenzeller Zeitung 1830b: 389ff.). However, they rejected more far-reaching popular participation, especially since they assumed that their demands would be realized by the majorities they expected to achieve in the cantonal parliaments. Popular decisions would only have implied a certain degree of unpredictability. Furthermore, the liberals pressed for a relaxation of restrictions to the franchise and for the equitable representation of the urban and the rural areas according to their populations. The new constitutions were meant to entrench the principles of division of powers, publicity of parliamentary debates and particularly the freedom of press, economic freedom and the freedom of trade (Heusler 1920: 356, 258, Kölz 1992: 228f., Schudel 1933: 98ff.). The elaboration of any new charter was to be conducted by directly elected CAs. Aware of the people's support and, in particular, its mistrust towards the old authorities, the liberals could furthermore reckon on winning a higher proportion of seats in the CAs than they held in parliament. Presumably, this new institution, which until then had not been provided anywhere in the whole of Switzerland, was taken from North American and French models.[10]

On the initiative of the movement's leaders, public meetings were held all over Switzerland starting from autumn 1830. In these, the poor peasant population whose support was crucial for the liberals expressed their preponderantly economic claims, which they addressed to the cantonal governments together with the political demands. Even though the authorities were aware of the necessity of reforms, they opposed them. Given the increasing pressure of the public, they eventually backed down and, despite the lack of legal regulation, initiated partial revisions of the constitutions. Only as the people, who aimed for far-reaching reforms, announced or even took more severe measures (in a number of cantons tumultuous or even civil-war like conditions broke out) the governments finally gave in and resigned.[11] Although the liberal causes only barely conformed to the

---

10    Appenzeller Zeitung 1830b: 389ff.; Erb 1962: 77ff.; Kölz 1992: 263, 305; Scherer 1954: 23; Soland 1977: 47, 56.

11    Feddersen 1867: 36, 64ff.; Heusler 1920: 357f.; Kloetzli 1922: 35ff.; Kölz 1992: 218ff., 228ff.; Nabholz 1911: 18ff.; NZZ 1980: 68; Schudel 1993: 98ff.

Federal Treaty, the Diet decided not to intervene in the cantons (Fazy 1890: 221, Heusler 1920: 357, Kölz 1992: 221, 357).

*Enactment and content of the new constitutions*    All revisions were carried out in breach of the old constitutional order. In most cantons, CAs, convoked in virtue of natural law (Kölz 1992: 220), were entrusted with the drafting of the new constitutions. In Argovia, St. Gallen, Vaud and Lucerne their members were elected directly, in Berne and Fribourg indirectly through electors. In Zurich and Thurgau new parliaments were elected.[12] Only in Solothurn and Basel were the new constitutions elaborated by the incumbent parliaments. The rules governing the voting process, most notably those with regard to the equal representation of urban and rural areas, took into account the liberal demands. In Zurich, for example, two thirds of the seats were granted to the rural population even though the principle of headcount was still not applied.[13]

In all cantons in which elections to CAs were held, these turned out successfully for the liberals. Upon invitation of these assemblies, the population handed in a huge number of petitions regarding the content of the new fundamental laws.[14] The constitutional drafts, which were elaborated in remarkably short periods,[15] were everywhere submitted to a referendum, except in Fribourg (Dorand 1998: 1043, Kölz 1992: 222, Schefold 1966: 106). In most cantons, they were accepted[16] with a clear majority.[17]

The new constitutions were based on the principle of representative democracy They guaranteed not only equality before the law but also, to a certain degree, political equality insofar as the representation of rural areas clearly increased. The franchise was expanded; however, women and paupers continued to be excluded from suffrage. In addition, certain fundamental rights such as the right of petition, the separation of powers or the publicity of parliamentary debates were granted. Often, economic claims were not embedded in the new constitutions, but rather, if at all, in later legislation (Kölz 1992: 232).

---

12    Solothurn: Feddersen 1867: 74 and Kölz 1992: 305; Basel: Feddersen 1867: 66; Argovia: Erb 1962: 77; St. Gallen and Vaud: Kölz 1992: 220; Vaud: Meuwly 1990: 117 ; Lucerne: Erb 1962: 125; Berne: Wahlprotokoll des Verfassungsrathes des Kantons Bern 1831, National archive of the Canton of Berne A II 4490 and Kloetzli 1922: 128; Fribourg: Rüegg 1989: 68, Footnote 3; Erb 1962: 78, 123; Zurich: Feddersen 1867: 71f.; Suter 2000: 48f.; Thurgau: Kölz 1992: 305.

13    Erb 1962: 80; Heusler 1920: 358; Kloetzli 1922: 128; Nabholz 1911: 1911: 21; NZZ 1931: first page; Schudel 1933: 105f.

14    Kölz 1992: 129, 222; Nabholz 1911: 21ff.; Soland 1980: 66, 92.

15    E.g. in Berne and Thurgau within four months (Kloetzli 1922: 129f.; Soland 1980: 61ff.).

16    In Schaffhausen, a first draft was rejected (Kölz 1992: 222; Schudel 1933: 114ff.).

17    In St. Gallen, a positive result was possible only thanks to the application of the veto principle (non-votes were counted as affirmative votes).

All cantonal constitutions contained new provisions with regard to their (total) revision.[18] Normally, the latter could be conducted only periodically or after the expiry of a fixed time period. Only the cantons of Thurgau and Lucerne prescribed the obligatory appointment of a CA for the elaboration of a constitutional draft (Heusler 1920: 358ff., Kölz 1992: 321ff., Schudel 1933: 119ff.). Both can be explained by the mistrust of the liberals towards the people and their endeavour to maintain power (Kölz 1992: 397, 394, Schudel 1933: 140). The mandatory constitutional referendum was established in all regenerated cantons but Fribourg. Other direct democratic instruments were introduced only exceptionally, for example, the popular initiative on constitutional amendments in Argovia, Lucerne, Schaffhausen and Thurgau and the veto in St. Gallen.

### The Conservative and Radical Movements in the 1840s

While various cantons still enacted new constitutions later in the 1830s,[19] the liberal movement increasingly lost momentum. In Wallis, the Prussian Neuchâtel and Geneva, the movement only achieved a breakthrough at the end of the decade or even later; in central (Uri, Obwalden and Nidwalden) and eastern Switzerland (Appenzell Inner Rhodes and Graubünden) it hardly had any effect at all – no new constitutions were enacted there in the 1830s (Kölz 1992: 224ff. 450ff., Fazy 1890: 224, 232ff.).

Almost contemporaneously to the expiry of the blocking period for constitutional amendments, a conservative backlash began in 1839. At the beginning of the 1840s this triggered another significant wave of constitutional changes, which – in a different context – continued throughout most of the entire decade. Altogether 16 new constitutions were put into effect between 1840 and 1849, eleven of which were elaborated by CAs. Eight thereof were elected (predominantly) directly by the people while in three cases the constitution was drawn up by newly elected parliaments. Later in this section, the cantons of Lucerne, Vaud and Berne are used as key examples for the outline of the relevant events and constitution-making processes.

*Legal framework*   The Federal Treaty (until 1848) and the earlier 'regeneration constitutions' constituted the legal framework for the cantonal constitution-making processes. Also after the enactment of the 1848 Federal Constitution and the consequent establishment of the federal state, the cantons passed their

---

18   No distinction had yet been drawn between a partial and total revision of a constitution.

19   Basel-Countryside 1832 (Heusler 1920: 363ff.), Schwyz 1833 (Kölz 1992: 223f.) and Glarus 1836 (Heusler 1920: 362; Kölz 1992: 226). In Basel and Schwyz, the conflict concerning the political representation resulted in a definitive (in the former case) or temporary (in the latter case) secession of the liberal parts of the canton. All constitutions emerging from these events were elaborated by CAs.

own constitutions. As a novelty, the Federal Constitution contained formal prescriptions in this regard: the cantonal constitutions had to be ratified by the people (mandatory constitutional referendum) and amended whenever petitioned by the latter (constitutional initiative). The enactment of a large number of cantonal constitutions by the end of the 1840s can be explained by their adjustment to the new federal constitutional order.

*Events*   In at least half of the cantons the liberals were in power during the 1830s whereas the majority of the other, predominantly Catholic cantons remained conservative. Here, liberal ideas found little support (Kölz 1992: 394). As a consequence of these power relations, the incumbent liberals oriented their style of governance towards the retention of power. This, in turn, aroused discontent among the people. Often and despite all promises, the latter's concerns had not even been implemented at the legislative level. Claims demanding further participation rights became louder (Kölz 1992: 233). Additionally, religious questions influenced political events at both the cantonal and the federal level.[20]

By combining democratic and religious concerns, the conservatives found great support. In 1839, they succeeded in overturning the liberal government in Zurich (Züriputsch) (Kölz 1992: 405ff., Schefold 1966: 65f., 70, Scherer 1954: 114ff., 297).[21] Initially, the Catholic and Protestant conservatives profited from these events, but from the mid-1840s the anti-church oriented radical movement also gained momentum. Its ascent was promoted by the reluctant attitude of the governments towards dealing with the Jesuit Order. In Geneva for instance, the hesitation of the government to vote for the expulsion of the Jesuits in the Diet, led to increased support for the radicals (Schefold 1966: 73, Kölz 1992: 484, 517ff.). Both the conservatives and the radicals demanded an extension of popular participation. Other than that, they had nothing in common. The conservatives, who were close to the Church, were principally hostile to any kind of reform. As a result, they were in favour of direct democracy mechanisms, such as the referendum and the veto, which they believed could obstruct such reforms. The radicals in contrast, strove for more profound changes. Their demands were similar to those of the liberals insofar as they included the protection of fundamental liberties, the separation of powers, and the transparency of the political system, but went further by promoting the introduction of the popular initiative, the right to recall and direct elections for members of the government. For the same reasons

---

20   Schefold 1966: 64; Scherer 1954: 11, 114. In 1834 several cantons enacted the 'Article of Baden', which in certain fields subordinated the church to the state (Kölz 1992: 400ff.). In 1835, the liberal government of Argovia dissolved several monasteries (Heusler 1920: 371). While the liberals founded defence associations and the Siebnerbund, which persisted until 1848 (Heusler 1920: 364f.; Kölz 1992: 396ff.), the Catholic cantons united in the Sarnerbund, which was dissolved by the Diet in 1833.

21   However, this did not trigger a constitutional revision.

the conservatives favoured the referendum, the radicals rejected it (Kölz 1992: 276ff., 290ff.).

*Enactment and content of the new constitutions*    Probably the most substantial transformation occurred in the Canton of Lucerne. By 1840, i.e. shortly before the expiry of the ten-year blocking period for constitutional amendments, the democratic-conservative opposition which had arisen during the 1830s pushed for constitutional reform (Bossard-Borner 2010: Note 35f.). On 31 January 1841 parliament submitted the issue to the people (Schefold 1966: 299). As provided for by the constitution a CA was elected on 11 March, after the positive outcome of the ballot. Owing to the clear majority they achieved, the conservatives nearly had a free hand in drafting the new charter. In the referendum of 1 May 1841, the people approved the new constitution which, in many ways, resembled its predecessor. The main innovations included changes with regard to political rights and relations between the church and the state (Heusler 1920: 370, Kölz 1992: 422f., 428f.).[22] Besides the constitutional initiative which could be lodged after the expiry of a one year blocking period, the new constitution introduced the premise that a mandatory referendum be held before any revision of the cantonal and the Federal Constitution (principle referendum). If the electors agreed to totally revise the cantonal constitution, a CA would have to be convoked. In addition, the 1841 constitution also provided for a veto against laws and other decrees.

In the Canton of Vaud, the people, upon the initiative of the radicals, called on the government to back the expulsion of the Jesuits in the Diet. Although the petition had been signed by at least one third of the eligible voters, neither the government nor the parliament complied with the demand. In response, the people gathered in Lausanne on 14 February 1845 where they decided to install a provisional government, to dissolve the parliament and to elaborate a new constitution. The following day, the government decreed the dismantling of the parliament and scheduled new elections, in which the radicals prevailed. As the new parliament was to act as a CA the people were invited to present their petitions regarding the content of the new constitution. These included demands for further democratic participation, the extension of the catalogue of fundamental rights as well as economic and social claims. Barely five months later the new fundamental law was approved by the constituent parliament and ratified by the people (Kölz 1992: 459ff., Meuwly 1990: 169ff.). Vaud was the first canton to provide for the legislative popular initiative as it is known today (Kölz 1992: 472, Schefold 1966: 276f., 308). In addition, citizens were empowered to submit constitutional initiatives, to decide on amendments to the constitution and on issues that the authorities had put to referendum. The revision of the constitution was to be conducted according to the regulations for legislative procedures. The

---

22    In particular, the constitution conceded pre-eminence to the Church in the field of education. The Jesuits were mandated to impart higher education.

only difference was that its ratification was reserved to the people. No profound modifications were made in the field of civil rights and liberties and the organization of the authorities (Kölz 1992: 477ff.).

Against the background of popular demands for reforms[23] and the radicals' positive results in the partial elections of October 1845, the Bernese parliament decided in January 1846 to suggest the revision of the constitution. The people, to whom the resolution was submitted contrary to existing constitutional provisions, rejected the proposal. Although the move was not sanctioned by the existing constitution the parliament decreed that a CA be convened. Its function was limited to the creation of a new fundamental law, which had to be submitted to referendum.[24] The radicals emerged victorious from the elections to the assembly. As in previous constitution-making processes the people were invited to hand in petitions with their wishes regarding the new constitution. After tough negotiations, the constitution was finally passed on 13 July and accepted by a clear majority of voters in the referendum of 31 July (Kölz 1992: 489f., 516). Furthermore, the people approved that the CA should remain in office as a regular parliament (Schefold 1966: 147). The most crucial reforms concerned the democratic system: the realization of universal male franchise (Kölz 1992: 495). Moreover, the new constitution provided for different direct democratic instruments; these included the mandatory referendum on amendments to the cantonal constitution and the Federal Treaty, the recall of the parliament and the extraordinary mandatory referendum. The revision procedure could be initiated at any time upon the initiative of the parliament or 8,000 citizens. Subsequently the principle of revision had to be submitted to a referendum. Therein, people were given the right to decide whether to assign the parliament or a CA with the elaboration of the draft.

*The Democratic Movement of the 1860s*

During the 1850s, several cantons were still adapting their constitutions to federal law. A new wave of revision broke out in the 1860s and led to eight successful constitutional revisions before the enactment of the Federal Constitution of 1874. Six thereof were elaborated by (predominantly) directly elected CAs. Amongst this group, the enactment of the new constitutions of Vaud and St. Gallen should be seen in the context of tensions between conservative and radical forces (Meuwly 1990: 229ff, Dierauer 1910: 99ff.). The revisions in 1867 in Obwalden and 1872 in Appenzell Inner Rhodes were of relatively little importance.

In the beginning of the 1860s, the democratic movement, which pursued the realization of popular sovereignty by expanding participatory rights, succeeded

---

23 'Vorstellungen für die Revision der Verfassung', National archive of the Canton of Berne A II 4518.

24 Decision of parliament of 14 January 1846, National archive of the Canton of Berne A II 4526.

in bringing about a political change in Basel-Countryside, Zurich and Thurgau (Gilg 1951, Kölz 2004: 7ff., Schaffner 1982: 23). Owing to the already achieved democratic improvements in the radical cantons, the movement spread over the rest of Switzerland only in the course of the following decades (Kölz 2004: 220, 451). Further democratization began only after the enforcement of the new Federal Constitution in 1874. Despite protests and mobilization of the people, the movements in Berne, Solothurn, Schaffhausen, Argovia and Lucerne had little impact. As no significant and effective democratic opposition emerged in these cantons, participation rights were introduced by means of partial revisions or by legislation.[25] The events and revision procedures in the cantons of Basel-Countryside, Zurich and Thurgau are described in the following section.

*Events*   In all three cantons the popular mobilization was triggered by the discontent and mistrust of the people, namely against the ruling radical party in Basel-Countryside and the bourgeois liberal elites in Zurich and Thurgau.[26] Mainly by suppressing the opposition and by nepotism the political elites had succeeded in concentrating political as well as economic power in their own hands. Moreover they remained indifferent with regard to the concerns of the middle and working classes suffering from the world economic crisis of 1857 (Gilg 1951: 14ff.). To the democratic forces, these circumstances provided the best evidence that representative democracy was imperfect and that fundamental political reforms were indispensable (Kölz 2004: 178ff., Weber 1932: 588). The democratic leaders mobilized the populace and organized assemblies where they highlighted the deficiencies of the current system. Unlike the radicals, the democrats demanded the full direct participation of the citizens in public affairs. Furthermore, they called for several measures of state interventionism to solve existing social problems. Revision programs were proposed and adopted by the people in popular assemblies.[27]

*Enactment and content of the new constitutions*   As prescribed by federal law, all three cantonal constitutions provided for the right to lodge a constitutional initiative and to participate in a constitutional referendum. Moreover, the citizens were empowered to decide by referendum on a total revision of the constitution and on a subsidiary question on the assignment of the organ responsible to elaborate a respective draft.

The total revisions of the constitutions were launched by popular initiatives in all three cantons and approved by vast majorities in the principle referendums. The elaboration of the new constitutional drafts was entrusted to (predominantly) directly elected CAs, in whose elections the democrats scored a major success over

---

25   Bosshard-Borner 2008: 519ff.; Gilg 1951: 41ff., 225ff.; His 1944: 127ff.; Kölz 2004: 94ff., 122ff.; Widmeier 1942, 85ff.; Ziswiler 1992: 146ff.
26   Blum 1977: 326ff.; Gilg 1951: 30f, 54ff.; Schaffner 1982: 27ff.
27   Blum 1977: 326ff., 355ff.; Burkhart 1963: 19ff.; Schaffner 1982: 47ff., 61ff.

their rivals. Within eight months the drafts had been passed in all three cantons. In Basel-Countryside the draft was rejected in the referendum, because it failed to provide for a possible future reunification with Basel-Town. After deciding in favour of the continuation of the reform process by a new CA, the people finally ratified the second draft on 22 March 1863. In Zurich, the people adopted the new democratic constitution on 18 April 1869, and in Thurgau on 28 February 1869.[28]

In substance the new constitutions introduced the changes proposed by the democrats. The representative systems were replaced by semi-direct democratic state institutions. The main claim for direct participation of the people in public affairs was realized by providing the holding of mandatory referendums with regard to legislation, treaties, concordats and financial issues. Moreover, the instruments of administrative referendum and popular initiative were entrenched in all constitutions. In Zurich the government was empowered to elaborate counter-proposals to popular initiatives and became the only canton to introduce the right to lodge an individual initiative. Democratic participation was extended even further as all three cantons introduced direct elections for the executive and the right of the people to recall the parliament.

The regulations relating to constitutional revision differed considerably from one canton to another. While in Zurich the revision process was initiated by popular initiative, the elaboration of the new constitution was assigned to a newly-elected parliament. In contrast, the initial referendum on the revision of the constitution, combined with a subsidiary question on whether to elect a CA was maintained in the Canton of Thurgau. Finally, the new constitution of Basel-Countryside provided for the obligatory establishment of a CA. Apart from that, the new constitutions introduced social measures to improve fiscal justice and assistance to the poor and established cantonal banks for the granting of favourable credits and the principle of government intervention to mitigate social inequities (Gilg 1951: 105ff.).

*The Wave of Constitutional Reforms in the 1870s*

The following two decades were characterized by a large number of constitutional reforms in the cantons. A total of 24 new constitutions were successfully enacted from the 1870s to the 1890s, twelve of which were elaborated by CAs. On the one hand the reform wave was related to the enactment of the new Federal Constitution on 29 May 1874 and the still persisting democratic movement in certain cantons. On the other hand, the First Vatican Council in 1869–1870 led to the outbreak of the so-called Culture War, which in several cantons resulted in decisive upheavals with regard to church policy.

---

28    Blum 1977: 341ff., 352ff., 364ff.; Burkhart 1963: 27f., 30ff., 182; Erb 1962: 21, 223; Gilg 32; Kölz 2004: 54, 181f.; Schaffner 1982: 39ff., 69ff.

*Events*   The democratic movement in the cantons affected the revision process at the federal level. Owing to the success of the democrats and radicals in the general elections to the national assembly in October 1869, a new constitutional draft could be elaborated. This was, however, rejected by the people and the cantons (Kölz 2004: 511ff., 520ff.). The decisions of the First Vatican Council, which aimed at strengthening the position of the Church and made papal infallibility part of official Church doctrine, gave added impetus for a revision of the federal constitution. As a result, all cantons in central Switzerland took ecclesio-political measures so as to protect their systems from the pretentions to power of the Roman Catholic Church. The liberal party, the radicals and the democrats adhered to their reform programs reflecting the democratic Zeitgeist and to the achievements of the Reformation. They demanded that measures be taken to ensure the superiority of the state in relation to the Church, a clear separation of Church and state and the enforcement of the individual guarantee of religious freedom (Stadler 1996: 336ff.). Indeed, the second draft of the proposed federal constitution included these measures. It introduced the institution of the optional legislative referendum at federal level, strengthened civil rights and provided for several social improvements. The draft was passed on 31 January 1874 by both councils and was adopted on 19 April 1874 by the people and the cantons. The results of both referendums clearly demonstrated a political cleavage of the federation into liberal and conservative regions.[29]

*Enactment and content of the new constitutions*   The federal regulations concerning the revision of cantonal constitutions remained the same even after the enactment of the 1874 Constitution. With some exceptions,[30] the cantonal constitutions contained provisions on the establishment of a CA. In Schaffhausen, Solothurn, Argovia and Basel-Countryside the total revision of the constitution could only be conducted by such an assembly.

The 1848 constitution of the Canton of Schwyz stipulated that a CA had to be convened if the initiative came from the people. However, in 1876 it was the parliament that proposed a total revision and was hence in charge of elaborating the new constitution. Substantially, these regulations were maintained in the new constitution. At the end of the 1890s the people asked for a further constitutional reform. On 13 February 1898 they rejected a first draft which had been elaborated by a constituent assembly. The parliament eventually adopted a second draft which was passed by referendum in October 1898 (Michel 2008: 82ff.).

In referendums to initiate constitutional change held in Berne, St. Gallen, Nidwalden and Uri, the electorate voted for the establishment of CAs. After Bernese citizens had rejected the assembly's draft on 1 March 1885 (Erb 1962:

---

29   The second draft was rejected by the conservative cantons (Kölz 2004: 623).

30   Zug and Glarus. In Graubünden a newly elected parliament was to be assigned with the elaboration of a constitutional draft as of 1880. In Ticino, the option to assign a CA was established in 1875.

218f.), they mandated the parliament to prepare a second on 20 November 1892. Considering its carefully tailored reform program, it came as no surprise that the people finally decided in favour of the parliament's proposal (Junker 1995).

In some other cantons, people convoked a CA by means of a referendum convoked by the parliament, even though no legal basis for such a procedure had been defined. In Vaud, for instance, the parliament had the exclusive competence to decide on whether the constitution should to be revised or not. However, when citizens submitted an initiative targeted towards democratization, the legislative instead decided to schedule a principle referendum on the initiation of revision procedures and on the organ to be entrusted with the elaboration of the new constitution.[31] Therein the people agreed to a constitutional reform and decided to have the draft elaborated by a CA. The new constitution was adopted by referendum on 1 March 1885 (Meuwly 1990: 233ff.). Also the Landsgemeinden of Appenzell Inner Rhodes (in 1868) and Appenzell Outer Rhodes (in 1875) decided to convoke CAs, and in the latter case the assembly remained in office as a legislative body until 1880 (Erb 1962: 134, Kölz 2004: 308ff., 320).

On some occasions, the legislature resisted the establishment of a CA. Contrary to the regulations for revision, according to which a CA was to be established if the initiative for total revision came from the people, the authorities of Solothurn tried to elaborate the draft themselves. However, when the banking crash of 1885 led to demands for the dismissal of the government and the parliament, the former proposed a popular vote and the election of a CA. The people adopted the proposal in May 1887 and ratified the resulting constitutional draft on 23 October 1887 (Angst 1986: 84ff.).

In Basel-Town it was the parliament that decided which body would elaborate the constitutional draft. In the end, both constitutions of 1875 and of 1889 were elaborated by parliamentary committees. The authorities of Lucerne and Wallis also used this means to prevent the establishment of CAs.

In general, the elections to the CAs were carried out in the same way as the general elections to legislative bodies. Everywhere, the people were included in the elaboration processes, either by submitting personal requests (Angst 1986: 171, Erb 1962: 195ff., Joos 2001: 42) or, as in St. Gallen, through public discussions of the CAs (Kölz 2004: 210). Finally in all cantons, the drafts were submitted to popular vote and, except for Berne and Schaffhausen, adopted.

In comparison with the total revisions conducted in the first half of the nineteenth century, the elaboration of the new drafts lasted considerably longer. An explanation may be the absence of pressure from the people to conduct reform, which had hitherto proven to have had an accelerating effect on the revision procedures. Moreover, party fragmentation within the CAs seems to have impeded the rapid passage of new constitutions (Erb 1962: 224f.).

At this stage, there was a clear trend to constitutionally prescribe the holding of an initial referendum on whether to initiate constitutional revision, together

---

31 Decree of 27 December 1883.

with a subsidiary question of whom to assign to carry out the revision.[32] With the exception of the constitutions of Appenzell Inner Rhodes and Zug, all cantons provided for the possibility to elect a CA or at least a new parliament for the elaboration of a new constitutional draft.

*The Newest Wave of Constitutional Revisions: From 1965 to the Present Day*

After only a few total revisions were conducted in the beginning of the twentieth century, almost all cantons have completely revised their constitutions since 1965. In ten cases CAs were established. Of the constitutions dating from the nineteenth and early twentieth century, only those of Zug, Appenzell Inner Rhodes and Wallis are still in force. The process continues today: The people of Schwyz adopted a new constitution on 15 May 2011. However, the Federal Assembly found the electoral system contradictory to the federal law and thus rejected the approval of the constitution.[33] In Geneva, the people accepted a new constitution in a vote held on 14 October 2012.

*Events*   Despite the historical events of the twentieth century, the constitutions adopted in the penultimate century, had or still have a far longer lifespan than their predecessors. Until 1965, neither the new conception of the state, which, in the wake of the Second World War, had undergone a substantial change from the liberal to the social and democratic constitutional state, nor the altered economic and social circumstances could trigger any total revision of cantonal constitutions. However, unlike in earlier years, certain needs for reform were satisfied by means of partial revisions. Thus, several cantons had progressively complemented their fundamental laws with (direct) democratic devices or refined the existing ones.

Contrary to the majority of the previous waves of constitution-making the latest was not based on a political (popular) movement but rather on the initiatives of the cantonal executives and parliaments. The arguments proposed in the booklets to the popular votes largely coincided: Neither in form nor in content did the existing cantonal constitutions comply with the valid federal constitutional order. The frequent partial revisions had undermined their logical structure and their language was outdated and often barely understandable. Some provisions were considered obsolete or even contrary to superior federal law. In certain fields regulation was completely lacking. The main reforms proposed by several cantons involved their relationship with the Confederation, their structure and organization, the autonomy of the municipalities, environmental protection and financial matters. Apart from

---

32   The subsidiary question was introduced in Appenzell Outer Rhodes, Basel-Countryside, Schaffhausen, in Ticino and Vaud. In Glarus and Graubünden the people had to decide whether to assign the incumbent or to elect a new parliament to elaborate the new constitution.

33   http://www.nzz.ch/aktuell/schweiz/krimi-um-kantonsverfassung-1.18044938 (12 April 2013).

that, the latest wave of constitution-making may be related to the initially fruitless attempts to adopt a new federal constitution in the 1970s and the enactment of the new Federal Constitution of 1999.

*Enactment and content of the new constitutions*   The federal regulations with regard to the revision of cantonal constitutions were not altered by the Federal Constitution of 1999 (cf. art. 51). In most cantons mandatory initial referendums were held on the conduct of a revision of the constitutions, while several contained the decision on the organ to draft the new constitution (CA or parliament). At the same time, in order to introduce new procedures of balloting such as voting on alternatives or parts of the new constitution, many cantons amended their provisions concerning constitutional referendums.

In Argovia, Basel-Countryside and Basel-Town the establishment of CAs was obligatory. The 1887 constitution of Solothurn provided for the election of a CA, if so requested by the parliament – as was the case in 1981 – or by the people. In Lucerne the procedure to alter the constitution was amended shortly before an initial referendum on whether to carry out a revision was held: The future constitution should not be drafted by a CA, but the so-called 'Projektorganization'.[34] The opposite trend could be observed in the cantons of Zurich and Geneva, where previously only the cantonal parliaments had been entitled to revise the constitution. Here the parliaments not only proposed a total constitutional revision but also suggested a modification of the provisions so as to allow a CA, rather than the legislature, to draft the new constitution. In both cases the electorate accepted the proposals. In Vaud and Fribourg, the electorate voted in favour of convening a CA, while voters in Berne, St. Gallen, Neuchâtel and Schaffhausen voted against. With the exception of Berne and Fribourg they followed their parliaments' voting recommendations. In several cantons the parliaments emphasized that the assignment of a CA would prevent the legislature from being overburdened and that broader popular support could be expected. Furthermore, they argued that this way parliament's daily business would influence the constitution-making process to a much lesser extent. In other cantons the legislature was considered to be better qualified to make constitutional changes given its experience and the easier coordination between constitution-making and legislation.

Unlike earlier experiences made, the revision procedures took several years. In all cantons the new constitutions were accepted by the electorate, although in Argovia and Schaffhausen a second vote was necessary. With regard to the new provisions on total constitutional revision, a CA is to be convened in Uri, Argovia, Basel-Countryside and Obwalden. Except for Uri, an initial referendum has to be held to approve the principle of constitutional revision. In most cantons the electorate still decides on the organ to be mandated with the elaboration of the new

---

34   The 'Projektorganization', elected by the cantonal government, was composed of five members of the cantonal parliament, five persons appointed from municipalities, courts and administration and ten persons who applied in written form.

constitution. Thus, a tendency to refrain from the compulsory establishment of a CA can be identified.[35]


## V. Conclusions

Under the influence of French liberalism revolutionary upheavals occurred in several cantons during the 1830s. In virtue of the principle of popular sovereignty, the people claimed constituent power. Despite the lack of a legal basis, they called for the election of CAs once the governments of the restoration period had been overthrown. The participation of broad sectors of the population and, in particular, the referendums completing the constitution-making process legitimized this process and the resulting constitutions. The CAs constituted an eligible means to translate the de facto situation into law. They permitted a quick replacement of the elites who could no longer be relied upon. As a result the new constitutions were based on the principle of popular sovereignty as the people had demanded. According to the liberal understanding, a representative democracy that was supplemented by the institution of the constitutional referendum could satisfy this principle. The use of such a referendum was integrated into the new constitutions with the sole exception of the Canton of Fribourg. In contrast, the institution of the CA was systematically incorporated into the constitutions only somewhat later in the history of cantonal constitutional evolution.

Similar considerations can be made with regard to the subsequent waves of revisions during the nineteenth century. For the most part they were initiated by popular movements calling for the convening of a CA. Whereas a part of the constitution-making processes conducted in the 1840s as well as the CAs that were established in this period can still be characterized as revolutionary, they were increasingly incorporated into the constitutional revision regulation in the later waves. With the assumption of power by the radicals, popular sovereignty became the fundamental principle of the cantonal and federal constitutional orders. The principle of democratic representation was progressively supplemented by instruments of direct democracy.

The establishment of the CAs was inextricably associated with the success of the popular movements and was considered one of the main features of change and democratization. However, a critical look at the new legal orders reveals that these were not indispensable for the democratization of the cantons. Democratization also occurred in those cantons where the new authorities refrained from convening a CA. The constitutions of Graubünden and Glarus were never drafted by a CA. Yet, as regards their content they were and are no less democratic than any other. This implies that, rather than the organ in charge, the postulates of the popular movements have been crucial to the introduction of instruments of direct

---

35　All voting results are based on the database of the Centre for Research on Direct Democracy, www.c2d.ch.

democracy. However, the institution of the constituent assembly as understood here is to be considered as an instrument which allows for democratic constitution-making processes.

The initiatives that led to the total revisions accomplished in the twentieth and twenty-first centuries invariably emanated from the authorities and not from a popular movement. The argument expressed by the government of Neuchâtel (page 2 of the voting booklet relating to the referendum of 10 March 1996), according to which the establishment of a CA only makes sense if the initiative for the revision process had been taken by the people, may explain why compared to previous processes, fewer CAs have been mandated to elaborate the new constitutions. Both the revisions and the establishment of the CAs were made out of rational considerations. Thus, the provisions regarding the total revision of the constitutions have often been amended before tackling the reform procedures.

In the course of the 180 years that is the focus of this chapter the temporal dimensions have changed. In the nineteenth century the elaboration of a new constitution was accomplished in a few months. Due to their intricacy, these processes nowadays take years, independently of the organ in charge. At the same time, the nature of the constitution-making body does not seem to have an influence on the durability of the constitutions (see Appendix Table A7.1).

CAs have proven to be crucial for constitution-making in the cantons. Since their appearance in the 1830s they have evolved from a revolutionary to a constitutional instrument, from a body established upon unilateral popular demand to a body convened upon consensus between citizens and authorities. However, the significance of this institution, which allows for a democratic constitution-making process, is still equally high.

# Appendix

(See following pages)

**Table A7.1    Overview on the constitution-making processes in the Swiss Cantons (1830–2012)**

| Canton | Year | Principle Referendum | | | Constitution-Making Body | Referendum | | Coming into Effect |
|---|---|---|---|---|---|---|---|---|
| | | Date | Result | Subsidiary Question | | Date | Result | |
| TI | 1830 | - | | | Newly elected Parliament | 04.07.30 | Yes | Yes |
| SO | 1831 | - | | | Parliament | 13.01.31 | Yes | Yes |
| FR | 1831 | - | | | Indirectly elected constituent assembly | - | | Yes |
| LU | 1831 | - | | | Mixed constituent assembly: 81 directly elected members, 20 members of the incumbent parliament | 30.01.31 | Yes | Yes |
| BA | 1831 | - | | | Commission (appointing body unknown)/Parliament | 27.02.31 | Yes | Yes |
| ZH | 1831 | - | | | Newly elected Parliament | 20.03.31 | Yes | Yes |
| TG | 1831 | - | | | Newly elected Parliament | 26.04.31 | Yes | Yes |
| AG | 1831 | - | | | Directly elected constituent assembly | 03.05.31 | Yes | Yes |
| SH | 1831 | - | | | Directly elected constituent assembly | 23.05.31 | No | No |
| | | | | | | 02.06.31 | Yes | Yes |
| VD | 1831 | - | | | Directly elected constituent assembly | 20.06.31 | Yes | Yes |
| BE | 1831 | - | | | Indirectly elected constituent assembly | 31.07.31 | Yes | Yes |
| SG | 1831 | - | | | Directly elected constituent assembly | Not known | Yes | Yes |
| BL | 1832 | - | | | Directly elected constituent assembly | 04.05.32 | Yes | Yes |
| SZ ÄL | 1832 | - | | | Directly elected constituent assembly | 05.05.32 | Yes | Yes |
| BS | 1833 | - | | | Parliament | 03.10.33 | Yes | Yes |
| SZ | 1833 | - | | | Directly elected constituent assembly | 11.10.33 | Yes | Yes |
| AR | 1834 | Not known | | | Directly elected constituent assembly | Not known | No | No |
| | | | | | Directly elected constituent assembly | 31.08.34 | Yes | Yes |
| SH | 1834 | 01.06.34 | Yes | No | Parliament | 14.12.32 | Yes | Yes |
| TG | 1837 | Not known | | | Directly elected constituent assembly | 17.06.37 | Yes | Yes |
| SG | 1837 | 02.04.37 | No | Not known | - | | | |

| Canton | Year | Principle Referendum | | | Constitution-Making Body | Referendum | | Coming into Effect |
|---|---|---|---|---|---|---|---|---|
| | | Date | Result | Subsidiary Question | | Date | Result | |
| GL | 1837 | 29.05.36 | Yes | Not known | Commission (appointing body unknown) | 01.10.36 | Yes | Yes |
| BL | 1838 | Not known | | | Directly elected constituent assembly | 26.08.38 | Yes | Yes |
| VS | 1839 | - | | | Parliament | 17.02.39 | Yes | Yes |
| VS | 1839 | - | | | Directly elected constituent assembly | 03.08.39 | Yes | Yes |
| AG | 1840 | Not known | | | Parliament | 04.10.40 | No | No |
| | 1841 | Not known | | | Parliament | 04.01.41 | Yes | Yes |
| SO | 1841 | - | | | Parliament | 10.01.41 | Yes | Yes |
| LU | 1841 | 31.01.41 | Yes | Yes | Directly elected constituent assembly | 01.05.41 | Yes | Yes |
| SZ | 1842 | 13.10.42 | Yes | No | Directly elected constituent assembly | Not known | No | No |
| GE | 1842 | - | | | Directly elected constituent assembly | 07.06.42 | Yes | Yes |
| SG | 1843 | Not known | | | | | No | |
| BL | 1844 | 22.09.44 | No | No | - | | | |
| VS | 1844 | - | | | Parliament | 20.10.44 | Yes | Yes |
| VD | 1845 | - | | | Newly elected Parliament | 10.08.45 | Yes | Yes |
| BE | 1846 | - | | | Directly elected constituent assembly | 31.07.46 | Yes | Yes |
| BS | 1847 | - | | | Directly elected constituent assembly | 08.04.47 | Yes | Yes |
| GE | 1847 | - | | | Newly elected Parliament | 24.05.47 | Yes | Yes |
| UR | 1847 | - | | | Parliament | 19.12.47 | Yes | Yes |
| GR | 1848 | - | | | Mixed: Executive and Parliament/Parliament | Not known | | No |
| ZG | 1848 | Not known | | | Constituent assembly of which 54 members were directly elected, eleven nominated by the assembly itself | 17.01.48 | Yes | Yes |
| SZ | 1848 | 15.12.47 | Yes | Not known | Directly elected constituent assembly | 23.01.48 | No | No |
| | | - | | | | 18.02.48 | Yes | Yes |
| FR | 1848 | - | | | Parliament | - | | Yes |

| Canton | Year | Principle Referendum | | | Constitution-Making Body | Referendum | | Coming into Effect |
|---|---|---|---|---|---|---|---|---|
| | | Date | Result | Subsidiary Question | | Date | Result | |
| NE | 1848 | | - | | Directly elected constituent assembly | 30.04.48 | Yes | Yes |
| VS | 1848 | | - | | Newly elected Parliament | 16.10.48 | Yes | Yes |
| TG | 1849 | 06.05.49 | Yes | Yes | Directly elected constituent assembly | Not known | Yes | Yes |
| SG | 1849 | 08.07.49 | No | Not known | - | | | |
| NW | 1850 | 13.05.49 | Yes | Yes | Directly elected constituent assembly | 01.04.50 | Yes | Yes |
| GR | 1850 | | - | | Mixed: Executive and Parliament/Parliament | Not known | No | No |
| | | | - | | Parliament | Not known | No | No |
| OW | 1850 | | - | | Executive/Parliament | 28.04.50 | Yes | Yes |
| UR | 1850 | ??.05.49 | Yes | Not known | Directly elected constituent assembly | 05.05.50 | Yes | Yes |
| SG | 1851 | 19.01.51 | No | Not known | - | | | |
| SO | 1851 | | - | | Parliament | 19.01.51 | Yes | Yes |
| BL | 1851 | | - | | Directly elected constituent assembly | 02.02.51 | Yes | Yes |
| AG | 1852 | 11.08.49 | Yes | Yes | Directly elected constituent assembly | 13.10.50 | No | No |
| | | 17.11.50 | Yes | Yes | Directly elected constituent assembly | 18.05.51 | No | No |
| | | | | | | 20.07.51 | No | No |
| | | 24.08.51 | Yes | No | Directly elected constituent assembly | 22.02.52 | Yes | Yes |
| SH | 1852 | 22.06.51 | Yes | Yes | Directly elected constituent assembly | 02.05.52 | Yes | Yes |
| VS | 1853 | 20.06.52 | Yes | Yes | Directly elected constituent assembly | 09.01.53 | Yes | Yes |
| GR | 1854 | | - | | Mixed: Executive and parliament/Parliament | 30.11.53 | Yes | Yes |
| AI | 1854 | Not known | | | | 06.02.54 | No | No |
| SZ | 1854 | 09.04.54 | No | Not known | - | | | |
| AR | 1854 | ??.??.54 | No | Not known | - | | | |
| SG | 1855 | 28.10.55 | No | Not known | - | | | |
| SO | 1856 | 30.03.56 | Yes | Yes | Directly elected constituent assembly | 01.06.56 | Yes | Yes |

| Canton | Year | Principle Referendum | | | Constitution-Making Body | Referendum | | Coming into Effect |
| --- | --- | --- | --- | --- | --- | --- | --- | --- |
| | | Date | Result | Subsidiary Question | | Date | Result | |
| FR | 1857 | - | | | Parliament | 24.05.57 | Yes | Yes |
| BS | 1858 | - | | | Directly elected constituent assembly | 28.02.58 | Yes | Yes |
| NE | 1858 | 21.06.57 | Yes | Yes | Directly elected constituent assembly | 25.06.57 | No | No |
| | | | | | | 08.08.58 | No | No |
| | | | | | | 21.11.58 | Yes | Yes |
| AR | 1858 | ??.??.58 | Yes | Yes | Directly elected constituent assembly | 03.10.58 | Yes | Yes |
| VD | 1859 | ??.??.59 | No | Not known | - | | | |
| SG | 1860 | 23.10.59 | Yes | Yes | Directly elected constituent assembly | 28.05.60 | No | No |
| SG | 1861 | 30.06.61 | Yes | No | Directly elected constituent assembly | 17.11.61 | Yes | Yes |
| VD | 1861 | 03.02.61 | Yes | Yes | Directly elected constituent assembly | 15.12.61 | Yes | Yes |
| AG | 1862 | 23.02.62 | No | Yes | - | | | |
| GE | 1862 | 25.05.62 | Yes | Yes | Directly elected constituent assembly | 02.12.62 | No | No |
| BL | 1863 | 18.05.62 | Yes | Yes | Directly elected constituent assembly | 02.11.62 | No | No |
| | | 23.11.62[1] | Yes | Yes | Directly elected constituent assembly | 22.03.63 | Yes | Yes |
| LU | 1863 | 31.10.62 | No | Yes | Parliament | 29.03.63 | Yes | Yes |
| SZ | 1866 | 10.06.66 | No | Not known | - | | | |
| OW | 1867 | ??.??.67 | Yes | Yes | Mixed: Executive and Parliament/Parliament | 27.10.67 | Yes | Yes |
| NE | 1868 | 15.03.68 | No | Not known | - | | | |
| TG | 1869 | 19.04.68 | Yes | Yes | Directly elected constituent assembly | 28.02.69 | Yes | Yes |
| ZH | 1869 | 26.01.68 | Yes | Yes | Directly elected constituent assembly (13 members were subsequently nominated by the assembly itself) | 18.04.69 | Yes | Yes |
| GR | 1869 | - | | | Mixed: Executive and Parliament/Parliament | 10.11.69 | No | No |
| AI | 1872 | ??.??.68 | Yes | Yes | Directly elected constituent assembly | ??.??.69 | No | No |
| | | | | | | ??.??.71 | No | No |
| | | | | | | 24.11.72 | Yes | Yes |

| Canton | Year | Principle Referendum | | | Constitution-Making Body | Referendum | | Coming into Effect |
|---|---|---|---|---|---|---|---|---|
| | | Date | Result | Subsidiary Question | | Date | Result | |
| LU | 1875 | | - | | Mixed: Executive and Parliament/Parliament | 28.02.75 | Yes | Yes |
| GR | 1875 | | - | | Mixed: Executive and Parliament/Parliament | 02 and 03.75 | No | No |
| BS | 1875 | | - | | Parliament | 09.05.75 | Yes | Yes |
| SO | 1875 | 21.02.69 | No | Not known | - | | | |
| | | 18.04.75 | Yes | Yes | Directly elected constituent assembly | 12.12.75 | Yes | Yes |
| BL | 1875 | 04.04.75 | No | Not known | - | | | |
| GL | 1876 | ??.??.74 | Yes | | Not known | ??.??.76 | No | No |
| ZG | 1876 | | - | | Mixed/Parliament | 14.12.73 | Yes | Yes |
| VS | 1876 | | - | | Mixed: Executive and Parliament/Parliament | 13.02.76 | Yes | Yes |
| SH | 1876 | 04.05.73 | Yes | No | Directly elected constituent assembly | 27.12.74 | No | No |
| | | | | | | 18.04.75 | No | No |
| | | | | | | 30.05.75 | No | No |
| | | | | | | 24.03.76 | Yes | Yes |
| UR | 1876 | | | | Not known | 29.10.76 | No | No |
| AR | 1877 | 24.04.75 | Yes | Yes | Directly elected constituent assembly | 30.04.76 | No | No |
| | | | | | | 15.10.76 | Yes | Yes |
| NW | 1877 | 14.05.76 | Yes | Yes | Directly elected constituent assembly and Parliament | 02.04.77 | Yes | Yes |
| SZ | 1877 | | - | | Mixed: members of the executive and the parliament, assigned by the executive | 11.06.76 | Yes | No[2] |
| | | | | | | 23.09.77 | Yes | Yes |
| GR | 1880 | | - | | Mixed: Executive and Parliament/Parliament | 23.05.80 | Yes | Yes |
| BE | 1885 | 03.05.83 | Yes | Yes | Directly elected constituent assembly | 01.03.85 | No | No |
| VD | 1885 | 16.12.85 | Yes | Yes | Directly elected constituent assembly | 01.03.85 | Yes | Yes |
| AG | 1885 | 09.12.83 | Yes | No | Directly elected constituent assembly | 07.06.85 | Yes | Yes |
| GL | 1887 | 09.05.86 | Yes | No | Mixed: Executive and Parliament/Parliament | 22.05.87 | Yes | Yes |

| Canton | Year | Principle Referendum | | | Constitution-Making Body | Referendum | | Coming into Effect |
|---|---|---|---|---|---|---|---|---|
| | | Date | Result | Subsidiary Question | | Date | Result | |
| SO | 1887 | 30.05.86 | No | Not known | - | | | |
| | | 15.05.87 | Yes | No | Directly elected constituent assembly | 23.10.87 | Yes | Yes |
| UR | 1888 | 01.05.87 | Yes | Yes | Directly elected constituent assembly | 06.05.88 | Yes | Yes |
| BL | 1889 | 27.03.87 | Yes | No | Directly elected constituent assembly | 20.01.89 | No | No |
| | | | | | | 31.03.89 | No | No |
| | | 26.05.89[3] | No | | - | | | |
| BS | 1890 | - | | | Parliament | 02.02.90 | Yes | Yes |
| SG | 1890 | 07.07.89 | Yes | Yes | Directly elected constituent assembly | 16.11.90 | Yes | Yes |
| TI[4] | 1891 | 05.10.90 | Yes | Yes | Directly elected constituent assembly | 08.03.91 | Yes | Yes |
| | 1892 | 14.06.91 | Yes | Yes | Directly elected constituent assembly | 02.07.92 | Yes | Yes |
| GR | 1892 | - | | | Mixed: Executive and Parliament/Parliament | 02.10.92 | Yes | Yes |
| BL | 1893 | 18.10.91 | Yes | No | Directly elected constituent assembly | 22.05.92 | Yes | Yes |
| BE | 1893 | 20.11.92 | Yes | Not known | Parliament | 04.06.93 | Yes | Yes |
| AR | 1893 | ??.??.93 | No | Not known | - | | | |
| ZG | 1894 | ??.??.94 | Yes | No | Parliament | 18.03.94 | Yes | Yes |
| NW | 1897 | 26.04.96 | Yes | Yes | Directly elected constituent assembly | 25.04.97 | No | No |
| SZ[4] | 1898 | ??.??.95 | Yes | No | Directly elected constituent assembly | 13.02.98 | No | No |
| | | - | | | Executive committee (mandated by the parliament)/ Parliament | 23.10.98 | Yes | Yes |
| SH | 1899 | 25.11.94 | Yes | Yes | Directly elected constituent assembly | 15.11.96 | No | No |
| | | | | | | 28.05.99 | No | No |
| OW | 1902 | 28.04.01 | Yes | Yes | Mixed commission appointed by the Parliament/ Parliament | 27.04.02 | Yes | Yes |
| AI | 1905 | | | | Not known | 30.04.05 | No | No |
| VS | 1907 | 19.06.04 | Yes | Yes | Executive committee appointed by the parliament/ Parliament | 12.05.07 | Yes | Yes |

| Canton | Year | Principle Referendum | | | Constitution-Making Body | Referendum | | Coming into Effect |
|---|---|---|---|---|---|---|---|---|
| | | Date | Result | Subsidiary Question | | Date | Result | |
| AR | 1908 | ??.??.03 | Yes | Not known | Directly elected constituent assembly | ??.??.05 | No | No |
| | | | | | Directly elected constituent assembly | 26.04.08 | Yes | Yes |
| NW | 1913 | Not known | | | Mixed | 27.04.13 | Yes | Yes |
| TI | 1921 | 26.05.20 | Yes | No | Directly elected constituent assembly | - | | |
| OW | 1948 | 04.05.47 | Yes | Yes | Directly elected constituent assembly | ??.??.48 | No | No |
| NW | 1965 | 26.04.64 | Yes | Yes | Parliament | 10.10.65 | Yes | Yes |
| TI | 1967 | - | | | Expert committee appointed by the Parliament/Parliament | 29.10.67 | Yes | Yes |
| OW | 1969 | ??.??.67 | Yes | Yes | Directly elected constituent assembly | 29.05.68 | Yes | Yes |
| JU | 1977 | 01.03.70 | Yes | No | Directly elected constituent assembly | 20.03.77 | Yes | Yes |
| AG | 1980 | 04.06.72 | Yes | No | Directly elected constituent assembly | 29.04.79 | No | No |
| | | 02.12.72[5] | Yes | Yes | | 28.09.80 | Yes | Yes |
| UR | 1984 | - | | | Mixed: Executive and Parliament/Parliament | 28.10.84 | Yes | Yes |
| BL | 1984 | - | | | Directly elected constituent assembly | 04.11.84 | Yes | Yes |
| SO | 1988 | 05.04.81 | Yes | No | Directly elected constituent assembly | 08.06.86 | Yes | Yes |
| GL | 1988 | 10.05.70 | Yes | No | Executive commission appointed by the Parliament/Parliament | 01.05.88 | Yes | Yes |
| TG | 1990 | - | | | Executive commission (appointed by the government)/ Parliament | ??.06.87 | Yes | No[6] |
| | | | | | | 04.12.88 | | |
| BE | 1995 | 06.12.87 | Yes | Yes | Parliament | 06.06.93 | Yes | Yes |
| AR | 1996 | ??.??.91 | Yes | Yes | Representative commission recruited by the Parliament and the Government /Parliament | 30.04.95 | Yes | Yes |
| TI | 1998 | - | | | Parliament | 14.12.97 | Yes | Yes |
| NE | 2002 | 10.03.96 | Yes | Yes | Parliament | 24.09.00 | Yes | Yes |
| SG | 2003 | 25.06.95 | Yes | Yes | Parliament | 10.06.01 | Yes | Yes |
| SH | 2003 | 06.04.97 | Yes | Yes | Mixed commission appointed by the Parliament/Parliament | 04.03.01 | No | No |
| | | | | | | 22.09.02 | Yes | Yes |

| Canton | Year | Principle Referendum | | | Constitution-Making Body | Referendum | | Coming into Effect |
|---|---|---|---|---|---|---|---|---|
| | | Date | Result | Subsidiary Question | | Date | Result | |
| FR | 2005 | 13.06.99 | Yes | Yes | Directly elected constituent assembly | 16.05.01 | Yes | Yes |
| VD | 2003 | 07.06.98 | Yes | Yes | Directly elected constituent assembly | 22.09.02 | Yes | Yes |
| GR | 2005 | 28.09.97 | Yes | No | Expert committee appointed by the Executive/Parliament | 18.05.03 | Yes | Yes |
| ZH | 2006 | 13.06.99 | Yes | No | Directly elected constituent assembly | 27.02.05 | Yes | Yes |
| BS | 2006 | 18.04.99 | Yes | No | Directly elected constituent assembly | 30.10.05 | Yes | Yes |
| LU | 2008 | 23.09.01 | Yes | No | Mixed commission appointed by the Executive/Parliament | 17.06.07 | Yes | Yes |
| SZ | 2013 | 25.09.05 | Yes | No | Mixed commission appointed by the Parliament/Parliament | 15.05.11 | Yes | Not yet |
| GE | 2013 | 24.02.08 | Yes | No | Directly elected constituent assembly | Not yet | | |

## Table Guide

*Swiss Cantons*

| | | | | | | | |
|---|---|---|---|---|---|---|---|
| AG | Argovia | FR | Fribourg | NW | Nidwalden | TG | Thurgau |
| AI | Appenzell Inner Rhodes | GE | Geneva | OW | Obwalden | TI | Ticino |
| AR | Appenzell Outer Rhodes | GL | Glarus | SG | St. Gallen | UR | Uri |
| BA | Basel | GR | Graubünden | SH | Schaffhausen | VD | Vaud |
| BE | Berne | JU | Jura | SO | Solothurn | VS | Wallis |
| BL | Basel-Countryside | LU | Lucerne | SZ | Schwyz | ZG | Zug |
| BS | Basel-Town | NE | Neuchâtel | SZ ÄL | Schwyz Outer Lands | ZH | Zurich |

*Year:* Refers to the year the constitution came into effect or, where appropriate, to the year the constitutional or principle referendum was held (see below).

*Principle Referendum:* Referendum in which the citizens decide whether they want the constitution to be totally revised or not. In some cases, it includes a

*Subsidiary Question:* which concedes the power to the people to determine the constitution-making body (see below). In most cases, the citizens chose between two different options (incumbent parliament or constituent assembly).

*Constitution-Making-Body:* Refers to the body that elaborated the new constitution. Please note that the designation of a parliament or a constituent assembly as the constitution-making body may include cases where the latter established internal commissions so as to elaborate the draft, i.e. a parliamentary commission.

*Referendum:* Constitutional referendum.

*Notes:* The second referendum was not a principle referendum in the above sense but about the question of whether to elect a new constituent assembly for the elaboration of a second draft.

1. At first the Constitution did not come into effect as the Federal Assembly refused to guarantee it.
2. The second referendum was about the continuation of the constitution-making process.
3. See above the main text, footnote no. 1.
4. The second referendum was held on the continuation of the constitution-making process and if yes, whether to mandate a new constituent assembly with the elaboration of the second draft.
5. At first, the new Constitution did not come into effect because the Federal Court, upon a complaint, had ordered that the poll should be repeated.

Chapter 8

# Popular Input, Territoriality, and the Constitution-Making Process: Comparative Reflections on the European Union's Supranational Experience

Fernando Mendez

## Introduction

A core theme addressed by this book is the extent of popular input during constitution-making processes. This chapter adds another component to this theme, territoriality. Chapters 1 and 2 have shown how popular participation can take a variety of forms, some direct others more indirect, and can be sequenced across three broad dimensions: i) the launching of a given constitutional exercise and in terms of choosing the representatives tasked with producing a constitutional document ii) the soliciting of opinions and participation of the public during the constitution drafting stages and iii) the degree to which the final constitutional document requires popular ratification. This gives rise to the variety of ways in which popular input can be sequenced in constitution-making exercises. This chapter's focus is on a subset of cases – with special reference to the EU – in which the popular participation dilemma is complicated by a territorial component. In what way do territorial concerns structure the constitution-making process?

At first glance, it may appear odd to try and compare the EU's constitution-making exercises let alone any forms of popular input that may be linked to such processes. To begin with the EU does not have a 'constitution' – though this need not be grounds for its exclusion from comparative assessment. Other political systems, such as the UK and New Zealand, do not have codified constitutional documents. None of this means that they are not governed by norms of constitutionalism. Better, therefore, to conceive a constitution more broadly as a governing set of principles that organize the political and social life of a polity rather than a particular document that is explicitly referred to as a 'constitution'.[1] In this latter sense the EU is certainly equipped with such a constitution (Weiler 1999). Furthermore, its governing principles are codified in a series of documents known as EU treaties. It could be argued that those documents are more akin to an 'international treaty'

---

1    This is the sense in which a constitution was understood by Aristotle in his *Politics*.

than a national constitution. However, the present EU polity is far from being an international organization and can be easily distinguished on many fronts from all other international organizations. No other international organization, for instance, has developed a competitive party system with direct elections to a legislative chamber nor penetrated the domestic politics of its member states to such a degree. Perhaps, then, the supranational label is more appropriate. Indeed, we have used the label in the title of this chapter to distinguishing it from other international organizations.

Leaving aside ontological debates about what type of political animal the EU is, it may be possible to move beyond the supranational template and compare the EU with other polities where territoriality matters. In other words rather than emphasize the EU's supranational uniqueness why not compare it to other multi-level polities. This is the step taken in this chapter. The key question asked is to what extent can the EU's supranational constitution-making experience, and the degree of popular participation therein, be compared to other political systems? And, if so, what insights can be drawn from its comparative treatment? In conducting the comparison the focus will be on a special form of political organization that is governed by principles of territoriality: a federal system.

We begin this chapter by looking at the EU's specific constitution-making model. This involves a degree of periodization since the EU polity has evolved considerably since the 1950s when it was originally founded. Despite significant transformations since its birth there are elements of the EU's constitutional DNA that can be traced back to its foundational moment. Therefore, in line with some of the conceptual distinctions made in Chapters 1 and 2, we also draw attention to the distinction between foundational and transformational constitutional moments. These aspects are covered in section 2 of this chapter. In section 3, we extend the analysis to cover a broader range of multi-level polities. The aim of the comparative assessment is to highlight similarities and differences across the six cases. In the concluding sections some reflections on the EU's constitution-making process, and in particular on the role of the people therein, will be offered.


## Modes of Constitution-Making in the EU

We have already noted that the EU is governed by a series of Treaties. As with most other polities, including many of those discussed in this chapter, foundational constitutional moments can generate significant institutional legacies. The EU is no different in this respect, although the legacies of its birth are perhaps more significant than in the other cases surveyed. What we presently refer to as the EU was born in some rather inauspicious circumstances. The project was narrowly conceived in the aftermath of the Second World War as a form of functional integration in two strategic industrial sectors – Coal and Steel – (Haas 1958). However, that treaty – the European Coal and Steel Community ratified by six member states in 1952 – was always seen as a precursor for further sectoral integration (Schultze 2003). This arrived a few years later when the six member states created the European Economic Community (EEC) when they signed the Treaty of Rome in 1957 and ratified it the following year. In terms of popular input into any of the aforementioned treaties the short answer is that there was none. The dominant logic in which those treaties where negotiated, signed, and ratified, was typically one of state-driven diplomacy.

By the 1960s it was becoming clear that this new supranational organization was intent on fulfilling its treaty Preamble obligation to 'lay the foundations of an ever closer union'. Soon renamed the European Community (EC), the new organization rapidly expanded in territorial numbers (more member states) and in scope (more policy areas). The immediate consequence of more member states joining – enlargements have taken place every decade since the 1970s when Denmark, Ireland, and the UK acceded – was the addition of new constitutional veto points. This mattered since the treaties are based on the constitutional principle of limited competences (Weiler 1999). Thus, as the member states wished to expand the supranational organization's policy remit into new areas (e.g. monetary affairs, foreign affairs, defence cooperation) that went beyond the original EEC treaty then it would be necessary to attribute the EEC/EC with specific new competences. Until the late 1980s most of the changes could be implemented via powers contained in the original treaties. The constitutional problems began as the EC sought to expand into areas beyond the internal market which requires treaty revision. This has given rise to that familiar process of 'semi-permanent' treaty revision which we have come to associate with EU constitutional politics since the late 1980s (de Witte 2002).

As mentioned above, the number of constitutional veto points increased as the EC/EU expanded to include more member states. This coincided with a desire to empower the EC to act in new policy areas that went beyond the original treaties. The route to achieve this since the 1980s has been mostly via revisions to the treaties. Such constitutional changes require unanimous agreement among the member states, however. For obvious reasons this was made more difficult as the number of member states grew. But the increase in the veto points was not merely quantitative. There was an important qualitative transformation to the changing nature of the constitutional veto points and it was one that had an important bearing on mechanisms of popular participation. Its potentiality had been lying mostly dormant during the foundational stages but was activated when the EC expanded from the original six to incorporate member states that provided for referendums as the constitutional route for ratification of EC/EU treaty revisions.[2] The crucial point is that how a member state ratifies a treaty revision is governed not by the EU but by the domestic constitutional order of the member states. Thus, the first in the series of 'semi-permanent' treaty revisions since the 1980s – the 1986 Single

---

2    It is important to note that the first referendum on European integration actually took place with the French referendum in 1972 on the expansion of the EC.

European Act – triggered a popular vote as the route to treaty ratification in one of the first enlargement member states, Denmark.

**Table 8.1￼Major constitutional moments in the European integration process**

| Treaty | Year signed | Year ratified |
| --- | --- | --- |
| European Coal and Steel Community | 1951 | 1952 |
| European Economic Community (Treaty of Rome) | 1957 | 1958 |
| European Atomic Energy Community (EURATOM) | 1957 | 1958 |
| Single European Act | 1986 | 1987 |
| Treaty of Maastricht (Treaty on European Union) | 1992 | 1993 |
| Treaty of Amsterdam | 1997 | 1999 |
| Treaty of Nice | 2001 | 2003 |
| Treaty Establishing a Constitution for Europe | 2004 | Rejected 2005 |
| Treaty of Lisbon | 2007 | 2009 |
| European Fiscal Compact | 2012 | – |

*Note*: That the list does not include amendments to the treaties to provide for accession of new member states.

Since the Single European Act there has been popular input, albeit in an asymmetric form involving some though not all member states, into every treaty revision. Whilst all the treaty revisions have been important, some have been significantly more so than others (see Table 8.1). This raises a question on the distinction between a foundational constitutional moment and a transformational one. There is little disagreement among scholars and observers about the importance of the Treaty on European Union (the Maastricht Treaty). Apart from the symbolically important change to its name – the European Union – the treaty gave birth to the Euro, and the institutional three pillar structure governing competences related to: (i) internal market (ii) justice and home affairs and (iii) foreign policy and defence cooperation. For some analysts, the Treaty on the European Union (TEU) is the moment when the EU struck a 'federal bargain' (Mckay 1999). There is no doubt that this was a transformational constitutional change and arguably of more significance than the ill-fated Constitutional Treaty or its Lisbon sequel.

In fact, the TEU could also be considered as a foundational constitutional moment. This would not be too dissimilar from the US case where both the Articles of Confederation signed in 1777 and the Constitution of the United States signed ten years later in 1787 are, in a sense, equally foundational. How we classify these constitutional events can therefore contain an element of arbitrariness – though none of this will impact in any significant way on the analysis conducted in this chapter. It is merely being noted at this stage before we direct our attention to two of the EU's major constitutional events: (i) the TEU and (ii) the Constitutional Treaty and its sequel the Lisbon treaty (the latter two events can be analysed together). There is little point in recounting the detailed narratives of either constitutional event (for an overview see Nugent 2010). The substantial constitutional changes brought about by the TEU have already been mentioned. In terms of the Constitutional Treaty signed in 2004 it certainly included some symbolic changes and institutional innovations, the most important of which were directly incorporated into the Lisbon Treaty when the former failed the popular vote ratification hurdle in 2005. The substantive content of the treaties is covered by an abundant literature (for detailed see Piris 2006; 2010) and is of little relevance to the book and this chapter's overriding themes, the modes of representation and ratification and the opportunities for popular input therein. In other words, our focus is on the process rather than the constitutional product.

In terms of the constitutional process and the various dimensions for popular input there is one salient characteristic of the EU constitution-making process that needs to be considered. The EU's rules of constitutional change are governed by a 'double unanimity requirement' (de Witte 2004). First, a treaty revision requires an intergovernmental conference (IGC) that needs to achieve unanimity among the heads of state (in the European Council). Now in terms of the mode of representation, the IGC is effectively constituted by the executive branch of the Member States that negotiate a treaty revision. In addition, no treaty revision can enter into force without a second stage in which all the Member States ratify according to their respective constitutional requirements. Both stages pay the utmost respect to the territorial principle. However, in the EU's ratification stage territoriality can generate considerable variance in procedures, from simple parliamentary majorities in some cases, to the need for super-majorities in others, and in others popular ratification via a referendum. Where political elites have avoided the popular ratification route (e.g. UK or Czech Republic) or there is no provision for ratification referendums (e.g. Germany) public opposition has on occasions resorted to the Courts and legal challenges.

The double unanimity requirement is a particularly rigid procedure for implementing the EU's functional equivalent of a constitutional change. Furthermore, this particular element of the EU's constitutional DNA has not been significantly altered since its 1957 foundational moment. What may appear to contemporary observers as a birth defect was unavoidable during the foundational moment but unlike other systems governed by territorial constitutional veto points, the EU has been unable to thus far overcome the double unanimity constraint (Trechsel 2005). There has been one important change in terms of the mode of representation however. This occurred during the process leading up to the rejected Constitutional Treaty of 2005 and it involved the specific institutional innovation of a Constitutional Convention.

Much has been written about the European experiment with a constitutional convention and in a few cases obvious parallels were drawn with the US Philadelphia experience (e.g. Fabbrini 2004). Most of the thick descriptions of the process leading up to the Convention need not concern us (for a comprehensive overview see Castiglione et al. 2008). What is relevant to note is that the Convention was born as a result of the 2001 Laeken Declaration, which provided a mandate from the highest political level (the European Council) to pursue constitutional reforms that, to name but two lofty goal from a longer wish list, would make the EU more democratic and transparent. To that end, the constitutional reformers hit upon the idea of adopting a Constitutional Convention – a model that had been successfully deployed in 1999–2000 for producing the EU Charter of Fundamental Rights (Piris 2006). Despite notable excitement among observers at the time, the overall constitutional model remained unaltered in important respects. An IGC involving the heads of state acting on the basis of unanimity at the end of the convention process was still required and, furthermore, the final product would still be subject to ratification according to domestic constitutional procedures in the member states.

It is important to note what the constitutional convention actually represents in terms of the dimensions structuring the book. There is a case for arguing that a change in the mode of representation occurred in terms of the procedure not being exclusively controlled by the state executives (and their legal advisors) – as had been the case for all treaty revisions prior to the Constitutional Treaty. In this respect, the convention's composition was expanded to include national parliamentarians and EU parliamentarians, as well as a small number of representatives from the regions, and European 'social partners'. The Constitutional Convention ultimately brought together 220 persons. However, no specific elections were convoked to directly select the delegates since the parliamentarians (from the member states and the European Parliament) had already been elected. Furthermore, the member states governments directly appointed a quarter of the representatives (Piris 2006: 46). In a sign of rare openness, the Convention was also open to the 10 acceding states (Central and Eastern European States) that had not yet joined the EU as well three candidate states. The Convention was therefore more 'representative' than the traditional route to treaty revision. It also broke new ground in terms of the style of deliberation. In this respect, there was a movement away from the secretive and elitist style of diplomatic bargaining that has characterized most EC/ EU treaty revisions. The debates were public and attracted media attention. This needs to be tempered by the fact that the work and the deliberations of the highest body within the convention, the Praesidium, were not public.

In terms of the mode of ratification the Constitutional Treaty was still governed by the domestic constitutional requirements of the member states. It is worth mentioning that, in order to maximize popular input into the whole constitution-making exercise, the Convention put forward the idea of submitting the Constitutional Treaty to a pan-European referendum (de Witte 2005). This was eventually rejected by the Praesidium. Nonetheless, a thus far unique dynamic was generated whereby nearly a dozen member states publicly committed themselves to ratification referendums on the Constitutional Treaty (Closa 2007). This all occurred in the context of an earlier, successful wave of accession referendums by the Central and Eastern European candidate countries (Albi 2005). But the Constitutional Treaty failed the popular ratification route. Following the negative referendums of France and The Netherlands in 2005, EU elites removed some of the Constitutional Treaty's more symbolic elements and repackaged it as the Lisbon Treaty. That treaty followed the ordinary route to treaty revision and triggered a sole referendum in Ireland, which was at first first rejected. The Lisbon Treaty was only ratified following a second referendum vote after the Irish had secured some additional protocols and opt outs to the treaty.

## Comparative Analysis

The EU's supranational model of constitution-making may appear unique given the brief overview of its main features described above. It is certainly the case that a very acute dilemma exists between the territoriality principle and demands for popular input. The dilemma affects how the EU polity is able to constitutionally adapt to the increasing demands placed on it. But are such dilemmas unique to the EU? In the section that follows we investigate this question by focusing on the so-called five classic federal systems. As a method of case selection the five classic federal systems are amongst some of the oldest federalized democracies and constitute what Lijphart (1999) has denominated 'strong federalism' by virtue of the strong autonomy granted to the territorial units making up the federations. Others have noted that these federal systems could be considered as examples of 'coming together' federalism by virtue of a founding dynamic whereby previously separate political units unite to form a federal union (Stepan 1999).[3] These two features, the territorial component and the coming together of previously separated units, are especially salient in the EU case. The question therefore is how does this affect modes of constitution-making. Given the obvious word constraints it will be impossible to cover in any detail the rich processes of constitution-making and constitutional change in the five classic federal systems. The best we can do is to flag some important constitutional events, both foundational and transformational, in order to provide a snapshot of ways in which territoriality can conflict with principles of popular participation.

### Foundational Moments

Let us begin with two of the earliest cases, the United States and Switzerland. In terms of the modes of constitution-making there are certain similarities between the two. It is possible to consider as foundational, the events of 1787 and 1848 which respectively gave rise to the federal constitutions of the United States

---

3   Coming together federalism can be contrasted with holding together federalism whereby more unitary systems federalise in order to maintain the union. Note the West German case in the 1940s is harder to classify as 'coming together' type.

and Switzerland. Both events altered the rules of previous foundational acts, the 1777 Articles of Confederation in the context of the American Revolution and the restoration of the Swiss confederacy in 1815, which followed the Napoleonic occupation.

In the US case the Philadelphia Convention was tasked with producing some minor revisions to the Articles of Confederation. In terms of the mode of representation, the territorial element involved all of the founding former colonies sending delegates to the convention. In most cases, the delegates were elected with the exception of Rhode Island which did not send any delegates to Philadelphia. When our attention is directed to the mode of ratification the interesting aspect is that, in what turned out to be a revolutionary constitutional act, the ratification rules were laid out in the new Constitution as opposed to the Articles of Confederation that were based on unanimity (Rakove 1997). Procedurally the ratification model was not so distinct from the EU model where ratification was left to the constituent units. There was, however, a subtle but important difference in that new Constitution expressly provided that ratification would take place via state wide conventions. According to Amar (2005) the whole process was much more an exercise in popular democracy than is commonly acknowledged. Whilst there were no direct referendums on the new constitution, there were specially convoked elections operating on a majority vote basis for state conventions that delivered ratification. The 'people' were involved to a much greater degree than mere ratification by ordinary state legislatures. Perhaps this accounts for some of the ratification problems experienced in a number of states. The most relevant was Rhode Island – the only colony to decide to submit the Constitution to a direct popular vote – which failed to deliver ratification. Interestingly, an alternative ratification route, the state convention method, was adopted for its second attempt.

The Swiss case too followed a similar territorial principle whereby the cantons, in the aftermath of a civil war, sent delegates to a body which came together in 1848 to draw up the modern Swiss federal constitution. As in the US, the constitutional package was then sent back to the territorial units for ratification. As in the EU, the precise mode of ratification was left to the Cantons themselves. The effect was that different ratification procedures were used, some involved the legislature/ executive and in other cases a popular vote was held. It is striking that in some Cantons that opted for the popular vote route the degree of opposition to the new Constitution was overwhelming (90 per cent rejection in some cases) (Kolz 1999). Nonetheless, the Swiss overcame the unanimity requirement by legal fiat when the highest political body (the Diet) voting on a majority basis decided to accept the constitution despite the rejections (Kolz 1999). In short, both foundational constitutional acts in the US and Switzerland involved pragmatic, negotiated compromises among delegates representing conflicting territorial interests that struck a federal constitutional bargain. In both cases too, ratification problems were experienced when territorial principles clashed with demands for popular participation.

Ratification problems during foundational constitutional moments were also experienced in Australia. In the context of decolonization from the British, a series of constitutional conventions was initiated during the 1890s among the colonies. As in the US, the mode of representation pursued was the convention method. The National Australasian Convention met in Sydney in 1891 and involved the colonies of Australia and New Zealand. The latter soon lost interest leaving the colonies of the Australian continent to continue their negotiations. A number of problems were encountered with the various constitutional drafts. At this point a novel idea was introduced in 1893 – the so-called Corowa Plan (La Nauze 1972). The drafting of the constitution would be entrusted to representatives from each colony elected for that special purposes and the final constitutional product was to be submitted to a popular vote as a mode of ratification (Aroney 2009). Crucially, the popular vote on ratification would need to respect the territorial principle – there was no Australia-wide referendum but rather separately sequenced series of referendums in each of the colonies.

Elections for the federal constitutional Convention were held in 1897 and a constitutional draft was quickly produced. The constitutional bargain quickly began to unravel due to problems encountered with the ratification process. Although the first three referendums were passed with an overwhelming majority, in the key state of New South Wales the requisite majority was not reached in the referendum on ratification. Some changes were made to the constitutional package to accommodate New South Wales and a new round of referendums took place. Despite some problems with one of the colonies, Western Australia (which later tried to secede from the federation), the new constitution was eventually ratified and entered into force in 1901.

In the cases of Canada and Germany the foundational constitutional moments occurred in quite different conditions to the cases discussed thus far. In the Canadian case a series of constitutional conferences were held in Canada and in Britain among selected territorial elites between 1864 and 1866 (Monahan 2006). The process was more akin to international diplomatic negotiations involving the territorial leaders and former colonial masters – a conference model that has been used in many cases of decolonization, i.e. especially in Africa. In this sense, the Canadian case differed from Australia's more open and bottom-up process involving a series of specially convoked elections to elect delegates to a constitutional convention and, most importantly, a ratification model predicated on a strong dose of popular input. None of this was present in the Canadian case. The Canadian constitution, adopted in 1867, remained firmly anchored to the British Crown until 1982.

In the German case the federal structure was externally imposed by the Allies in the immediate aftermath of the Second World War. As in the US (and Australia) a constitutional convention was convened – the Herrenchiemsee Convention – to prepare a federal constitution (Kommers 2006). With due respect to the territorial principle, the delegates were elected by the legislatures of each Lander. What is more pertinent to our inquiry is that in terms of the mode of ratification a decision to avoid the popular vote was consciously taken. There was some pressure to subject the document to a popular vote on ratification but this was abandoned in favour of the state legislature route. In fact, the eventual constitutional product banned referendums at the federal altogether.[4] Ratification took place via a Constituent Assembly (known as the Parliamentary Council). As with all other cases with the exception of Canada there were ratification failures – Bavaria – in the West German case. Nonetheless, despite the rejection the new constitution was able to surpass the supermajority threshold required to enter into force.

*Transformational Constitutional Change*

The main focus of this subsection is on the process of constitutional change and the degree of popular input therein. In some of the examples it is meaningful to talk of significant constitutional changes that take place at a given historical juncture (i.e. German reunification) whilst in other cases the concept is less relevant due to the more evolutionary process that has governed major constitutional change (i.e. in the United States). How, then, are significant constitutional changes undertaken? As with the EU, foundational moments can leave institutional legacies. Switzerland and Australia can be grouped together in this respect for they share similar models of constitutional change. In both cases the foundational constitutional act incorporated a specific bargain that provided for direct popular input with respect to any future changes to the constitution. In this regard, the two polities share similar modes for ratifying constitutional changes: a popular vote that requires a double majority of the people and of the states. The latter requirement satisfies the territorial principles of 'one territory, one vote' whilst the majority of the people criterion satisfies the democratic principle of 'one person, one vote'.

There are various ways in which it is possible to institute constitutional changes across the two polities on the basis of initiatives from the legislature and/ or executive. In terms of the mode of representation for instituting constitutional changes, Australia has resorted to the constitutional convention method on a number of occasions. In the 1973 Constitutional Convention delegates were directly appointed by the government and the legislature. That convention failed. A more recent, salient example was the 1998 Constitutional Convention, which was mandated with discussing whether Australia should become a republic. In terms of its composition, half of the delegates were elected and the remaining half were directly appointed. Australia remains a constitutional monarchy after the convention's proposal was rejected by both a majority of the people and of the states. This is hardly surprising since most constitutional changes fail the popular ratification hurdle in Australia.

The contrast between Australia and Switzerland in relation to constitutional change is rather illuminating. Most proposals for amendments – referred to

---

4   There was a legal basis for a territorial referendum in the case of reunification however.

as 'partial revisions' of the constitution – that have been put forward by the Swiss authorities are able to surmount the popular vote challenge. This was not always the case. One of the earliest attempts by the Executive to implement what in constitutional terms is referred to as a 'total revision' of the constitution was rejected by a popular vote in 1871. A new constitutional package was negotiated to satisfy some of the cantons that had rejected the earlier version. The second time round the new constitutional package managed to pass the double majority threshold for the popular vote and entered into force in 1874. The second total revision of the constitution occurred in 1999 and was passed smoothly.

In terms of the mode of representation there is a unique mechanism available to the Swiss people. Put simply, the people can themselves launch constitutional changes (both partial and total revisions) without the need for intermediary institutions such as legislatures. The basis for such constitutional measures is the popular initiative which is predicated on the collection of signature that must pass a numerical threshold (typically 100,000 signatures). In recent years there has been increasing recourse to popular initiatives for implementing constitutional amendments (partial revisions) and whilst most of these fail there have been some recent controversial cases which have succeeded at the final stage: the popular vote on ratification. The people can also launch a total revision of the constitution. No constitutional change has taken place via this procedure though there was one occasion, during the rise of the National Front movement in the 1930s, when a proposal for a total revision was put to the people but resoundingly rejected in the popular vote.

In the US case, the constitution has been difficult to amend in practice. This has not prevented the constitution from adapting to a changing internal and external environment but this has occurred less through formal constitutional amendments than via the federal legislative route or through judicial interpretation. Nominally, the US constitution has been amended 27 times but 10 of these amendments (the Bill of Rights) were implemented during the ratification process of the US constitution. Thus the US constitution has been amended 17 times since the 1790s. In terms of the modes of representation and ratification, most of these amendments took place through the intermediary institutions of the federal and state legislatures. What is striking about the US case is that although it still exists as a formal procedure of constitutional change, the Convention method has only been used once since the federal Constitution was adopted (for the repeal of Prohibition in 1921). We already noted the popular dimension to the Convention method in terms of electing state delegates and in terms of further state elections for ratifying the constitutional proposal. The latter being the closest US equivalent to a federal level referendum.

Germany, like the US, does not have any provisions for popular votes at the federal level. There is one exception to that rule however, and it relates to territorial changes. Referendums have been used to alter the number of constituent units in the federation but none has triggered a federation wide referendum. The most obvious case where such a form of popular legitimation could have been used was for the momentous constitutional transformation symbolized by German reunification. The legal basis for ratifying such a change via a popular vote certainly existed. But it was conspicuously avoided by German elites in favour of an expedited Reunification Treaty signed in 1990. No doubt for those seeking an expedited route the stakes were too high to risk unification to a popular vote on either side. There was subsequently a serious debate, including the appointment of a commission on constitutional reform to consider a proposal to put the Constitution to the people – in the end those proposals were rejected. Paradoxically, the process of EU integration is an important driver of growing calls within Germany for a procedure to provide for the referendum as a route to ratification of further EU treaties (this occurred especially during the ratification process of the Constitutional Treaty and, at the time of writing, during the Eurozone crisis).

Of all the cases considered perhaps the most relevant for the EU is the dynamic unfolding in Canadian constitutionalism. For some observers Canada has been involved in an odyssey since the 1980s to implement constitutional changes that involve, amongst other things, trying to bring the province of Quebec firmly into the constitutional order (Russell 2004). Part of the problem may be related to Canada's mode of constitution-making, a legacy of the past and its foundational moment when territorial leaders negotiated with their former colonial masters in constitutional conferences in both London and Canada. As in the EU case, Canada's constitution-making process resembles an exercise in state diplomacy with territorial elites negotiating behind closed doors in the proverbial smoke-filled rooms over the weekend. Constitutional packages are thrashed out at the eleventh hour only to be submitted for ratification to the provinces. This was the mode for the first attempt at significant constitutional change, the so-called 1987 Meech Lake Accords. Popular mobilization against the deal played a significant role in the rejection of the constitutional package, which occurred when the territorial legislatures did not ratify the package within the prescribed time limits.

In recognition of the criticisms surrounding Meech Lake's secretive, executive-dominated style of constitutional negotiations, Canadian political elites experimented with a novel method. First, the state executive-led negotiating style was tempered by introducing mechanisms for popular input through a series of broadly open and transparent popular consultations. Second, the eventual constitutional package – the 1992 Charlottetown Accord – was to be put to the people in a federal referendum. The latest proposed constitutional overhaul failed the popular ratification hurdle. In a further set of developments that does not bode well for future constitutional reform, changes at the province level are expanding the nature of the constitutional veto points. Put simply, some territorial units have enshrined a mandatory referendum on future constitutional changes. This is not unlike the case of the EU where some of the territorial units (notably Denmark,[5]

---

5   Under special conditions.

Ireland, and most recently, the UK) have mandatory requirements for referendums on treaty ratification.

## Discussion

The comparative analysis touched upon the three dimensions of popular input structuring this book. However, it did so in a rather unbalanced fashion. Relatively little was said about the style of constitutional negotiations and the role of popular input therein. We did, however, point to some instances where a polity has experimented with new styles of constitutional negotiations. This occurred with the Convention that drafted the EU's Constitutional Treaty and during Canada's second major attempt at constitutional reform in 1992. In both these polities – which traditionally share similar styles of secretive, diplomatic style constitutional bargaining – there was a deliberate attempt to open up aspects of the constitution-making process. However, both experiments were ultimately vetoed by the people in referendums. In most instances of constitution-making, especially foundational moments, the style of constitution-making has been rather closed and involved pragmatic compromise among territorial elites.

Our focus has therefore mostly concentrated on the mode of representation and the mode of ratification, with a particular emphasis on the latter. What can we say about the cases at some notional, aggregate level? The two cases of Canada and the EU are instructive in this respect and appear to conform to one of the findings in Chapter 2 concerning a general trade-off facing constitutional designers: the dilemma between sequencing popular participation as a form of input legitimacy (i.e. during the launch of a constitution-making exercise) or focusing on output legitimacy (i.e. popular input for ratifying the constitution). Generally, it is hard to maximize popular participation on both fronts. The trade-off can be seen quite clearly in the case of both Canada and the EU were there has been a general dissatisfaction with the mode of representation in the constitution-making process, considered mostly as secretive and executive driven, and this has fuelled demands for greater popular input.

Demands for greater popular input on the ratification side can be compounded by a territorial principle when some territorial units submit ratification to a popular vote while others do not. This can cause greater institutional uncertainty and can also lead to mimetic effects. In Canada this was overcome by holding a one-off, polity-wide ratification referendum in 1992. But future constitutional packages need not trigger a polity wide referendum. Instead, ratification will be left to the territorial units, some of which now have mandatory referendums in place for ratifying constitutional changes while others do not. The emergence of such asymmetric territorial veto points based on ratification referendums is precisely the constitutional setting in which the EU presently finds itself. Indeed, territorial popular veto points in the EU appear to be expanding – a recipe for greater institutional paralysis.

In the cases of Australia and Switzerland potential future dilemmas about territoriality and popular input were settled, in certain respects, by their foundational constitutions. This was accomplished by instituting a popular veto point for ratifying future constitutional changes on the basis of both the democratic principle and the territorial principle (the double majority). The two cases differed quite markedly in how their foundational moment was configured, however. The Swiss case in 1848 is not very different from present day EU constitutional negotiations. Territorial elites met behind closed doors and negotiated a constitutional package that was sent back to the Cantons which ratified according to their domestic constitutional orders (some using the popular vote device and others not). That is the present EU model with an important difference: when the Swiss encountered ratification problems in 1848, the highest political body decided to overcome unanimity and adopt the constitution. The European Council has never done this. Of all the cases, Australia's foundational moment enjoyed the greatest degree of popular input both in terms of the mode of representation and the mode of ratification. But it failed on its first attempt and had to be renegotiated and resubmitted to the people. Indeed, rejection by popular vote seems to be a rather common outcome, and it has occurred in relation to foundational moments and significant constitutional reforms in Australia, Canada, Switzerland and the EU. In all cases, elites repackaged the constitutional document and resubmitted it for ratification – though in Canada the second attempt also failed.

One of the most interesting, yet comparatively rare, modes of representation and ratification is the US Convention method. It generates a high degree of popular input, elections for appointing the delegates and a subsequent series of elections for ratifying the constitution. But it has only been used once during the foundational moment, and as mechanism for ratifying the constitutional amendment that repealed Prohibition in 1921. Most formal constitutional changes have taken place through the federal legislature, albeit with a supermajority requirement. This is how the German case operates too. For the moment at least, it is unlikely we shall see greater popular input with regard to either the mode of representation or ratification in the US or Germany.

The cross-polity comparative analysis has revealed that the territorial principle of 'one territory, one vote' matters during constitution-making exercises. It could hardly be otherwise, especially during the foundational moments of so-called 'coming together' federal polities. Indeed, in Canada and the EU there was little else during the foundational moment and no attempt to provide for popular input. Over time however pressures for greater popular input are likely to emerge. The problem then becomes one of how to reconcile the principles territoriality and popular participation. Both Australia and Switzerland provide an example of how to achieve this with a high degree of popular input on the ratification side. An alternative model is provided by Germany and the US, where there is no direct popular input in terms of constitutional changes – it is largely accomplished through intermediary institutions (legislatures and the Courts). For the moment at least, Canada and the EU, have yet to find a viable model of constitutional change.

It seems that the EU may, after all, not be as unique as it is commonly assumed and there are certainly comparative lessons to be drawn from investigating how other multi-level polities have reconciled some of the dilemmas of territoriality and popular participation.

# Chapter 9
# Conclusion

Jonathan Wheatley

The overall aim of this book was that set out in Chapter 1: namely, to examine the extent to which constitution-making processes matter in terms of their impact on the stability of the constitutional order, in terms of democracy and in terms of the peaceful regulation of conflict. We attempted to get to the bottom of this puzzle by using a comparative method of analysis: first, by looking at a large number of critical constitution-making events across the world (Part 1), later by looking at constitution-making processes across time in a number of more nuanced, small-n case studies (Part 2).

The first task of this book was to explore how the various elements of the constitution-making process related to one another and which of these elements (if any) has a critical impact on the outcomes in which we are interested, i.e. constitutional stability, democracy and conflict resolution. A close examination of how these elements interacted during 160 critical constitution-making events suggested to us that we had to disaggregate two main components: the mode of representation and the mode of legitimation. The mode of representation correlated closely with the style of constitution-making, to the extent that directly elected constitution-making bodies tended to deliberate in public, while appointed bodies tended to negotiate behind closed doors. On the other hand, perhaps paradoxically, the mode of representation and the mode of legitimation were found to be inversely correlated; if the constitution-making body was directly elected there was a somewhat reduced chance that the constitution would be ratified by means of a referendum in comparison with cases in which the body was appointed by the executive.

Through the use of Qualitative Comparative Analysis (QCA), we found that certain modes of constitution-making, defined both by the mode of representation and the mode of legitimation, occurring during certain time periods and under certain socioeconomic conditions tended to be associated with either continuing authoritarianism or a greater likelihood to democratize. We identified a significant cluster of events in which constitutions were elaborated by a body appointed by the incumbent political elite, subsequently ratified by a referendum, and in which the effect of this process was merely to consolidate authoritarian control. This finding led us to conclude that the use of a referendum was not necessarily a feature of an open and democratic constitution-making process. Often authoritarian regimes use the referendum as an empty gesture designed to give a stamp of legitimacy to the politics of domination. Indeed frequently referendums are used to legitimize constitutional changes that give almost unconstrained power to the executive, most often the president. Often they are manipulated or even rigged.

Overall, however, evidence from the large-n study of 160 constitution-making events was insufficient to convince us that the constitution-making process had a necessary effect on subsequent democratization. An alternative explanation is that *both* the constitution-making process *and* the subsequent evolution of events were conditioned by the underlying political context; in other words, an authoritarian dynamic of power may engender *both* a closed, undemocratic process of constitution-making (possibly 'legitimized' by a rigged referendum) *and* yet more authoritarianism. Similarly a democratic context smay engender both a democratic style of constitution-making and a democratic style of governance; in Chapter 7 we saw how the ideological framework engendered by the 1830 revolution in France set the scene for both the first liberal constitutions in a number of Swiss cantons and for the gradual development of liberal and democratic governance.

One fundamental puzzle that this book aims to address is the relationship between the constitution as a text and the principles of constitutionalism. This corresponds to North's (1990) distinction between formal and informal institutions. The constitution itself is a formal instrument that defines the formal parameters of the legal and political order. However, the informal institutions of constitutionalism are as, if not more, important than the constitutional text. These institutions determine how the text is interpreted and whether constitutional provisions are followed or ignored and, more importantly, place limits on executive power, not in a formal sense, but in terms of defining what is acceptable behaviour by leaders. In Chapter 4 we saw how constitutional texts could be amended almost beyond recognition to serve the will of a president; principles of constitutionalism involve an informal understanding amongst elites and citizens alike that this cannot happen. In short, these principles represent a consensus on the limits of government.

Returning to our earlier point, sometimes the existence or non-existence of such a consensus around the principles of constitutionalism determines the context that influences both the nature of the constitution-making process and the subsequent evolution of the political regime. A constitution that is written in a context in which consensus is absent is unlikely to respect the interests of all political and social forces and is likely to lead either to the domination of one such force over another or to prolonged conflict or instability. The central question is whether the exercise of writing a constitution can help build such a consensus and internalize the informal principles of constitutionalism. In other words, can the constitution-making process act as a kind of catharsis that leads most, if not all, groups to agree on a common set of rules of the game, or does it instead represent the imposition of the will of one leader or faction over others?

Let us for a moment focus on that group of cases in which at least a minimal consensus is achieved on the basis of a set of (typically) informal principles that here we refer to as constitutionalism. The question here is which comes first: the constitution as a document or constitutionalism as a set of principles? Or can the principles of constitutionalism be agreed upon without any (formal) constitutional change? Our research suggests all combinations are possible. First, the adoption of a new constitution can indeed represent a cathartic moment in which an understanding is reached on the principles of democratic governance. Spain and South Africa seem to more or less fit this scenario. Second, the adoption of a new constitution may mark only the beginning of a gradually-evolving consensus around certain democratic principles. The cases of Brazil and Ghana appear to represent the slow consolidation of constitutionalism and the constitution itself marked only the beginning of a developing consensus amongst the main political forces. Third, it may be that constitutionalism predates the constitution. To a certain extent, this could be said to apply to a number of Swiss cantons by the 1840s, although not as yet to Switzerland as a whole. It could also be said to apply to Poland, where a broad consensus on democracy was achieved at the end of the 1980s and the constitutional wrangling during the mid-1990s represented little more than an irrelevant sideshow to most observers. Finally, in order to take root consensus does not necessarily need a written constitution at all. Britain and New Zealand represent cases in which the principles of constitutionalism are rather well-established but there is no written constitution. Similarly, the 'cathartic moment' at which a set of fundamental principles are agreed to may be marked by nothing more than a little known constitutional amendment, as was the case in Sweden in 1909 or the Netherlands in 1917.

This issue of the path of causality is also highly relevant to the impact of constitution-making on conflict resolution. Constitutions that are drafted in the aftermath of conflict more frequently reflect the interests of the winners of the conflict than they do the interests of peace-making. Only in rather rare cases are constitutions drafted to reflect the interests of all sides as part of a peace process. Moreover, as the case of Bosnia demonstrates, constitutions that are elaborated as part of a peace-making process risk being unwieldy and inflexible once the peace is actually established. In rare cases, a conflict resolution settlement can form the basis for a consensus that gradually takes root in the years following the settlement. This is most likely to happen if the conflict is not so severe that divisions within society remain implacable. Sometimes, but not necessarily, the settlement is enshrined in a new constitution or a new set of constitutional amendments. The South African case is a good example of such a settlement, as is the ratification of the Swiss constitution in 1848, which came a year after the 27-day Sonderbund War. Although the civil war in Switzerland ended in victory by the radical cantons over the conservative, Catholic cantons, the new constitution represented compromise between central control and cantonal authority and even Lucerne, Fribourg and Zug, which had been amongst the most important cantons in the Sonderbund, accepted the compromise. The Swiss constitution gradually gained acceptance from all sides, formed the basis for modern Swiss democracy and put an end to civil conflict. However, such cases form the exception rather than the rule; in most cases post-conflict constitutions are victors' constitutions.

If a constitution-making event is to either represent a cathartic moment in which elites and society agree upon a set of binding principles, or mark the beginning of a gradually consolidating consensus, it would seem that the optimal format for the constitution-making body is that it is: a) at least representative of society or the main political forces within it and b) relatively open, to the extent that the public is at least informed as to what is going on. In the terminology that we have used in this book, therefore, probably the optimal design is that the mode of representation either be that of direct election or indirect selection, while the style should be either open or partly open. If the constitution-making body is appointed by elites and deliberates behind closed doors, the constitution that it spawns is unlikely to form the basis for consent, irrespective of whether there is a referendum. However, even a directly elected constitution-making body that deliberates in the full glare of publicity with maximum public input does not guarantee that deep divisions are overcome or that a culture of constitutionalism is cultivated. As we saw in Chapter 4, the open and democratic constitution-making process that appeared to build the foundations of consent in Benin failed to do so in Congo-Brazzaville, where inter-factional divisions remained insurmountable. Even in Venezuela, Bolivia and Ecuador (see Chapter 6), despite the existence of (minimally) democratic institutions, a highly inclusive and open process (at least superficially) masked a bitter power struggle between a newly-elected president and the vested interests of the existing political system. While the adoption of the constitution marked a victory for the former, there were few indications that these divisions had been overcome. In all three cases, the new constitution resulted in a further accrual of power to the president. In Venezuela in particular, large sections of society did not participate in the constitution-making process at all.

# Bibliography

Acosta, A. et al. 2008. Entre el quiebre y la realidad. Constitución de 2008. Quito: Abya-Yala.

Albi, A. 2005. *EU Enlargement and the Constitutions of Central and Eastern Europe*. Cambridge: Cambridge University Press.

Alcántara Sáez, M. 1992. Las transiciones a la democracia en España, América Latina y Europa Oriental. Elementos de aproximación a un estudio comparativo. *Revista del Centro de Estudios Constitucionales* 11.

Amar, A.R. 2005. *America's Constitution: A Biography*. New York: Random House.

Angst, M. 1986. *Der Solothurner Bankkrach und die Verfassungsrevision von 1887* Olten: Walter.

*Appenzeller Zeitung* (1830a) no. 39, 25 September.

*Appenzeller Zeitung* (1830b) no. 47, 20 November.

Aristotle (translation by T.A. Sinclair). 1962. *The Politics*. Harmondsworth: Penguin 1962.

Aroney, N. 2009. *The Constitution of a Federal Commonwealth: The Making and Meaning of the Australian Constitution*. Cambridge, Cambridge University Press.

Asare, S.K. and Prempeh, H.K. 2012. Amending the Constitution of Ghana: Is the Imperial President Trespassing? *African Journal of International and Comparative Law* 20(1), 141–54.

Aubynn, A.K. 2002. Behind the Transparent Ballot Box: The significance of the 1990s Elections in Ghana, in *Multi-party Elections in Africa*, edited by M. Cowen and L. Laakso. Oxford: James Currey.

Basabe Serrano, S. 2009. Ecuador: reforma constitucional, nuevos actores políticos y viejas prácticas partidistas. *Revista de Ciencia Política* 29(2), 381–406.

Blum, R. 1977. *Die politische Beteiligung des Volkes im jungen Kanton Baselland 1832–1875*. Liestal: Kantonale Drucksachen- und Materialzentrale.

Boafo-Arthur, K. 2008. Democracy and Stability in West Africa: The Ghanaian Experience. *Claude Ake Memorial Papers* 4. Available at http://nai.diva-porta.org/smash/get/diva2:279373/FULLTEXT01 [accessed 11 August 2011].

Bosshard-Borner, H. 2008. *Im Spannungsfeld von Politik und Religion. Der Kanton Luzern 1831 bis 1875*. Basel: Schwabe.

Bowen, C. 1966. *Miracle at Philadelphia: The Story of the Constitutional Convention, May to September 1787*. Boston: Little Brown.

Brewer-Carías, A.R. 2002. *Golpe de Estado y proceso constituyente en Venezuela*. México: Universidad Nacional Autónoma de México.

Brewer-Carías, A.R. 1999. El desequilibrio entre soberanía popular y supremacía constitucional y la salida constituyente en Venezuela en 1999. *Revista Anuario Iberoamericano de Justicia Constitucional* 3, 31–56.

Brewer-Carías, A.R. 2004. Constitución, Democracia y Control el Poder. *Venezuela: Universidad de los Andes, Consejo de Publicaciones, Editorial Jurídica venezolana, Centro Iberoamericano de Estudios Provinciales y Locales, Mérida*, 245–90.

Buchanan, J.M. and Tullock, G. 1962. *The Calculus of Consent, Logical Foundations of Constitutional Democracy.* Ann Arbor: University of Michigan Press.

Burkhart, M. 1963. *Die Entstehung der thurgauischen Verfassung von 1869.* Weinfelden: XV, 194 S. (Diss. Zürich 1958.): unpublished PhD thesis.

Castiglione, D., Schönlau, J., Longman, C., Lombardo, E., Perez-Solorzano, N. and Aziz, M. (eds). 2008. *Constitutional politics in the European Union: The convention moment and its aftermath.* Basingstoke: Palgrave Macmillan.

Castro, C. 2000. *The Military and Politics in Brazil: 1964–2000.* University of Oxford Centre for Brazilian Studies, Working Paper Series.

Centre pour la Gouvernance Démocratique (CGD). 2008. *Constitutionalism and Constitutional Amendments in West Africa: A Case Study of Benin, Burkina Faso and Senegal.* Paper for Open Society Initiative West Africa.

Choudhry, S. (ed.) 2008. *Constitutional Design for Divided Societies : Integration or Accommodation?* Oxford and New York: Oxford University Press.

Chrusciak, R. 2007. The Small Constitution of 1992. *Przeglad Sejmowy* (The Sejm Review) 5(82), 89–110.

Closa, C. 2007. Why convene referendums? Explaining choices in EU constitutional politics. *Journal of European Public Policy* 14(8), 1311–32.

Colomer, J.M. 1994. Teorías de la transición. *Revista de Estudios político*s 86, 243–53.

Colomer, J.M. and Pascual, M. 1994. The Polish Games of Transition. *Communist and Post-Communist Studies* 27(3), 275–94.

Conaghan, C.M. 2008. Ecuador: Correa's Plebiscitary Presidency, in *Latin America's Struggle for Democracy*, edited by L. Diamond, M.F. Plattner and D. Abente Brun. Baltimore: Johns Hopkins University Press.

Cordero Carraffa C. 2005. La representación en la asamblea constituyente, in *Cuaderno de Análisis e Investigación N° 6*, edited by Corte Nacional Electoral Bolivia. La Paz: Weinberg.

Dardanelli, P. 2011. The Emergence and Evolution of Democracy in Switzerland, in *Achieving Democracy: Democratization in Theory and Practice*, edited by M. Malone. New York: Continuum.

de la Fuente Jeria, J. 2010. El difícil parto de otra democracia: la Asamblea Constituyente de Bolivia. *Latin American Research Review* 45, 5–26.

de Witte, B. 2002. The Closest Thing to a Constitutional Conversation in Europe: The Semi-Permanent Treaty Revision Process, in *Convergence and Divergence in European Public Law*, edited by P. Beaumont, C. Lyons and N. Walker. Oxford: Hart.

de Witte, B. 2004. Treaty Revision in the European Union: Constitutional change through international law. *Netherlands Yearbook of International Law* 35, 51–84.

de Witte, B. 2005. The Process of Ratification and the Crisis Options: A Legal Perspective, in *The EU Constitution: The Best Way Forward?*, edited by D.M. Curtin, A.E. Kellermann and S. Blockmans. The Hague: TMC Asser Press.

Diamond, L. 2001. How People View Democracy: Findings from Public Opinion Surveys in Four Regions. *Presentation to the Stanford Seminar on Democratization. January 11, 2001.* Available at http://http://democracy. stanford.edu/Seminar/Diamond2001.htm [accessed 16 October 2012].

Diamond, L. 1992. Economic Development and Democracy Reconsidered. *American Behavioral Scientist* 35, 450–99.

Dierauer, J. 1919. Politische Geschichte des Kanton St. Gallen, in *Der Kanton St. Gallen 1803–1903*, edited by Regierung des Kantons St. Gallen. St. Gallen: Verlags-Eigentum des Kantons St. Gallen.

Dorand, J-P. 1998. La Constitution de 1857, annexe au message n° 110 du 29 septembre 1998 accompagnant le projet de décret engageant la procédure de révision totale de la Constitution cantonale. *Feuille officielle*, Nov. 1998.

Elkins, Z., Ginsburg, T. and Melton, J. 2009. *The Endurance of National Constitutions*. Cambridge: Cambridge University Press, 2009.

Elster, J. 2006. Legislatures as Constituent Assemblies, in *The Least Examined Branch: The Role of Legislatures in the Constitutional State*, edited by R.W. Bauman and T. Kahana. Cambridge: Cambridge University Press.

Elster, J. 1999. Arguing and Bargaining in Two Constituent Assemblies. *The Journal of Constitutional Law* 2(2), 345–421.

Elster, J. 1995. Forces and Mechanisms in the Constitution-making Process. *Duke Law Review* 45(2), 364–96.

Elster, J., Offe, C. and Preuss, U.K. 1998. *Institutional Design in Post-Communist Societies: Rebuilding the Ship at Sea.* New York: Cambridge University Press, 1998.

Erb, M.R. 1962. *Der Verfassungsrat im schweizerischen Staatsrecht.* Aarau: H.R. Sauerländer.

Fabbrini, S. 2004. Transatlantic Constitutionalism: Comparing the United States and the European Union. *European Journal of Political Research* 43(4), 547–69.

Fazy, H. 1890. *Les Constitutions de la République de Genève.* Geneva/Basel: Georg.

Feddersen, P. 1867. *Geschichte der Schweizerischen Regeneration von 1830 bis 1848.* Zurich: Verlags-Magazin.

Fitzsimmons, M.P. 1994. *The remaking of France: the National Assembly and the Constitution of 1791.* Cambridge: Cambridge University Press, 1994.

Fleischer, D. 1995. *Brazilian Politics: Structures, Elections, Parties and Political Groups (1985–1995)*. University of Brasilia, February 1995.

Fung, A. 2007. Democratic Theory and Political Science: A Pragmatic Method of Constructive Engagement. *American Political Science Review* 101(3), 443–58.

Gamboa Rocabado, F. 2009. *Dilemas y conflictos sobre la Constitución en Bolivia*. La Paz: Konrad Adenauer Stiftung.

Garcia-Guadilla, M.P. and Hurtado, M. 2000. Participation and Constitution Making in Colombia and Venezuela: enlarging the scope of democracy? Paper prepared for the *XXII Congreso internacional de Latin American Studies Association (LASA)*, Miami, FL.

Gargarella, R. 2003. The Majoritarian Reading of the Rule of Law, in *Democracy and the Rule of Law*, edited by A. Przeworski and J.M. Maravall. Cambridge: Cambridge University Press.

Ghai, Y. 2006. The Role of Constituent Assemblies in Constitution Making. *International IDEA* (2006). Available at http://www.constitutionnet.org/files/the_role_of_constituent_assemblies_-_final_yg_-_200606.pdf [accessed 27 April 2012].

Gilg, P. 1951. *Die Entstehung der demokratischen Bewegung und die soziale Frage*. Affoltern am Albis: unpublished PhD.

Ginsburg, T. (ed.) 2012. *Comparative Constitutional Design*. Cambridge: Cambridge University Press.

Ginsburg, T. 2009 (ed.). *Administrative Law and Governance in Asia: Comparative Perspectives*. Routledge University Press.

Ginsburg, T. 2008. Constitutional Afterlife: The Continuing Impact of Thailand's Post-Political Constitution. *International Journal of Constitutional Law* 7(1), 83–105.

Ginsburg, T. and Dixon, R. (eds) 2011. *Comparative Constitutional Law*. Cheltenham, UK and Northampton, MA: Edward Elgar.

Ginsburg, T., Elkins, Z. and Blount, J. 2009. Does the Process of Constitution-Making Matter? *Annual Review of Law and Social Science* 5, 201–23.

Ginsburg, T., Elkins, Z. and Melton, J. 2007. The Lifespan of Written Constitutions. Draft Paper. Available at www.yale.edu/macmillan/ruleoflaw/papers/Ginsburg-Lifespans-California.pdf [accessed 16 October 2012].

Gomes, S. 2006. O Impacto das Regras de Organização do Processo Legislativo no Comportamento dos Parlamentares: Um Estudo de Caso da Assembléia Nacional Constituinte (1987–1988). *DADOS – Revista de Ciências Sociais* 49(1), 193–224.

Gómez Calcaño, L. 2000. Sociedad civil y proceso constituyente en Venezuela: encuentros y rivalidades. Paper prepared for the *XXII Congreso internacional de Latin American Studies Association (LASA)*, Miami, FL.

Haas, E.B. 1958. *The Uniting of Europe: Political, Social and Economic Forces, 1950–1957*. Stanford CA: Stanford University Press.

Hamber, B. 1999. Have no doubt it is fear in the land: An exploration of the continuing cycles of violence in South Africa. *Zeitschrift für Politische Psychologie* 7(1–2), 13–128.

Harel-Shalev, A. 2009. The problematic nature of religious autonomy to minorities in democracies: The Case of India's Muslims. *Democratization* 16(6) 1261–81.

Hart, V. 2001. Constitution-making and the Transformation of Conflict. *Peace & Change* 26(2), 153–76.

Heilbrunn, J.R. 1993. Social Origins of National Conferences in Benin and Togo. *The Journal of Modern African Studies* 31(2), 277–99.

Heusler, A. 1920. *Schweizerische Verfassungsgeschichte*. Basel: Frobenius.

His, E. 1944. *Luzerner Verfassungsgeschichte der neuern Zeit 1798–1940*. Lucerne: Reuss-Verlag.

Horowitz, D. 1985. *Ethnic Groups in Conflict*. Berkeley: University of California Press.

Huber-Schlatter, A. 1987. *Politische Institutionen des Landsgemeindekantons Appenzell Innerrhoden*. Berne/Stuttgart: Verlag Paul Haupt.

Huntington, S.P. 1991. *Democratization in the Late Twentieth Century*. Norman: University of Oklahoma Press.

Jillson, C.C. 1988. *Constitution making: conflict and consensus in the Federal Convention of 1787*. New York: Agathon Press, 1988.

Joos, E. 2001. Ein Stadtstaat erfindet Kantonsstrukturen, in *Schaffhauser Recht und Rechtsleben*, edited by Verein Schaffhauser Juristinnen und Juristen. Schaffhausen: unpublished PhD thesis.

Junker, B. 1995. *Geschichte des Kantons Bern seit 1798, Vol. III*. Berne: Historischer Verein des Kantons Bern.

Karl, T.L. 1990. Dilemmas of Democratization in Latin America. *Comparative Politics* 23(1), 1–21.

Karl, T.L. and Schmitter, P.C. 1991. Modes of Transition in Latin America, Southern and Eastern Europe. *International Social Science Journal* 128, 269–84.

Kingman, S. 2008. Entre la asimilación y la diferencia: la Asamblea Constituyente y los territorios indígenas. *Iconos* 32, 25–9.

Kloetzli, H. 1922. *Die Bittschriften des Berner Volkes*. Zurich: Buchdruck Neue Zürcher Zeitung.

Kölz, A. 2004. *Neuere Schweizerische Verfassungsgeschichte, Vol. II: Ihre Grundlinien in Bund und Kantonen seit 1848*. Berne: Stämpfli.

Kölz, A. 1999. *Le origine dell costituzione Svizerra*. Traduzione Italiana. Locarno: Armando Dado.

Kölz, A. 1992. *Neuere Schweizerische Verfassungsgeschichte, Vol. I: Ihre Grundlinien vom Ende der Alten Eidgenossenschaft bis 1848*. Berne: Stämpfli.

Kommers, D. 2006. "Germany: Balancing Rights and Duties", in *Interpreting Constitutions: A Comparative Study*, edited by J. Goldsworthy. Oxford: Oxford University Press.

Lagos, M. 2003. World Opinion: Support for, and Satisfaction with, Democracy, *International Journal of Public Opinion Research* 15(4), 471–87.

La Nauze, J. (1972). *The Making of the Australian Constitution*. Melbourne, Australia: Melbourne University Press.

Lazarte, J. 2008. La Asamblea Constituyente de Bolivia: de la oportunidad a la amenaza. *Nuevo Mundo Mundos Nuevos, Cuestiones del tiempo presente*. Available at http://nuevomundo.revues.org/42663 [accessed 18 July 2011].

Levitsky, S. and Way, L.A. 2010. *Competitive Authoritarianism: Hybrid Regimes After the Cold War*. Cambridge: Cambridge University Press.

Lijphart, A. 1999. *Patterns of democracy: Government forms and performance in thirty-six countries*. New Haven: Yale University Press.

Lijphart, A. 1977. *Democracy in Plural Societies*. New Haven: Yale University Press.

Linz, J. 1990. Transiciones a la democracia. *Revista Española de Investigaciones Sociológicas* 51, 7–33.

Linz, J. and Stepan, A. 1996. *Problems of Democratic Transition and Consolidation: Southern Europe, South America, and Post-Communist Europe*. Baltimore: Johns Hopkins University Press.

Lipset, S.M. 1994. The Social Requisites of Democracy Revisited: 1993 Presidential Address. *American Sociological Review* 59, 1–22.

Lipset, S.M. 1959. Some Social Requisites of Democracy: Economic Development and Political Legitimacy. *American Political Science Review* 53, 69–105

Lutz, D. 2007. *Principles of Constitutional Design*. Cambridge: Cambridge University Press.

Magnusson, Bruce A. and John F. Clark. 2005. Understanding Democratic Survival and Democratic Failure in Africa: Insights from Divergent Democratic Experiments in Benin and Congo (Brazzaville). *Comparative Studies in Society and History* 47(3), 552–82.

Maingon, T., Pérz Baralt, C. and Sonntag, H. 2000. La batalla por una nueva Constitución para Venezuela. *Revista Mexicana de Sociología* 62(4), 91–124.

Marshall, G. 1987. *Constitutional Conventions: The Rules and Forms of Political Accountability*. Oxford: Oxford University Press.

Mayorga, F. 2010. Acerca Del Estado Plurinacional. BuenasTareas.com. 05. Available at www.buenastareas.com/ensayos/Acerca-Del-Estado-Plurinacional/272915.html [accessed 16 October 2012].

McIlwain, C.H. 1939. *Constitutionalism and the Changing World*. Cambridge: Cambridge University Press.

McKay, D. 1999. *Federalism and European Union: A Political Economy Perspective*. Oxford: Oxford University Press.

McQuaid, D. 1993. The Parliamentary Elections: A Postmortem. Report on Eastern Europe, 8 November, 15–21.

Meuwly, O. 1990. *Histoire des droits politiques dans le Canton de Vaud de 1803–1885*. Lausanne: unpublished PhD thesis.

Michel, K. 2008. *Skizzen der Schwyzer Verfassungsgeschichte*. Lachen: unpublished PhD thesis.

Mitchell, J. 1988. *The French Legislative Assembly*. Leiden: Brill.

Moehler, D. 2008. *Distrusting Democrats: Outcomes of Participatory Constitution-Making*. Ann Arbor: University of Michigan Press.

Monahan, P. 2006. *Constitutional Law*. Toronto: Irwin Law.

Morales Viteri, J.P. 2008. Los nuevos horizontes de la participación. *Neo-constitucionalismo y Sociedad*, Quito: Ministerio de Justicia y Derechos Humanos.

Moreira Alves, M.H. 1988. Dilemmas of the Consolidation of Democracy from the Top in Brazil: A Political Analysis. *Latin American Perspectives* 15(3), 47–63.

Movimiento Al Socialismo (MAS). 2007. Visión de País: Desde las naciones indígenas y originarias, los movimientos sociales organizados y la sociedad civil.

Movimiento Al Socialismo. Instrumento Político por la Soberanía de los Pueblos (MAS-IPSP). 2006. Refundar Bolivia para vivir bien. Propuesta para la Asamblea Constituyente. La Paz.

Nabholz, H. 1911. *Die Eingaben des zürcherischen Volkes zur Verfassungsreform des Jahres 1830*. Zurich: Orell Füssli.

*Neue Zürcher Zeitung* (NZZ; 1931) evening edition no. 517, 20 March.

*Neue Zürcher Zeitung* (NZZ; 1980) no. 213, 13/14 September.

North, D. 1990. *Institutions, Institutional Change and Economic Performance*. Cambridge: Cambridge University Press.

Nugent, N. 2010. *The Government and Politics of the European Union* (7th ed.). Basingstoke: Palgrave Macmillan.

Nwajiaku, K. 1994. The National Conferences in Benin and Togo Revisited. *The Journal of Modern African Studies* 32(3), 429–47.

O'Donnell, G. and Schmitter, P.C. 1986. *Transitions from Authoritarian Rule: Tentative Conclusions about Uncertain Democracies*. Baltimore: Johns Hopkins University Press.

Ogowewo, T.I. 2000. Why the Judicial Annulment of the Constitution of 1999 is Imperative for the Survival of Nigeria's Democracy. *Journal of African Law* 44(2), 135–66.

Ortiz Crespo, S. 2008. Participación ciudadana: la Constitución de 1998 y el nuevo proyecto constitucional. *Iconos* 32, 13–17.

Osiatyński, W. 1997. A Brief History of the Constitution. *East European Constitutional Review* 6, 66–76.

Pérez Loose, H. 2009. Ecuador y su metamorfosis constitucional, in *Procesos constituyentes contemporáneos en América Latina*, edited by J. Serna de la Garza, José. Ciudad de México: Universidad Nacional Autonónoma de México, Instituto de Investigaciones Jurídicas.

Piris, J-C. 2006. *The Constitution for Europe. A Legal Analysis*. Cambridge: Cambridge University Press.

Piris, J-C. 2010. *The Lisbon Treaty: A Legal and Political Analysis*. Cambridge: Cambridge University Press.

Poplawska, E. 2008. Constitution- making in Poland: Some reflections on popular involvement. *Zbornik radova Pravnog fakulteta u Splitu* 45(2), 279–86.

Praça, S. and Noronha, L. 2012. Políticas públicas e a descentralização legislativa da Assembleia Constituinte Brasileira, 1987–1988. *Revista Brasileira de Ciencias Sociais* 27(78), 131–47.

Pylee, M.V. 2007. *An Introduction to the Constitution of India*, 5th ed. New Delhi: Vikas.

Ragin, C.C. 1987. *The Comparative Method: Moving Beyond Qualitative and Quantitative Strategies*. Berkeley and Los Angeles: University of California Press.

Rakove, J.N. 1997. *Original Meanings: Politics and Ideas in the Making of the Constitution*. New York: Vintage.

Rauschenbach, R. 2011. Processes of direct democracy on the federal level in Brazil: An inventory and a research outlook. C2D Working Paper Series, 40/2011. Available at http://www.c2d.ch [accessed 16 October 2012].

Rawls, J. 1971. *A Theory of Justice*, Cambridge MA: Belknap Press of Harvard University.

Reilly, B. 2001. *Democracy in Divided Societies*. Cambridge: Cambridge University Press.

Reynold, David (ed.) 2002. *The Architecture of Democracy: Constitutional Design, Conflict Management, and Democracy*. Oxford: Oxford University Press.

Riker, W.H. 1964. *Federalism: Origin, Operation, Significance*. Boston, MA: Little, Brown.

Robinson, P.T. 1994. The National Conference Phenomenon in Francophone Africa. *Comparative Studies in Society and History* 36(3), 575–610.

Rüegg, P. 1989. *Über den Verfassungsrat in der heutigen Schweiz*. Zurich: Schulthess Juristische Medien.

Russell, P.H. 2004. *Constitutional Odyssey: Can Canadians Become A Sovereign People?* Buffalo: University of Toronto Press.

Rustow, D.A. 1970. Transitions to Democracy: Toward a Dynamic Model. *Comparative Politics* 2(3), 337–63.

Salazar Elena, R. 2009. El referéndum en Bolivia, in *Armas de doble filo*, edited by Y. Welp, and U. Serdült, Uwe. Buenos Aires: Prometeo.

Schaffner, M. 1982. *Die demokratische Bewegung der 1860er Jahre: Beschreibung und Erklärung der Zürcher Volksbewegung von 1867*. Basel/Frankfurt am Main: Helbing und Lichtenhahn.

Schedler, A. 2001. Taking Uncertainty Seriously: The Blurred Boundaries of Democratic Transition and Consolidation. *Democratization* 8(4), 1–22.

Schefold, D. 1966. *Volkssouveränität und repräsentative Demokratie in der schweizerischen Regeneration 1830□1858*. Basel/Stuttgart: Helbing und Lichtenhahn.

Scherer, A. 1954. *Ludwig Snell und der Schweizerische Radikalismus 1830–1850.* Fribourg: Universitätsverlag.

Schmitter, P.C. and Karl, T.L. 1991. What Democracy is ... and is not. *Journal of Democracy* 2(3), 75–88.

Schudel, R. 1933. *Geschichte der Schaffhauser Staatsverfassung 1798–1834.* Thayngen: unpublished PhD thesis.

Schütze, R. 2009. *From Dual to Cooperative Federalism: The Changing Structure of European Law.* Oxford: Oxford University Press.

Seely, J.C. 2005. The Legacies of Transition Governments: Post-Transition Dynamics in Benin and Toga. *Democratization,* 12(3) 357–377.

Sisk, T. 1996. *Power Sharing and International Mediation in Ethnic Conflicts.* Washington, DC: United States Institute of Peace.

Soland, R. 1977. *Joachim Leonz Eder und die Regeneration im Thurgau 1830–1831.* Weinfelden: Rudolf Mühlemann.

Souza Santos, B. de. 2010. Refundación del Estado en América Latina. Perspectivas desde una epistemología del Sur. Quito: Ed. Abya Yala.

Stadler, P. 1996. *Der Kulturkampf der Schweiz: Eidgenossenschaft und katholische Kirche im europäischen Umkreis 1848–1888.* Zurich: Chronos.

Steinberg, J. 2006. *Why Switzerland?* Cambridge: Cambridge University Press.

Stepan, A. 1999. Federalism and democracy: Beyond the US model. *Journal of Democracy* 10: 19–34.

Stepan, A. 1998. *Rethinking Military Politics.* Princeton: Princeton University Press.

Suter, M. 2000. *Kleine Zürcher Verfassungsgeschichte.* Zurich: Chronos.

Tilly, C. 2003. *Contention and Democracy in Europe, 1650–2000.* Cambridge: Cambridge University Press.

Trechsel, A.H. 2005. How to federalize the European Union… and why bother. *Journal of European Public Policy* 12, 401–18.

Von Flüe, N. 1998. Obwalden 1848–1888. Die Einordnung in den Bundesstaat in *Obwaldner Geschichtsblätter 25/1998.* Sarnen: Verlag des Historischen Vereins Obwalden.

Weber, K. 1932. Entstehung und Entwicklung des Kantons Basel-Land, in *Geschichte der Landschaft Basel, Vol. II,* edited by K. Weber and K. Gauss. Liestal: Kommissionsverlag Lüdin.

Weber, P. 1986–1987. The Constitutional Convention: A Safe Political Option. *Journal of Law and Politics* 51, 57–8.

Weiler, J. 1999. *The Constitution of Europe.* Cambridge: Cambridge University Press.

Weingast, B.R. 1997. The Political Foundations of Democracy and the Rule of Law. *The American Political Science Review* 91(2), 245–63.

Wheatley, J. 2008. Direct Democracy in the Commonwealth of Independent States: The State of the Art. *C2D Working Paper Series* 28. Available at at http://www.c2d.ch/files/C2D_WP28.pdf [Accessed 28 August 2012].

Widmeier, E. 1942. *Die Entwicklung der bernischen Volksrechte 1846–1869*. Zurich: E. Lang.

Widner, J. 2008. Constitution writing in post-conflict settings: an overview. *William & Mary Law Review* 49, 1513–40.

Widner J. 2007. Proceedings: Workshop on Constitution Building Processes. *Princeton University, May 17–20, 2007, Bobst Center for Peace & Justice, Princeton University, in conjunction with Interpeace and International IDEA*. Available at http://www.princeton.edu/bobst/docs/Constitutions_Edited_ Proceedings_1_(2).doc [accessed 31 August 2011].

Zaverucha, J. 1998. The 1998 Brazilian Constitution and its authoritarian legacy: formalizing democracy while gutting its essence. *Journal Third World Studies* 15 (1), 105–24.

Ziswiler, H.U. 1992. *Die Demokratisierung des Kantons Aargau zwischen 1830 und 1885*. Zurich: unpublished PhD thesis.

# Index

References to figures are shown in *italics*. References to tables are shown in **bold**. References to notes consist of the page number followed by the letter 'n' followed by the number of the note, e.g. 81n8 refers to note no. 8 on page 81.